HARLEY-DAVIDSON
EVOLUTION
MOTORCYCLES

GREG FIELD

MBI Publishing Company

First published in 2001 by MBI Publishing Company, 729 Prospect Avenue, PO Box 1, Osceola, WI 54020-0001 USA

MBI Publishing Company books are also available at discounts in bulk quantity for industrial or sales-promotional use. For details write to Special Sales Manager at Motorbooks International Wholesalers & Distributors, 729 Prospect Avenue, PO Box 1, Osceola, WI 54020-0001 USA.

Library of Congress Cataloging-in-Publication Data

Field, Greg.
    Harley-Davidson Evolution Motorcycles / Greg Field.
        p. cm.
    Includes index.
    ISBN 0-7603-0500-5 (hc: alk. paper)
     1. Harley-Davidson motorcycle—Motors. 2. Harley-Davidson motorcycle.
3. Harley-Davidson Incorporated. I. Title.
    TL448.H3 F52 2001
    629.227'5—dc21   00-060095

On the front cover: The Evolution engine powered Harley-Davidson's recovery from the brink of insolvency, partly due to brilliant marketing on Harley's part. By using the same engine design in different types of motorcycles such as the Softail, Harley created a diverse lineup. Shown are a 2000 FXR4, a 1987 1100 Sportster, and a 1986-1/2 Heritage Softail.

On the frontispiece: The blacked-out risers towering above the classically-styled dash let you know that this Springer Softail is a Bad Boy.

On the title page: Although the Dyna chassis was available only in the limited edition Sturgis model during its first year, the Dyna split to form its own line in the following years, replacing the FXR models one by one.

On the back cover: *Left:* Compared to the blacked-out Evolution engine of the Dyna Sturgis, the Dyna Wide Glide's engine was a display of chrome.

Right: In 1993, the front fender and its linkage to the fork on the Softail Springer was revised to lower the fender closer to the tire, reducing the dreaded "motocross" look shown on this machine.

Endpaper: The three faces of Evo: FXR, Sportster, and Softail.

Edited by Darwin Holmstrom
Designed by Tom Heffron

Printed in China

Contents

Introduction

When the Evolution engine came out, we wanted the dealers and the buyers to recognize that this, by God, was a new engine!

—**Vaughn Beals, former chairman and CEO**

I hesitate to put it this way because I don't want to take away from the mystique of the Evolution engine, but there really was never an Evolution engine.

—**Mark Tuttle, former vice president of engineering**

Why two seemingly contradictory quotes to start this book? Because they perfectly punctuate the dichotomy that is and always has been Harley-Davidson, particularly through the Evolution era, model years 1984 through 1999 for the V^2 Evolution Big Twin engine and model years 1986 through at least 2001 for the V^2 Evolution Sportster engine.

To see why, you have to think back nearly 20 years to the dire days of the early 1980s. The Motor Company was newly independent of AMF (American Machine and Foundry, which had owned Harley-Davidson since 1969) but teetering on the brink of bankruptcy because of a sagging motorcycle market, a reputation for poor quality, and a long lack of innovation. Several new chassis gave hope, but the company was still building ancient, iron-barreled engines reviled as much for their oil consumption and failure rate as they were loved for their loping exhaust note and bottomless torque.

The company needed an updated version of its old V-twin engines to restore the confidence of the company's "old faithful" customers and to draw in the legions of the potential "new faithful"—folks who had always loved the sight and sound of a Harley and might buy one if Harley could just make them less leaky and more reliable. This is what Beals was talking about.

However, the company's more astute managers and engineers knew that Harley dare not change the engine too much. No matter how much they improved the new engine, if it didn't look, sound, and *feel* like a Harley motor, neither legion of the faithful would be interested. For that reason (and a lot of others), the company revised the venerable Big Twin motor "from the base gasket up, with minor revisions below," in Mark Tuttle's words, which is why the engineers didn't really think of the new engine as a new engine.

New or not, once the V^2 Big Twin engine proved itself reliable and oil-tight, those who needed to, saw that this, by God, *was* a new engine. At the same time, those who needed to, saw (and heard and felt) that this, by God, was still a *Harley* engine. Harley repeated the trick on the Sportster engine two years later, putting the words *new* and *Sportster* together in a way they hadn't been since 1957.

But the story of the Evolution engines is much more than the story of a bunch of engineers doing what they do best. Rather, it's the story of a company written off as dead getting an injection of life from top to bottom and amazing the motorcycling world. Between 1980 and 1986, Harley-Davidson released four all-new chassis and the two new motors. With every passing year, the bikes and engines got better and more new models emerged.

The result? Everyone saw that this, by God, was a new Motor Company. In the past, progress had been measured by decades, vibration on the Richter scale, and failure rates in the double digits. Now, the Evo motor powered The Motor Company further than anybody thought possible.

All that didn't happen merely because a bunch of Harley engineers developed a couple of new engines. The real story here is the evolution of Harley-Davidson as a company. At the start of the Evo years, Harley-Davidson was ridiculed as the dying dinosaur of a niche market. As this book goes to press in late 2000, Harley-Davidson is acclaimed as a forward-thinking builder of mainstream objects of desire, and its business model is studied and emulated around the world. With this book, I tried to do justice to both the Evolution engine and the evolution of The Motor Company.

Why a book on the Evos when the Big Twin has only been out of production for a year and the Evo Sportster is still in production? Because the guys who designed the Evolution engines and all the great bikes they powered are still alive, as are the executives who engineered the evolution of the company. In my previous books on the Knucklehead and Panhead Harleys, I often found myself wondering why Harley's engineers and execs did some of the things they did. Most of them have long been residents of Harley heaven, so I had to resort to the motorcycling equivalent of archeology. That is, looking at the artifacts and trying to guess the whys and hows. Sometimes archeology reveals the right answers, but more often it does not.

In researching this book, I was fortunate to have the help of many of the most important contributors to The Motor Company's revival, and I relied heavily on their recollections of the events to tell the Evolution story. If you can ask the guy who did something why he did it that way, you're more likely to get the truth than if you look at the part 50 years later and try to guess. This approach carries its own inherent risks of inaccuracies because of the vagaries of human memory, but the first-person anecdotes that resulted are often funny and always insightful, giving an inside look at the motorcycles, the company, and the personalities.

You may wonder why I relied only on only former employees. The answer is that Harley chose not to support this book, so I honored the company's request that I not talk to current employees. Before support was withdrawn, I had interviewed some of them, but that material was left out of the book.

In the case of Bill Davis, inventor of the Softail, who works for Harley on a consultant basis, I limited my questioning to work he completed before he began to work for The Motor Company.

A note on the organization of this book: All the engine stuff is in chapter 1. Then, each major model line gets its own chapter. I know many of you will jump right to the chapter on your favorite model, so I tried to make each chapter stand on its own as much as possible, with a few references to key information in other chapters. Since most of the chassis discussed in this book predate the Evo engine, I give a little heritage lesson on each, so you can understand how each got to be what it was when the Evolution engine was bolted in. Then, I take you through the Evo years for each model.

Acknowledgments

Many thanks to the following former Harley-Davidson employees who were kind enough to spend many hours with me on the phone: Vaughn Beals, chairman and CEO; Rit Booth, engineer and product manager; John Davidson, president; Tom Gelb, senior vice president of operations; Hank Hubbard, engineer; Ray Miennert, engineer; Dick O'Brien, racing manager; Bob Sroka, engineer; Mark Tuttle, vice president of engineering; Don Valentine, chief engineer; and David Webster, engineer. Beals, Booth, and Tuttle were also kind enough to review the manuscript.

A whole host of other folks were extremely helpful, too. If I have forgotten anyone, I hope they will forgive the oversight.

First, many thanks to Allan Girdler. Whenever I'm stuck and discouraged, he always seems to be able to pat me on the head and point me in the right direction.

Employees of several Seattle-area Harley-Davidson franchises were enormously helpful in helping me to locate motorcycles and in sharing information. In alphabetical order, they are Jim Boltz of Lynwood Cycle Barn; Lyle Burns, James Lee, Greg McGoff, Jon Martin, and Scott Moon of Eastside Harley-Davidson; Dave Nelson of Lynwood Cycle Barn; and Carmen and Russ Tom of Downtown Harley-Davidson. Special thanks to Casey Wing and Mike Gosson of Eastside Harley-Davidson, who were especially helpful throughout the whole effort and who were also kind enough to review the manuscript. Thanks also to Mike Shattuck of Sacramento (California) Harley-Davidson; Jerry Benson of Valley Harley-Davidson, Stockton, California; and Mike Hillman of Milwaukee Harley-Davidson.

For allowing me the opportunity to photograph their motorcycles, I'd like to thank the following owners: Steve Acord, 1985 FLT; Johann Aggenbach, 2000

The Evolution Big Twin engine, introduced for model year 1984, put Harley-Davidson onto the road to recovery. By late 1985, Harley-Davidson was still heavily mortgaged and operating at the pleasure of its bankers, who weren't very pleased and were intending to foreclose. New financing in the last days of 1985 saved the company, and a public sale of stock in mid-1986 gave Harley control of its own destiny. The rest is history, or heritage, and it's all part of this book.

FXR[4]; Patrick and Patricia Bennett, 1995 XLH 883; Peter Bratz, 1985 FXSB; Dan Carroll, 1996 FXSTB; Willie Chase, 1998 FLTRI; John Clark, 1990 FLSTF; Claus Clifton, 1989 FXRS; Louis Coulson, 1988 FLHTC; Bill Frenette, 1999 FXR[2]; Lois Lundquist, 1987 XLH 1100; Albert McCaleb, 1985 FXST; Chuck Myers, 1986 Liberty FLHT; Ronald G. Rall, 1998 FXDWG; Steve and Laura Richardson, 1984 FXST, 1998 FLHTCUI, and 1988 FLT/FLHS with sidecar; Susan Roberts, 1998 FXDL; Jerry Sanden, 1986 FLST, 1991 FXSTS, and 1996 FLHR; Jeff "AK" Sincic, 1986 FXWG; Bruce Smith, 1987 XLH 1100; Welder Mike, 1984 FXRT; Steven Womack, 1999 XLH 883; Howard Zang, 1999 FXSTB.

For the great photos of Vaughn and Eleanore Beals, thanks to my good buddy Nolan Woodbury. Special thanks also to Stephan Byarlay for lending some critical materials at a critical time; Tom Murphy for all his contacts; Buzz Buzzelli, *American Rider* magazine for some crucial photographs; Dan Quintanares; Kip Woodring; and to Rob Carlson of Kokesh Motorcycles, Spring Lake Park, Minnesota, and Ron Kay for supplying the Sub Shock advertisement.

For rolling out of bed long before the cold butt crack of dawn to get their bikes on location for the cover-photo shoot, my thanks to Johann Aggenbach, Jerry Sanden, and Bruce Smith. Special thanks to my buddy Kevin Cruff for getting there early and lending gear and much-needed advice. For help on the afternoon effort, thanks also to Steven Womack.

For contributing in myriad ways, thanks to the following individuals: Kevin Cruff and Teri Majka; Rick Mahnke of Moto Guzzi Cycle, Brooklyn, Wisconsin; Brock and Debbie Radloff of Classic Iron Works, Redmond, Washington; Gerry and Susan Olson; Chuck, Sandy, and Julie Cossè; Bill and Sandy Banfield; and Dave Cotton.

For long-term encouragement and support, to my parents, Larry and Laurie; my siblings, Scot, Shawn, Dawn, and Heather; my grandparents, John and Gladys Field, Leo and Marge Miller, and Lawrence and Ruth Murdock; and my good friends, Jerry Beach, Todd Blakely, Owen Herman, Martyn Jessup, Kevin Lentz, Tim Lien, Mike McCoy, Barry Mercer, Tom Samuelsen, John Scharf, and Joe Sova.

For putting me up and putting up with me while in Milwaukee: Annie, Tobie, and Heidi Golembiewski; Ray, Carol, Tracie, Becky, Vicky, Katie, and Nicole Karshna; Ed and Jean Kwiecinski; and Jeff, Jackie, and Olivia Ciardo.

For tolerating my "fluid" deadlines, to Zack Miller, Lee Klancher, and Darwin Holmstrom, and the rest of the staff at MBI Publishing.

Finally, to Jeni, who put up with so much obsessive behavior and gave up so much so that I'd have time to finish the manuscript.

CHAPTER 1

The Evo Big Twin and Sportster Engines

1984 – 2001

SOUL IN THE NEW MACHINE

"It was clear that the V-twin we had was running out of gas. . . . [Our] idea was, "Let's take whatever the current technology is and make a better V-twin."

—**Vaughn Beals, former Chairman and CEO of Harley-Davidson, Inc.**

Initially Harley-Davidson only offered a plain silver version of the Evo engine, without chrome covers. As The Motor Company refined its finishing processes, it began offering special editions, such as the FXRDG and FXRC with chrome engine covers. In 1986, the new FXSTC Softail Custom was the first regular production model to be fitted with a black-and-chrome version of the Evo engine. Before long, the black-and-chrome engine would be standard in most models.

The new era for Harley-Davidson began in April 1976, at a management retreat at the Pinehurst Country Club in North Carolina. The mission? To get to know one another better by relaxing and playing golf, and to think strategically about Harley's future.

Except for two important newcomers, everyone there was an old-timer. Both newcomers—Vaughn L. Beals Jr. and Jeffrey Bleustein, Ph.D.—had been brought in during 1975 by Ray Tritten, the AMF group executive in charge of Harley-Davidson, and both were key players in the resurgence of the company.

Tritten had hired Beals as deputy group executive in charge of Harley. Beals was well qualified for the job, too, by training and by experience. After

When the Evolution engine debuted for model year 1984, it was bolted into the rubber-mounted FLT and FXR chassis, as well as the then-new FXST Softail chassis. Shown here is a 1985 FXST. The solid-mount FLH and FX models for 1984 came with the old Shovelhead engine.

getting a master's degree in aeronautical engineering from the Massachusetts Institute of Technology (MIT), Beals had worked for North American Aviation and Cummins Engine Co. as an engineer and executive. Following his entrepreneurial bent, he became part owner and CEO of a logging equipment manufacturing company in Seattle, Washington. Forced from that job by the majority owners, Beals was recruited by AMF. That he knew nothing about motorcycles and had never even ridden one didn't scare him in the least.

Bleustein earned a doctorate in mechanical engineering from Columbia University and had taught engineering at Yale before joining AMF as a member of its elite corporate research and engineering unit. Tritten brought him in to recommend ways to improve Harley-Davidson's engineering department. After giving his recommendations, Bleustein was asked to step in as vice president of engineering.

Of the Pinehurst retreat, Beals remembers:

"Basically, four months before that retreat, I didn't know what a motorcycle was. I got there just before the end of 1975. The first task I was given was to prepare a product plan and a business plan.

"As a means of doing that, I took, oh, a half-dozen key people—Jeff Bleustein, Willie G. (head of design), John Davidson (essentially head of marketing), and a couple of others—to a resort for the better part of a week. Basically, from that meeting we stitched together a long-range product plan for the company.

"The basic plan that came out of Pinehurst was, 'Let's ride two horses at once.' We needed two powertrains. One was the Evolution engine, and the other was a modern water-cooled V-configuration family of engines that would allow us to compete with what everybody else was doing. Vibration isolation and some new chassis were built into the plan, too.

"It was clear that the V-twin we had was running out of gas. It was not able to give us the durability, and it was not able to adapt to progressively more difficult emissions requirements, so we had to do something to bring it into the twentieth century. The idea was, 'Let's take whatever the current technology is and make a better V-twin.' The key design requirements were that it be designed to meet the future emissions and noise requirements, have a bigger displacement, and more power. And it wasn't supposed to fall apart!

"We all felt the V-twin was our history—that it would have been stupid to abandon it. That's what Indian did, and it bankrupted the company! And down deep, we all hoped that the V-twin would be our future, too, but we were looking at much more sophisticated water-cooled engines from our competitors, so we also felt that having the V-twin as the sole product strategy of the company was too risky at that time. That's where the idea for the water-cooled engine came from. It would have been unwise to say, let's just fix up the V-twin and go from there."

On their return from the retreat, they fleshed out their plan and calculated the cost. By September of 1976, the plan was ready, and boy was it a doozy. "We figured it was gonna cost 100 million bucks, which was bigger money back then than it is now," Beals remembered. "I had looked at the prior strategic product plans that had been submitted, and 'BS' is the only appropriate way to describe what was in them. The numbers were like a third of what we came up with. To go in and tell the boss that the price tag is three times what he thought it was going to be is not something we contemplated with pleasure."

When Beals presented the new plan to AMF senior management, "It was a long, cold shower for them," according to Beals. "AMF never really understood Harley-Davidson." Beals noted that AMF resulted from an antitrust action in the early part of the century, forcing tobacco makers to cease manufacturing the machinery that processed tobacco and made cigarettes. "Their fundamental old business was in tobacco-manufacturing equipment, which didn't really change very rapidly," Beals said. "That was a good, classical, old, heavy-industry kind of business that kind of ran along in the background." Then AMF began acquiring leisure businesses, and by the time Beals was hired, leisure accounted for two-thirds of the company's revenue.

No other AMF division was remotely comparable to the size and complexity of Harley. "At the time, AMF was probably $1.5 billion revenue, and they had 40 companies," Beals said. "Harley-Davidson's revenue was probably in the high 200s (millions). They also didn't understand long-lead-time, capital-intensive stuff, because it doesn't take five years to develop a new pair of skis or a tennis racket."

AMF wanted a third party to look at the plan Beals presented. "That didn't surprise me, and I was fully supportive of it," Beals said. AMF decided to hire an outside consulting group to examine Harley-Davidson's product plan and make recommendations.

For 1985, all the Big Twins came with the Evolution engine, including the few solid-mount, exposed-shock models that remained: FXEF Super Glide Fat Bob, FXSB Low Rider, and FXWG Wide Glide. Even with the new engine, the Low Rider, Wide Glide, and Softail still came fitted with a charming relic of the past: a kickstarter. Shown is a 1985 Low Rider.

JUST ANOTHER BAND OUT OF BOSTON

In late 1976, AMF hired the Boston Consulting Group (BCG), a research firm that had previously done a study for the British government on how or whether government action could revive that country's dying motorcycle industry, as one after another of the legendary British makers went bankrupt or was taken over by the British government to prevent loss of industry jobs.

BCG did an extensive study, surveying dealers and customers in depth. "They endorsed our plan and said that what we proposed was a reasonable thing to do," Beals said. "With some fine tuning, that plan was what we then went to execute."

With BCG's endorsement and AMF's money, work began on the planned update of the Big Twin and Sportster engines, the new liquid-cooled engines, and several new chassis in early 1977. (Eventually, the main author of the BCG study, Richard Hermon-Taylor, was asked to join Harley-Davidson's board of directors.)

While the BCG study is still a controversial subject among many at The Motor Company (many scoff that it had predicted that the traditional Harley V-twin would die out), one thing's certain: It convinced AMF to bankroll Harley's future, and without that, there probably would not have been a future.

"WE DIDN'T HAVE THE FIRST ENGINEERING DEPARTMENT"

The plan called for reworking the Big Twin engine in-house and contracting an outside firm to design the water-cooled engine, with a planned debut for both engines in the early 1980s, and an updated Sportster engine to follow. Why not do both in-house? "The fundamental problem was that in 1976 we didn't have the first engineering department," explained Beals. "We needed to make [the Nova] engine from scratch. Thinking that we could make one from scratch and simultaneously develop two new engines—I don't think that would have been good judgment."

With that, Bleustein began building Harley's "first engineering department" and selecting a firm to design the other engine. "AMF invested heavily in human resources during that time," explained Mark Tuttle, former vice president of engineering. "Without that investment, Harley-Davidson could not have recovered."

One of Bleustein's key acquisitions was a new leader for the powertrain section, Don Valentine, who had managed engine development for Waukesha Motors, American Bosch, and Cummins (where he had worked for Beals). Valentine's first efforts were focused on improving the Shovelhead, but later, he played a key role in designing the Evos.

Meanwhile, Bleustein had been in contact with Porsche Design in Germany, Ricardo in England, and at least one other firm. Eventually, Harley-David-son picked Porsche to pen the engine that would be called "Nova." For the next several years, Nova's development continued in parallel with the Evo.

"What became the Evolution engine was really started as a response to a changing environment, and it *evolved*," explained Tuttle, then chief engineer of motorcycles. "The way customers were using our motorcycles was changing. Speeds were up, distances traveled were greater, emissions regulations were getting tighter, and they were reformulating gasoline. As a result, our Shovelhead started having reliability problems, in particular, oil consumption and valve-train problems. We were already developing the technologies to fix these problems and they evolved into the Evolution engine."

Tuttle said the time was ripe for a new engine—the Evolution. But as alluded to earlier, the Evo was not really a new design. "It was primarily from the crankcases up," said Tuttle. "It was cylinders, pistons, cylinder heads, intake manifolds, cams, and so forth, but the crankcases did not really change dramatically. The reason for that was, first, we could not afford to do a complete engine. Second, all of our reliability issues were taking place from the base gasket up."

In an early effort to cope with the changing environment (and the fast-moving aftermarket) Harley bored out the Shovelhead cylinders for an 80-cubic-inch displacement. "The 80-cubic-inch was a field-upgrade kit that was available through some speed shops," explained Dave Webster, former Harley powertrain engineer, "and it was extremely successful. We thought, 'Well let's try it!'" This led to the 80-inch Shovelhead that was first produced during the 1978 model year—and it led to a lot of problems.

"It became very obvious, very quickly, that the cylinder arrangement was not compatible with 80 cubic inches because we started breaking the base flanges on the cast-iron cylinders," explained Don Valentine.

"We had a few 'missile launches' along the way," remembered Webster. "The early prototypes were made from current iron parts. Once we thought we knew what we wanted, we had the patterns changed and new castings made. The parts were still just about warm from the molds—they weren't 'aged'—when they were put on an engine and tested. The flange would let go, and the jug, head, and rocker covers would embed itself in the ceiling of the test cell."

Eventually, Engineering developed some load-distribution plates for use between the bolts and base flange that helped on the Shovelhead, but the real lesson learned was that a more modern cylinder design was needed.

HANK HUBBARD AND "THE CONCEPT"

That lesson was carried through when Jerry Long (Harley's manager of engine design) approached engineer Hank Hubbard in November 1977 and asked him to design an updated Harley engine. The basic assignment? "Redesign the engine from the crankcases up for state-of-the-art oil control, increasing the bore to get more power out of the engine, and for cost reduction," remembered Hubbard.

At the time, Hubbard was Harley's main engine "concept man" —the guy who brainstormed the fundamentals of future designs. True to form, Hubbard came up with a design concept by the end of November that proved remarkably similar to the production Evo engine. Major changes compared to the

Shovel were his use of aluminum cylinders (with iron liners) sandwiched between the crankcase and heads by long studs. "Missile launches" were not part of his concept.

Hubbard's stud design had one handy feature that paid big dividends later: "I used two-piece studs with a female thread at the top end," he explained. "The long stud screwed down into the crankcase, and then the cylinder-head bolts screwed into that stud from above. You didn't have to lift it up very far to take the cylinder head out. I also had two-piece rocker covers. The idea from the beginning was you could get the two-piece covers off with the engine in the frame, and then get the head and cylinder off, too."

The through-stud cylinder design wasn't new or unique to Harley (other manufacturers had used it for decades, and even Harley had, on the alloy-engine XR-750 of 1972), but it had many advantages. First, the cylinder didn't have to carry all the structural load of the whole top end, so the cylinder could be made of aluminum, a material that is lighter and transfers heat far more rapidly than cast iron. Cases and heads were already aluminum, so the new cylinders would expand and contract at the same rate as the heads and cases, reducing the "scrubbing" and subsequent leaking of head and base gaskets that had been such a problem on the Shovelhead.

Second, the stubby bolts between the base flange and case and between the top flange and heads didn't have to carry all the clamping loads. Instead, the long, springy studs helped carry the structural and clamping loads, distributing them more evenly across the cylinder. This even distribution of loads reduced distortion of the cylinders (for better ring sealing) and prevented "missile launches." Also, steel studs don't elongate as much as the aluminum cylinders under heat, so the clamping load increases on the base and head gaskets, helping to keep a tight seal.

Hubbard's concept also included major changes to the heads. "We changed the valve angles considerably. The reduced valve angle lent itself to better intake and exhaust porting." That reduced angle also affected many later decisions made about the cylinder heads.

Hubbard's finished concept was put onto a D-sized drawing. Then, according to Hubbard, "two other guys, Bob Sroka and Dave Webster, gave birth to it."

"NITTY-GRITTY" DESIGN WORK

Sroka and Webster were tasked with developing Hubbard's concept into a finished design. "At that time," remembered Webster, "Jerry Long told us the game plan was to maintain or, if possible, to improve power, reduce cost, improve durability, and cut back on the oil leaks. From there, things just began to evolve."

Said Sroka, "Webster and I went into the nitty-gritty details of making [Hubbard's concept] feasible from the standpoints of power output, reliability, and manufacturing requirements. And then we wanted to renovate the oiling system to get the oil consumption to the level of 1,000 miles or better per quart."

Was the engine that was to power the company's future given a stealthy code name, like the "P22" that was used for the later Twin Cam 88? Apparently not. "We referred to it as 'Evolution' from the start," Sroka remembered. "The name stuck with it when it went into production. It's just one of those things that seemed like it was always there."

In the years ahead, Sroka and Webster played primary roles in Evo development, first refining the concept drawing with all the detail necessary to build prototypes, then turning those drawings into actual prototypes.

Vaughn Beals was president and one of the main men behind Harley's astonishing return to quality and profitability in the 1980s. *Nolan Woodbury photo*

EARLY PROTOTYPES

The first prototypes were made by grafting the improved pieces onto Shovelhead engines and wringing them out on the dyno. "The old 80-ci was modified as the forerunner of the Evolution," said Sroka. "We got performance information from that, if you want to call it a prototype." Added Webster, "On the first prototypes, the cylinder was a sand-cast aluminum part that we bored out and shrink-fit an iron sleeve. The heads were sand-cast, too." So, was it a repeat of the "rocket launches" when the prototypes were brutalized on the dyno? "We blew up surprisingly few of the Evolution prototypes," Webster continued. "We dropped a few valve seats, but beyond that, the prototypes ran pretty well."

Before long, the proto-Evos were installed in bikes and tearing up the local roads. "A lot of the durability testing was being done locally when we began, on the streets around Milwaukee," said Webster. "I had a personally assigned prototype for my own use. When we were about halfway through the program, we switched to road and high-speed testing at the track at Talladega [Alabama]."

TEAM EVO

The foundation design work was all done by 1980 but thousands of additional details still needed to be finalized. "Through the Evolution engine, we wanted to get back the customer base we were losing because of the problems with the Shovelhead," said Don Valentine. "The engine had to be leak-free and relatively trouble-free (we were looking for a 100,000-mile engine). And we had to do it on a shoestring budget. Money was very tight—especially in the early 1980s."

Shoestring budget? What happened to that hundred mil from AMF?

Well, it was spent on a lot of things, including design of the FLT (see chapter 3), *two* redesigns of the Sportster chassis (see chapter 5), design of the FXR (see chapter 4), the Nova, and upgrading the manufacturing facilities.

Using what money it did have, a whole team of engineers from the powertrain section got to work, under chief Don Valentine and his new manager of engine design, John Favill (who replaced Jerry Long). Favill, a Briton, came to Harley-Davidson from Norton, where he had helped design the Commando and other models. Other important contributors included Roger Bascomb, Bruce Dennert (from the Applied Mechanics/Design Analysis Department), and many others. For the purposes of this book, we'll refer to them collectively as "Team Evo."

Over the next three years of slaving over hot dynos, in front of glowing computer terminals, and around nearly a million miles of testing, Team Evo refined the design for production. Being engineers, members of Team Evo went methodically but creatively about their task, looking at the list of traditional Big Twin problems and finding solutions. "We'd look at problems one at a time and grind them out," remembered Valentine.

Soon, the engineers from Powertrain were joined by a mass of talent from throughout the company. "The Evolution project was a collaboration," explained Mark Tuttle. "It was really the beginning of the program to involve more people in the design and development of our products. Historically, the handoff from engineering to manufacturing has sort of been, 'Here's the perfect design; now you figure out how to make it,' versus working in collaboration to balance manufacturing needs with functional needs with styling needs and so forth." Even a terse summary of all that coordinated activity would fill dozens of books this size, so instead, let's take a look at the design features that made it onto the final design and *why* they made it into production.

NEEDING SOME SQUISH: THE EVO CYLINDER HEADS

"Cylinder heads were the biggest challenge," explained Valentine. "There was a learning curve because the heads were all new. We even had to develop a new casting process for them."

Why all new, when the Shovelhead engine already had aluminum heads? Because the Shovel's heads used the venerable "hemi" design—the combustion chambers were formed in a hemispherical, or domed, shape. "Hemi" became a performance buzzword in the 1950s and 1960s among the car crowd, but the Harley-Davidson overhead-valve (OHV) Big Twin had always been a hemi, from the first Knucklehead built in 1936, through the last Shovelhead produced in 1984. For a lot of reasons we don't have room to discuss, hemis made sense when the Knucklehead engine was designed in the 1930s but were considered archaic when the Evo was being designed.

Starting from scratch, Dave Webster came up with the basic cylinder-head design that was refined into the production heads. State-of-the-art *efficiency* was the goal, rather than max power. Thus, he stuck with two valves per cylinder, rather than the four-valve-per-cylinder designs then coming into vogue, and went with the latest "textbook design" in setting the shape of the combustion chambers, piston crown, and ports, as well as the valve angles.

Efficiency encompassed a lot of things, from cool running to low exhaust and noise emissions, to high gas mileage. Contemporary thought on cylinder-head design dictated three keys for obtaining peak efficiency: (1) minimize combustion chamber and piston crown area so the engine absorbs the absolute minimum of the heat energy released by combustion; (2) induce turbulence or "swirl" among the gases in the combustion chamber to get a more complete burn; and (3) put the spark plug's electrode as near the center of the chamber as possible to minimize the distance the resulting flame has to travel to reach all corners of the chamber.

To minimize piston area, Webster settled on flat-top pistons. To minimize chamber area, he "lowered the roof" for a flatter chamber area. The lower and flatter chamber roof required lessening the angle between the valve stems. Instead of the 90-degree valve angle on the Shovel, Webster settled on a 58-degree angle for the new engine—27 degrees from vertical for the intake valve and 31 for the exhaust. Why 58 degrees? "Pure fit," he remembered.

That got two parts of the efficiency formula, but how to get the swirl? And even more important, how to get an acceptably high compression ratio without a dome on the piston? "We were needing some squish," said Dave Webster, "which we got from the D-shaped design."

By "squish," Webster referred to the "squish area" designed into the heads. On the Evo heads, the squish area is a flat shelf on one side of the combustion chamber, resulting in a chamber that is shaped like a "D." Harley's term for the shape is Side Squish Combustion Chamber (SSCC).

That shelf takes up chamber space to raise the compression ratio to 8.5:1, versus the 7.4:1 ratio on the last Shovelheads. Harley was able to avoid detonation with the higher ratio because the rest of the engine ran so

Even Sportster fans had cause to rejoice in model year 1986, because the Evolution Sportster model made its debut, in the $3,995 Sportster 883 and the $5,199 Sportster 1100. Replacing the iron barrels and heads of the old Sportster were new aluminum cylinders and heads on the Evo. The Evo Sportster engine proved as reliable and oil-tight as the Big Twin. The next major update came in 1991 with the release of the five-speed Sportster powerplants. *Joe Ford photo via Buzz Buzzelli*

much cooler. The shelf also promotes swirl in the chamber because as the piston rises in the bore, gasses are compressed against the shelf. When the flat-top piston tops out just below the shelf, most of those gasses are squished out to the side, really stirring things up in the main chamber. To touch off those squished and swirling gasses efficiently, Team Evo placed the spark plug as close to the center of the heads as the intake and exhaust valves would allow.

Those valves, and the ports through which they breathe, were made smaller than those on the old Shovel, again following then-current theories of engine design. Smaller valves run cooler (all else being equal) and smaller (to a limit) ports actually give better power in the low-revving Harley Big Twin engine, because they force the gases to flow at higher velocities for a ram-air effect.

Though the new studs clamped the head securely to the cylinders, the Team added locating dowels to keep the head from "walking" around and causing head-gasket leaks. Dowels were also added to the cases to preserve base-gasket sealing.

Manifold connections to the heads were completely redesigned. The metal spigots formerly used to connect the Y-shaped manifolds to the heads were replaced by bonded-rubber spigots that could flex a bit to stay sealed, despite engine vibration and slight misalignment from production variability.

TRAINING VALVES: THE EVO VALVE TRAIN

Like the heads, the whole valve train was redesigned from scratch. Most of the changes were required to use an internal oiling system for the top end,

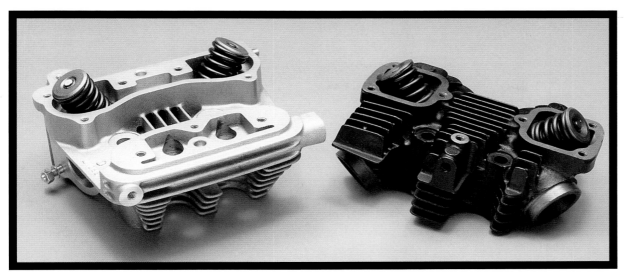

The hydraulic lifters also contributed to the tracking problem. For the Evo engine, Webster chose one-piece lifters similar to those used on General Motors diesels and had Eaton (the supplier of the tappets) revise them to reduce leak-down. Further problems with the tappet rollers were solved by using a larger roller, of a different material, and new bearings. In the end, the system worked with automotive reliability.

A redesigned profile for the rocker valve tips encouraged the valves to spin, evening out wear and dissipation of heat from the exhaust valve, which is usually the hottest part of the engine.

Though the updates were primarily from the base gasket up, the case-mounted cams also got plenty of attention. Again, the goal was efficiency, along with quieter operation to help meet ever-tighter noise limits. Over literally thousands of hours of dyno testing, they devised new cam profiles that gave

eliminating the clunky looking external oil lines to the heads, which were a common source of leaks. Other changes were required to get the proper rocker geometry to go with the narrower valve angles, and still others were made after testing showed that the valves were not smoothly following the opening and closing inputs from the cams.

The oiling system was lifted from automotive practice. Instead of an external oil line or internal passage, oil to the heads was fed from the hydraulic tappets through the hollow pushrods to an oil passage in the rockers, which metered oil out to lubricate the rocker bushings and valve stems. "That oiling system was a carryover from a system that I had used when I worked at Wisconsin Motors and copied from, I believe, Chevrolet division of General Motors from the late 1950s or early 1960s," remembered Bob Sroka.

Oil drained back to the crankcases through holes in the low (exhaust) side of each head, through passages in the cylinders. As a means of getting quicker oil return, the breather system was revised to equalize pressure between the crankcase and heads by means of a passage through the redesigned lifter blocks, via the pushrod tubes.

The problem of the valvetrain not tracking with the cam inputs took some innovative testing to solve. All that stuff's moving faster than the eye can follow and is covered up, so how to find the problem? "We used Linear Displacement Velocity Transducers (LVDTs) to monitor the valve motions," explained Dave Webster. "We mounted them above the end of the valves to give us a display of valve-tip motion. We could then compare that to the lifter motion and see when the valves began to float or bounce." From this information, Bruce Dennert suggested softening the cam profiles so the valves had an easier time tracking.

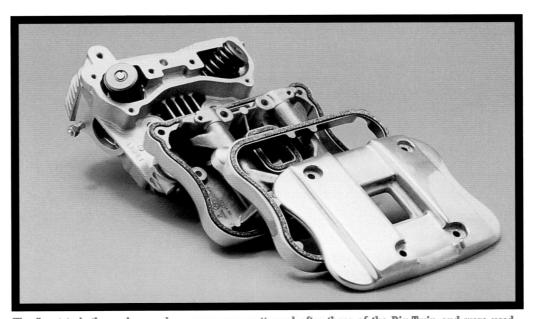

what they felt was the best balance of torque and horsepower for an engine that would be used in a broad range of motorcycles, from a 600-pound sporty bike like the FXRS to a near-900-pound full-dresser like the FLT, while still meeting emissions regulations. Since they really weren't after extra gobs of horsepower, they went with very conservative amounts of valve lift and overlap.

On the preproduction Evolutions, the rocker-cover assemblies were made in two pieces—upper and lower. Unfortunately, these didn't seal well and they made it difficult to get the covers off with the engine in the frame, which meant you couldn't get the heads and cylinders off, either. The eventual fix for this is discussed later.

IRON HEART: THE EVO CYLINDERS

Team Evo's overall conservative approach to design is typified by its choice of cylinders. Yeah, they were deeply finned and made of aluminum, but they also had iron liners. Team Evo chose this well-proven, low-tech cylinder design over what was then the latest and greatest: all-aluminum cylinders with a wear surface of Nikasil or other coating plated directly on the aluminum. Such cylinders are even lighter and shed heat better than lined cylinders, so why did

Harley-Davidson stick with iron, especially when the chosen developer of the pistons for the Evo engine (the German company Mahle) was also the developer of the Nikasil plating process?

"Mahle tried hard to convince us to use Nikasil bores," remembered Webster, "but we basically said no from a serviceability standpoint. Once the bore was coated it was not serviceable or rebuildable. One of the big requirements of the Evolution program was that the engine be serviceable."

Although conservative in its choice, once Team Evo decided on iron liners, it took them to a whole new level, working with the companies that make the liners and cylinder castings to get the best possible cylinders. The team tried many liners that didn't bond well enough with the alloy. Eventually, the team found that liners made with the SPINY-LOK® system not only bonded better than any others, but cooled better as well. The heart of the system is a range of peaks and valleys cast into the outer surface of the liner that increases the surface area where the iron meets the aluminum, for better cooling. When the aluminum is cast around these liners in a high-pressure die-casting process, those same peaks and valleys give the aluminum something to grab hold of.

Despite the SPINY-LOK® system, Harley had trouble with liners popping loose in the prototype stage. "There were some growing pains in getting

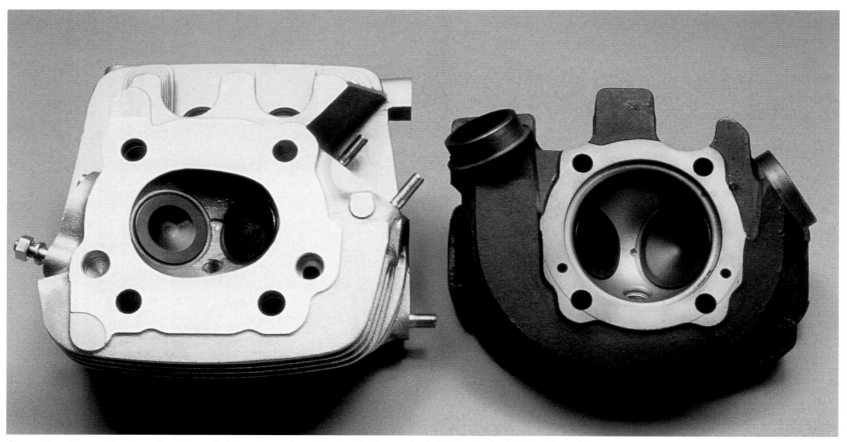

Comparing the combustion chambers of old and new Sportster heads shows the "shallow bathtub" chamber of the Evo Sportster and the hemi head of the iron Sportster. The bathtub heads were replaced by modified hemi heads during 1987. *Joe Ford photo, via Buzz Buzzelli*

The Evo Sportster engine retained the four-cam setup that the original Sportster engine inherited from its Model KH predecessor. *Joe Ford photo, via Buzz Buzzelli*

cast-iron sleeves bonded to aluminum cylinders," said Don Valentine. "But fixing that was strictly a matter of developing better methods for surface preparation and cleanliness and finding the right temperatures. In the end, we had to sandblast the exteriors of the raw cylinders." With the revised techniques, though, the liners stay bonded to the casting, and the cylinders cool and wear extremely well.

The design of the complex, variable-ovality pistons Harley-Davidson wanted for the Evo engine is the realm of specialists. Team Evo chose the German company Mahle to design and manufacture them. Mahle used a process called "diamond turning," in which a diamond cutter carves the shape while the piston is simultaneously rotated on two axes, to get the complex shape necessary to ensure that the pistons were cylindrical at operating temperatures.

With the whole top end designed to maximize cooling and pistons designed to have the right shape when hot, Harley's engineers were able to go with 0.0014-inch piston clearance, the tightness of which reduces noise and cools the piston by keeping it in close contact with the cylinder wall.

BASE GASKET DOWN

Despite the original goal of "minor revisions below the base gasket," the Evo's lower end was substantially revised because Team Evo wanted 100,000-mile reliability out of the whole engine, and the connecting rods and crankpin just weren't up to the job. All too often on high-mileage engines, the connecting rods would crack or the crankpins would "spall" (shed chips of metal) or develop cracks. On the Shovelhead, when you sometimes needed to rebuild the top end every 10,000 or 20,000 miles, it wasn't that big a deal to have rods and a crankpin that were good for only 50,000 miles, but the Evo needed better.

Rod cracks came from "stress risers" inherent in the old design, so the Evo connecting rods were redesigned completely to eliminate the problem. Harley claimed the new rods had 10 times the fatigue strength.

Crankpin spalling was a consequence of having the oiling hole right in the center of the bearing track, where it acted like a tiny pothole to the bearing rollers passing by thousands of times a minute. Over time, that pothole would start chunking off metal into the bearing. A partial fix was to move the hole off to the side of the roller track.

Cracking of the crankpins was also caused by microscopic "checking" from the intense heat generated during the manufacturing process. The fix was a refinement of the process developed during World War II called "Superfinish," which uses finer grinding tools while the crankpin is immersed in an oil bath to keep it cool and prevent surface checks.

Team Evo also sought to simplify manufacture of the five-piece crankshaft assembly by eliminating the keys and keyways on the main shafts and crankpins, using just the tapers. That system proved problematic and was fixed just prior to mass production. The cases, of course, got some revisions, too, to incorporate the studs for the cylinders, the new lifter blocks, and other changes.

A new electronic ignition that Harley called V-Fire III touched off the mixture in the Evo engine. It used a vacuum-operated switch to select between two advance curves programmed into the ignition's "black box." One curve was optimized for high-vacuum conditions like steady-state cruising, using more advance to return better gas mileage. The other curve has less advance, and kicks in when you whack open the throttle suddenly and vacuum drops (pressure rises). Both curves include rev-limiting circuitry to prevent revving the engine past 5,200 rpm. Best of all, no maintenance required.

ROUNDING OUT THE LOOK: THE AIR CLEANER

The round shape of the air-cleaner cover in the V of the engine's right side had been a trademark of the Harley look from 1937 until the 1970s, when ever-tightening noise regulations resulted in the large "ham-can" air box. For the Evo, the styling department wanted the round cleaner back.

Team Evo had to be clever to get small-air-cleaner looks with large-air-box quietness. To get the volume necessary to quiet down the intake, the team designed a large plastic reservoir and hid it within the V, so that only the chrome-plated round air-cleaner cover showed from the outside. The new system cost a bit of power and torque, but the classic look was more of a marketing advantage than the extra performance would have been.

THE EAGLE SOARS ALONE

If the budget had been "shoestring" in the beginning, two events during Evo design further choked the finances. The first of these occurred when a group of 12 Harley executives, plus Tim Hoelter (the outside general counsel), bought the company from AMF in June 1981, for about $80 million, according to Vaughn Beals. Beals became chairman and CEO of the newly formed

The early Evo Sportster engines were as plain as the early Big Twin engines. Shown is a 1987 Sportster 1100.

Harley-Davidson Motor Company, Inc. The new owners shouted "The Eagle Soars Alone" from ads and posters.

Obscenely in debt, and no longer having a "sugar daddy" to cover any shortfalls in revenue, Harley-Davidson could only spend what it made—and it wasn't making much. Sales throughout the motorcycle industry in the United States were down, but Harley felt it more than most. Sales for 1981 fell 14 percent, to the lowest total in a decade. Realizing the Evo was its future (but also realizing there would be no future if it spent itself into bankruptcy in the process), Harley spent what little it had to continue work on the Evolution engine and a few other important projects. Everything else was "de-funded." "While we were part of AMF," said Vaughn Beals, "we were not necessarily constrained by good sense. After we bought the company, though, every dollar and every sale was precious."

To make the most of every sale and every dollar, manufacturing chief Tom Gelb spread the philosophies of just in time (JIT) manufacturing and statistical process control (SPC) throughout the company's manufacturing operations. These were the ideas of American efficiency and quality expert W. Edwards Deming, adapted to motorcycle production by the Japanese, and borrowed back and adapted by Harley as its Materials As Needed (MAN) system. Here are the basics of how it works: (1) If you adapt your production methods to small-batch production and get your suppliers to deliver just the number of parts you need when you need them, you can save a lot of money in inventory costs and warehousing; and (2) if you have just the number of parts on hand that you need, every single one of them had better be good, so you have to statistically evaluate the quality of the parts you're building to spot problems before the parts get out of tolerance, and then you can tighten the specifications and further increase quality.

In 1982, the first full year of MAN, the company saved more than $20 million, and that may have saved the company. Said Vaughn Beals, "In essence, the cash freed up from inventory offsets the operating loss for 1982. Absent that, I'm absolutely certain our lenders would not have supported us." MAN and SPC also resulted in noticeable quality improvements.

As the emphasis switched to improving quality in manufacturing, the quality bar was also raised on the nearly completed Evolution *design*. "After the buyback," said Bob Sroka, "the decree was given that with the Evolution, we would put the Harley engine back to its reputation before AMF took over. We were also told, as far as oil seepage was concerned, the engine was to be dry to the point where misting was not permitted. In other words, no area of the motorcycle could have oil mist on it that would collect dust."

Here, we come to a parting of engine development programs. "The Sportster design was done at the same time as the Big Twin," said Dave Webster, "but it was just on paper." The emphasis had always been on getting the Evolution Big Twin done first, but with money for development getting ever scarcer, work on the Sportster was stopped about the time of the buyout, to concentrate more engineering resources on the Big Twin, with the goal of introducing the engine in late summer 1982, for the 1983 model year.

OPERATING AT THE PLEASURE OF THE BANKS

All the great changes that were under way at Harley-Davidson—Evolution engine, MAN, SPC, and all—almost came to an end in the spring of 1982. "A semirecession had hit automotive earlier," explained Gelb, "and all of a sudden in March 1982, it hit us. At the time, the Japanese motorcycle manufacturers had about 18 months worth of finished inventory in this country, and they were selling two- and three-year-old bikes right out of the crate and discounting them, so the bottom fell out of the market. I remember we had a policy meeting, and in the next weeks we cut our production rate in half, laid off 40 percent of our work force, and cut all the salaries of the officers by something like 12 percent and the salaried work force by 10 percent."

All that was bad enough, but worse was looming during the rest of 1982. Those production cuts put Harley-Davidson in violation of the production-level covenants of its asset-based loans, meaning the bankers could foreclose at will. "We were operating at the pleasure of the banks," said Gelb. His MAN system had already so transformed Harley's production and warehousing operations that even though Harley was losing money, the company actually had positive cash flow. At the same time, Vaughn Beals began the process of convincing the U.S. government to give Harley-Davidson some breathing room by instituting a tariff against the company's Japanese competitors.

DELAYED EVOLUTION

Unfortunately, the Evolution Big Twin engine, the one thing the company needed most (besides an infusion of cash) to pull itself out of the pit of 1982, wasn't quite ready. Despite doing more in less time and with less cash than anyone thought possible, Team Evo was still confounded by two vexing problems. "We had some crankshaft problems and rocker-box leakage problems," remembered Don Valentine.

As a result, the Policy Committee made the tough decision to delay introduction of the Evo. "I don't think we ever made a tougher decision than when we finally had to delay the Evolution," said Beals. "We had planned to introduce it at the start of model year 1983, but the one vow we took, because of the reputation we had, was that when the Evolution engine came out, we wanted the dealers and buyers to recognize that this, by God, was a new engine! That it was durable, oil-tight, bulletproof.

"We finally decided that the 1983-model introduction was too risky, because we weren't yet confident that it was bulletproof—so we reluctantly decided to delay the introduction until Daytona, which is in March, halfway through the model season. As time went on, we decided to put it off for a whole calendar year. Man, we needed it badly at that time because the market was terrible, which meant that we needed the engine sooner rather than later."

Many of those who survived the layoffs of spring 1982 soon jumped what they saw as a sinking ship. Dave Webster, one of the principal designers of the Evo, was among them. "I left in August 1982," he remembered, "and for about the previous six months there had been constant cutbacks, layoffs, programs being put on hold. Probably for the last three or four months I was there, my job was to house-clean files because development had basically stopped. By then, we had cut back close to 50 percent of our engineering staff, and at the plant, seniority was cut back to about the 25-year point."

Sure, cleaning out files is boring, but what really caused Webster to leave a good job in the middle of a recession? "I belonged to the Kiwanis Club, and one of my friends at the club was on the board with one of the banks that held the loan. He called me one day and said, 'Harley has about 30 days before they'll have to close the door. Beat the rush.' At that point, I left."

By the time Webster left, Harley had just completed its first full model year (1982) of independence, and the results were not encouraging. Production for 1982 (30,262) fell by over 27 percent compared to 1981 (41,586 built), and 1981 had seen the lowest production in a decade. Few thought the company would survive 1983.

In 1986, two important new Softail models were released: the Softail Custom at the beginning of the model year and the Heritage Softail in midyear. Shown is a 1986 Heritage Softail.

LAST-MINUTE FIXES

The few engineers who weren't laid off used the extra time well, devising fixes for the problems that originally delayed production and refining the tooling and processes for manufacture.

To fix the rocker-cover oil leaks, team members devised ingenious three-piece, horizontally split rocker covers. Once unbolted, the three pieces slide off the heads like cards from a deck, leaving room to remove the heads and cylinders while the engine is still in the frame.

The fix for the crankshaft problems wasn't nearly as clever, but it worked nonetheless. Basically, the team put back the keys and keyways, as on the Shovel crankshaft.

GETTING THROUGH THE SPRING

While the last refinements to the Evo design were being made, the tariff battle really heated up. As point man, Beals was the focus of scathing criticism from the motorcycling press and from the buyers of Japanese bikes. He never dreamed Harley-Davidson, Inc. would actually win its case, but started the action to "get us through the spring." That is, spring of 1983, until the Evo engine was ready.

Nevertheless, by early 1983, anyone could see that there was real substance to Harley's charges. Unsold models were piling up at an accelerating rate in the Japanese manufacturers' stateside warehouses and dealerships. And with the recent release of such new models as the FLT, FXRS, new Sportster chassis, FLHT, and FXRT, it was equally obvious that Harley-Davidson was improving its products.

All of this influenced the tariff commission, but the Japanese manufacturers made one strategic blunder that ultimately was a major deciding factor in the decision against them: "They had one attorney represent all four companies, which was tangible evidence of Japan Inc.," said Beals. "I can't conceive of anyone dumb enough to do that, but they were." As a result, the tariff commission recommended a 45 percent tariff on imported value (not retail). President Ronald Reagan modified the commission's recommendations some before approving them. The tariff would take effect April 15, 1983, and the percentage would decrease every year for the next five years.

Even before its tariff win, Harley-Davidson began playing its tariff card by offering to drop its tariff bid if the Japanese would give Harley loan guarantees of $15 million to $18 million that would allow it to finish development of the Nova project. After the victory, Harley offered to ask for an easing of the tariffs in exchange for the loans. Harley denied these reports in April 1983 and then confessed in July. Ultimately, Harley didn't get the loans, so the Nova and later Trihawk projects were canceled.

Gratifying though the tariff was, it came too late to help Harley much for the 1983 model year. Anticipating the possibility that they might lose, the Japanese manufacturers had stepped up production and shipment of their large 1983 models to get them to U.S. shores before the tariff took effect. As a result, Harley's sales for 1983 were hurt even worse than in 1982. Despite the lower sales, Harley-Davidson was able to "eke out a small profit by forcing more bikes on dealers than they needed," according to Vaughn Beals. Harley's bankers held off on foreclosure, but everyone involved knew that if the situation did not show real improvement soon, it was all going to fold.

HEDGING FOR 1984

While all the drama of the tariff hearings was going on, Beals and company decided the form of the 1984 line-up. Foremost among their decisions was whether the Shovelhead would go out of production at the end of 1983 in favor of the Evo, or whether both would be built.

The question for Harley became whether the new Evo would be "Harley" enough to get the old Shovel guys to trade up, while being improved enough to get the non-Harley guys to cross over. Confidence was high on both accounts, but there was no room for error. Harley needed to show its bankers some improvement in 1984, or there would not be another chance.

But there was an even more compelling dilemma facing Vaughn Beals and the cash-strapped company: What if big problems surfaced with the new motor? They had delayed it a year already; should they bet the whole year's production that the new Evo would be trouble-free and accepted? Harley-Davidson did the only sensible thing: It decided to keep the old engine in production, along with the new one.

By keeping the old Shovelhead engine in production, H-D had a fall-back in case the Evo bombed. At the same time the company had something to offer both the traditionalist and the hoped-for newer buyer, giving both of them reasons to believe in the new Harley-Davidson. To those who wanted modern refinement, Harley would offer the new Evo motor in its newer, rubber-mounted chassis—the FLTC Tour Glide Classic and FLHTC Electra Glide Classic (both in chapter 3), and the FXRS Low Glide and FXRT Sport Glide (both in chapter 4). To the traditionalist, Harley would offer the Shovel motor in its solid-mount, exposed-shock FLH and FX chassis. To those who wanted a little modern and a lot of tradition, Harley would offer up an all-new model, the FXST Softail (see chapter 2), with the Evo engine.

A few select dealers and moto-journalists were given their first looks at and rides on the Evo-powered Harleys (including the all-new Softail) in June 1983 at Harley's test facilities in Talladega, Alabama, and at the assembly plant at York, Pennsylvania. This bit of publicity was perfectly timed so that the teaser test reports were in all the major motorcycle magazines by the time the machines started arriving at Harley dealers across the country. Initial reports were mostly glowing.

NEW GUTS FOR OLD GLORY: DEBUT OF THE EVOLUTION ENGINE

When the Evo was finally released in late summer, Harley billed it as "New Guts for Old Glory" in a special brochure that described all the updates that made it so new, and exhorted the old faithful and all those sitting on the fence to come ride it in Harley's Super Ride program. Those who didn't want an Evo had plenty to choose from, too—the FLH, Wide Glide, Fat Bob, and so on. The strategy achieved its intended effect, and sales began to rise.

Evo engines in all the "sport" models came with staggered shorty dual exhaust and a return to the round-style air cleaner. Engines in the FLTs and FLHTs came with the larger "ham can" air cleaner and dual exhaust, which actually gave these larger machines more horsepower and torque to better move the extra bulk.

When the magazine test reports came in, they were just the sort of reviews Harley needed. *Cycle* magazine tested an FXRT in the November 1983 issue and raved that compared to the Shovelhead, the new V^2 Evolution engine started easier, ran cooler, vibrated less, and gave higher power and a flatter torque curve, especially at low engine speeds. In *Cycle*'s tests, power peaked at 54.64 horsepower at 5,000 rpm, and torque peaked at 68.16 ft-lbs at 3,500 rpm. Best of all, the Evo proved to be oil-tight. "In one 1,000-mile trip," *Cycle* said, "the engine consumed about 12 ounces of oil, and only a slight amount of oil mist weeped from the clutch-actuating arm. It never leaked a drop while in our hands." While Team Evo may not have lived up to the letter of the "no misting" directive, it'd made the Evo more oil-tight than many thought a Harley could ever be.

Motorcyclist magazine (January 1984) also tested the Evo-powered FXRT and was similarly pleased. Basically, the editors felt that the new motor brought out the potential in the then-recent and excellent FXRT chassis. Their final pronouncement? "For those who wanted to see if Harley could build a real, honest-to-Davidson 1984 motorcycle, feast your eyes. The '84 season is here—and Harley is right here with it."

That same issue of *Motorcyclist* also named Vaughn Beals as 1983's Motorcyclist of the Year. Because of his handling of the whole tariff issue, plus the astonishing resurgence of Harley-Davidson in late 1983, Beals was the unanimous choice of the magazine's editors for the award. This was just the kind of publicity the company needed in the months following the Evo introduction. Sales continued to rise and even held through the winter months.

DISC GLIDE AND WET CLUTCH

After the great reception of the Evos, and increased sales, times were better at The Motor Company, but they were still far from good. Needing every sale it could get, Harley released a limited-edition model, the FXRDG Disc Glide, which gave a glimpse of Harley's future because it had chrome on a whole bunch of its aluminum engine castings. (See chapter 4 for more details.)

The Evolution's dry clutch was substantially the same clutch as had been in use since the late Knucklehead days—and in those days, Harley clutches

In 1991, a revised version of the Evo motor and five-speed transmission made its debut on the Dyna Glide Sturgis. The Sturgis featured new cases that allowed the engine and tranny to bolt rigidly together. Other features included the new mounting boss for the oil filter on the front of the engine and an oil sump in a new casting underneath the transmission. Shown is a 1991 Sturgis.

were operated by a foot pedal. What the weight of a leg could easily operate, the grip of a hand had trouble with. High lever effort wasn't the only problem, though. "The dry clutch when it worked was a tremendous clutch," said Mark Tuttle. "By 'when it worked' I mean when it was kept dry. The issue was in keeping it dry while getting adequate lubrication to the primary chain."

The obvious fix was to use a "wet" clutch design (a clutch designed to run in an oil bath), so that lube for the chain and the clutch plates could live together in harmony. Design work was started long before the Evo engine was finished, but it proved a long, difficult, and controversial project.

One problem was that the "old guard" at Harley insisted that any new clutch be as powerful as the old dry clutch. "Some of this gets to be a little bizarre," explained Tuttle, "but I remember arguments because the CHP would use our motorcycles to push stalled cars off the expressway. The people in the Experimental Department said the wet clutch should continue to have enough reserve capability that you could actually push a car with our motorcycles. The designers were saying, 'Well that's unreasonable; we don't build our motorcycles for that purpose.' They said, 'OK, but they're *doing* it *now*. How can you give them a new motorcycle and say, "Oh by the way this has got the new, improved wet clutch but you can't do what you did last year"?' Also, some of our customers wanted to use sidecars. I can remember the first time we put a sidecar on a wet-clutch motorcycle. The clutch wouldn't carry the incremental load of that sidecar."

After several iterations, the designers finally got a wet clutch that performed well enough to (mostly) measure up to the dry clutch. It went into production as a running change during the 1984 model year. It worked well and had a much lighter "pull," courtesy of the diaphragm spring that replaced the coil springs in the old clutch. Even that refined version didn't have the reserve capacity it needed, however, so it was eventually updated several times during the Evo years.

All the FLT-based bikes were revised for 1993 to use Dyna-style cases. Many popular new models followed. Shown is a 1998 FLHTCUI.

IT WAS A VERY GOOD YEAR

Long before the 1984 model year ended, Beals and company knew they had a winner. The all-new, solid-mounted, Evo-powered Softail (a bike for the Harley traditionalist) was outselling everything else, and the Evo-powered versions of the rubber-mounted Harleys (bikes for the less traditional) were also selling at record pace. Both the "old faithful" and "new faithful" were embracing the Evolution engine because it looked and sounded like a Harley engine, but it didn't leak or burn enough oil to cause concern, didn't need much more maintenance than a car engine, and it didn't rattle itself apart. Harley could now give the old Shovelhead its well-earned retirement, which apparently happened in June 1984.

When all was tallied at the end of the year, Harley's domestic sales were up 31 percent, to 38,741—a phenomenal increase in a year in which the U.S. motorcycle market accelerated deeper and deeper into a death spin that would continue through the 1980s. Yamaha, for example, lost an astonishing $150 million in the United States for the year ending April 30, 1984, as it dumped thousands of Visions and XS650s for a fraction of retail. To put Yamaha's loss in perspective, it's nearly twice what Beals and friends had paid for H-D in June 1981. Ominously for Harley, though, the only bike Yamaha had no trouble selling that year was the Harley-style Virago, which was selling so quickly that some of the magazines couldn't even get one to test.

That Evo-fueled sales increase gave Harley the cash to get through 1984. Perhaps more importantly, though, the Evo-fueled quality increase completely changed Harley's reputation, which was one of the keys to the company's eventual return to prosperity. How completely and how quickly is revealed by the following story told by Mark Tuttle:

"Toward the end of the Shovelhead era, we were getting 500–600 miles per quart oil consumption, so if you were going to go ride 2,000 miles, you were going to have to carry four quarts of oil. They used to laugh that one saddlebag was reserved for oil!

"I led a ride up from San Antonio, Texas, for the 85th anniversary (in 1988). The Evolution engine had been out at that time four years, and there was only one Shovel in a group of 32 that made the trip. Every day we had a rider's meeting where we discussed the route and where we'd stop for lunch and so on. At one of those meetings, on a whim, I asked, 'How many of you are carrying any oil on your motorcycle?' They all started laughing. Nobody had any oil with him.

"The Evolution engine took oil consumption from being a significant problem to nonexistent. You needed a quart of oil when it was time to change the oil because it got 2,500–3,000 miles per quart. The Evolution engine took the user-friendliness and the reliability of our motorcycles quantum steps forward."

THE EVO TAKES OVER AND GETS BELTED

When production began for model year 1985, all the Harley Big Twins were Evo-powered. The 1985 Evo was essentially the same as the late-1984 Evo engine, with the wet clutch and either solid mounting and a four-speed transmission or rubber mounting and a five-speed transmission. Other changes included a revised starter relay, and (finally) evaporative emissions canisters on California models. The real news for 1985, though, was in the final drive, because all the Harley Big Twins except the FXEF Super Glide Fat Bob were fitted with rubber-belt final drive.

Belt-Drive Development

Why belts? Because Harley customers had long wanted an alternative to the maintenance-intensive exposed drive chain. In the late 1970s, the competition turned to shaft drive. Harley even toyed with shafts, but only very briefly because the crossways crankshaft of the Harley engine would have required two power-robbing 90-degree bends in the driveline. "We didn't have the horsepower to spare," said Vaughn Beals.

Harley's first stab at an alternative drive was the enclosed chain of the FLT for 1980. The system kept both chain and bike clean and also kept the chain well lubed and in adjustment, but it was ugly and bulky, so it was suitable only for bikes with saddlebags to hide it.

Along came the aftermarket, which began offering belt drives to replace both primary and secondary chains in the late 1970s. About the same time, Gates developed its aramid-fiber (Kevlar) belts, and according to former Harley engineer Rit Booth, Gates "wanted to make a big splash by having every Harley powered by their belts."

Harley first used rubber belts (two, final and primary) on the FXB Sturgis of 1980. Unfortunately, it took quite a while to get every Harley running belts because Harley and its suppliers had yet to perfect the process for hard-chroming mass quantities of aluminum belt sprockets. "We had a lot of problems at first with the chrome being too thin and wearing through, or being too thick and flaking off," affirmed Mark Tuttle.

As with chrome on its engines, Harley started using the belts on a limited-edition model and gradually expanded the offering to the other models. Once the initial problems were sorted out, the belts worked better than anyone had imagined. "Our design objectives were much less than what we ended up with on the belt drive," said Vaughn Beals. "We just wanted something you didn't have to oil or adjust, that didn't spray oil all over you. We got all that, but the belts also lasted much longer and looked better, too."

Rubber drive belts had been put on most of the four-speed line by 1984. For 1985, even the five-speed models had the belts. Now, it's difficult to imagine a Harley with any other final drive.

At the end of the 1985 model year, Harley's sales were down slightly (but everybody else in the industry fared much worse). Sales of the Evo Big Twins were up, some by substantial margins. The brief downturn in sales was primarily the result of slow Sportster sales and because the old rigid-mount FLH had been dropped from the line-up.

Another Money Crisis

Nevertheless, in 1985, Harley was still "operating at the pleasure of the banks," and the main banker, Citicorp Industrial Credit, was no longer pleased. Harley's main loan officer, who had been supportive through the really hard times, was replaced by another officer, one who from the start had been opposed to Citicorp's financing of Harley. "He didn't think we were gonna make it," explained Tom Gelb. Citicorp informed Harley that as of the first of 1986, Citicorp would no longer supply overadvance money to help Harley-Davidson through temporary shortfalls. "That meant we were gonna die," continued Gelb.

Rich Teerlink, then the company's chief financial officer (who recently retired as CEO) began working with Steve Deli of Dean Witter trying to put together financing to replace that of Citicorp. Teerlink and Deli eventually hooked up with Heller Financial, and at Heller found a strong ally named Bob Koe.

Harley and Dean Witter made their formal pitch to Heller just before Christmas and were turned down. While Teerlink, Deli, and Koe continued to try to put together a deal, everyone else started implementing the plans made earlier in preparation for Chapter 11 bankruptcy "because at the end of the year, we didn't have any choice," Gelb continued, "I think it was the day before the banks closed for the New Year that Heller finally agreed to make the deal, and all the money got transferred. We still operated at the pleasure of the banks, but at least we had breathing room and weren't paying this tremendous amount of interest on the overadvances. We were relieved when we found Heller, because finally we were with someone friendly."

Little-known fact: Heller Financial was then a recently acquired subsidiary of Japan's Fuji Bank. Pro-Harley forces call this bailout of Harley by a branch of a Japanese bank "ironic," while the Harley-bashers suspect that it was really just the continuation of earlier efforts to get loan guarantees to complete the Nova in exchange for Harley's requesting an early end to the tariff. More than a year later, Harley did request an early end to the tariff, but few really believe that was a result of the Fuji-Heller refinancing. Another little-known fact: The State of Wisconsin invested $10 million from its employee pension fund, as a cornerstone of the refinancing.

DESIGN OF THE EVOLUTION SPORTSTER ENGINE

If the Big Twin Evo engine was long overdue, what can you say about the Sportster engine? After all, the Big Twin had had aluminum heads and hydraulic lifters since 1948, while the Sportster had made due with iron heads and mechanical tappets since its intro in 1957. Nevertheless, a new engine had been in the works at H-D for a while, but Sportster fans had to wonder where it was.

As discussed previously, preliminary design of the Evolution Sportster engine was done in parallel with that of the Big Twin, but the Sporty was put on the back burner while all the rest of the development work was completed on the Big Twin. After the Big Twin was polished for production, serious work began on bringing the new Sportster engine to market, under engineer Bill Erdman.

Certainly, Harley-Davidson needed the new engine sooner rather than later, but the U.S. Environmental Protection Administration (EPA) supplied one big push that made the new engine mandatory for model year 1986: On January 1, 1986, the noise limit for new motorcycles would drop from 83 decibels to just 80. Big deal, 3 decibels, right? Well, 3 decibels translates to 50 percent, and it's a big job to reduce an engine's noise level by 50 percent. With its mechanical tappets and all, the old Sportster engine just wouldn't make it.

As on the Big Twin, the basic goal for the Sportster was to redesign everything from the base gasket up (with minor revisions below) to make the engine more reliable, more oil-tight, less needy of maintenance, less expensive to build, and quiet and clean-burning enough to meet all the noise and emissions requirements on the horizon—all without changing its fundamental character. Because of all that Harley's engineers had learned on the Big Twin redesign, the Sportster redesign progressed rapidly. "It took us about 18 months," said Don Valentine.

Unlike with the Big Twin, however, a low selling price was a major goal from the start. Through a series of sales necessary to clear out overstocks in 1981 and 1982, Harley had learned that when the price of the Sportster dropped below $4,000, sales as much as doubled. (For a more complete account of the story, see chapter 5.) As a result of that lesson, Harley-Davidson management decided the new Sportster would be built in two displacements, 883 cc and 1,100 cc, with the explicit goal of bringing the 883 in at a retail price of under $4,000. "I remember vividly on the 883, they gave me a price target of $3,995 retail," said Valentine. "The 883 was probably the toughest job I ever had because of that price limit."

Why 883 and 1,100 cc, when the latest iron Sportsters were 1,000 cc? "They wanted the old 55-cubic-inch, 883-cc displacement because that's what the first Sportsters had been," Valentine continued. "We went with 1,100 cc for the other because that's about all we could get in at the time. The whole purpose of the 883 was to go after the young, entry-level crowd and get them into a Harley-Davidson dealer and onto a Harley. If they then migrated to an 1100, that was fine. If they migrated to a Big Twin, that was even better. The 1100 was more for the traditional Sportster buyer."

Basically, the two versions of the engine would be similar enough that they could be made on the same tooling, yet different enough that there was reason enough to buy an 1100 if you wanted more power. "The 1100 and 883 we wanted to be substantially different," said Valentine. "My concern that I voiced to management was that if you use the same cylinder heads on the 883 and 1100, people are going to buy $3,995 motorcycles and just buy a set of 1100 jugs and pistons to make a cheap 1100."

As Valentine implied, the main differences would be limited to the cylinders, pistons, and cylinder heads. Both to save pennies and to punctuate the differences between the two Sportsters, the 1100 was given larger valves to further enhance its performance. "The 883 would have loved to have the bigger valves," he continued, "but there's a cost penalty in going to bigger valves and seats."

For the heads, pistons, and cylinders, the Sportster engineers used the same tricks as on the Big Twin: redesigned aluminum heads with smaller combustion chambers, a large squish area, a narrow 58-degree valve angle, and smaller ports; iron-lined aluminum cylinders; and flat-top pistons—all topped off by three-piece rocker covers.

Since the Evo Big Twin had been designed, a new combustion-chamber shape had come into vogue—the "shallow bathtub." This design distributes the squish area on both sides of the valve pockets, rather than putting it all on one side, as on the Big Twin's D-shaped chambers. The result is a small, bathtub-shaped chamber wrapped tightly around the valves, and that's what the Sportster engineers used.

With these more-efficient top-end parts, the engine ran cooler and cleaner. Still, a new air box was needed to further quiet intake roar, so Harley's engineers designed one just for the Sportster. The Sporty's was oblong, rather than round, but it cut the noise without strangling the 34-millimeter Keihin carb fitted to both the 883 and 1100.

Minor revisions planned for the bottom end actually turned into fairly major redesign, mostly to reduce mechanical noise. One step toward that goal, and toward reducing maintenance, was to fit hydraulic lifters, and that required replumbing the oil passages in the cases. While they were modifying the oiling system, they also increased oil-pump capacity and rerouted the oiling circuit so that the front-mounted filter strained out the dirt before the oil went to the engine, rather than on its return. Oiling to the top end was patterned after that of the Big Twin, going from the lifters, through hollow pushrods, and to the rockers.

The other major concession to the upcoming stricter noise standard was to use microphones and the valve-train modeling programs developed on the Big Twin project to try to quiet down all the gnashing of teeth from the Sportster's six-gear cam train. Ultimately, the solution to controlling cam-gear noise was more manufacturing refinement than redesign. Tom Gelb, manufacturing chief, said, "The four single camshafts were a nightmare, because the gear drive was four cam gears, the pinion gear, and an idler gear. To keep the noise down with the capabilities we had back in the 1980s was a son of a gun."

"There's kind of a funny story about that valve train that probably only I know," he continued. "In 1964 when I was plant superintendent trying to assemble all these things and couldn't get anything to fit, I went back to the engineers and said, 'Why the hell did you guys design those four camshafts? Why not a single cam or a double cam or something?' The story I got from one of the engineers was, when they designed the Sportster, they copied the Servicar engine's cam train. In 1959, they had a lot of problems manufacturing that thing, so they had a Product Planning meeting where they discussed getting rid of those four camshafts. The result was, they decided not to do it because they figured the Sportster wouldn't live that long anyway. Here it is over 40 years later, and the Sportster's still going strong, and those cam gears are still a bitch to make!"

Gelb and his production team found that precision fitting of the gears to each other and to the cam cover was the key to quieter operation, so manufacturing developed a process for automatically measuring the gears and covers in a climate-controlled room and matching them for best fit and lowest noise.

To help keep the overall height of the engine down and make it easier to remove the top end with the engine in the frame, connecting rods were shortened by a half-inch, while retaining the 3.81-inch stroke. The bore for the 883 was 3.00 inches, and that of the 1100 was 3.5 inches.

In the end, Harley claimed that of the Sportster engine's 426 parts, 206 were all new, and that there were 29 fewer overall. It was also about 9 pounds

The next big Sportster update came for 1991, when the whole engine was revised to make room for a five-speed transmission. Shown is a 1995 Hugger.

Through the Evolution years the Softail line was expanded again and again. The Softail led to the Custom and the Springer and then to the Bad Boy, built for model years 1995–1997. Shown is a 1996 model. Similarly, the Heritage led to Heritage Classics and Fat Boys and then Heritage Springers.

lighter than the old iron engine. And Valentine and the Sportster team hit its price goal. "I don't think we missed it by more than a couple bucks," he remembered. He and the team also hit their other goals as well, but that wasn't proven until the new Sportsters hit the field.

INTRODUCTION OF THE EVOLUTION SPORTSTERS

By spring of 1985, the 883 was ready to go. Dealers and the motorcycling press were given notice in April, and the $3,995 bikes started getting to dealerships in midsummer and riding out under new customers almost as quickly. The 1100s followed about a month and a half later, at a retail price of $5,199.

For the extra money, the 1100 buyer got the bigger motor, a dual seat and passenger pegs, buckhorn bars, a tachometer, different tank graphics, a bit more polish, flashier paint options, about 10 more horsepower, and a bit more vibration.

Big Twins built after December 31, 1985, had to meet the reduced noise limit of 80 decibels. Since the Evo Big Twin design effort made these engines quiet already, Harley was able to meet the standard on all its 1986 models through use of redesigned "tuned" intakes with a revised plastic resonance chamber hidden behind the air cleaner and quieter mufflers. The FXSTC Softail Custom was released as the first regular-production Evo with chrome engine covers and crinkle-black cylinders and heads. And for 1986, even the FLT and FLHT were fitted with the small round air cleaner. Goodbye ham-can!

GOING PUBLIC

Near the end of the model year, six months after the last-second Heller financing saved the company from bankruptcy, Harley-Davidson "went public" by selling its stock on the NASDAQ stock exchange. The offer was successful, so Harley-Davidson no longer operated at the pleasure of the banks. "When Steve Deli from Dean Witter told us we should go public," remembered Tom Gelb, "we all said, 'You're crazy!' But he was right. From then on, we controlled our own destiny." Over time, Harley-Davidson stock has proven a fantastic investment, rising in value and splitting again and again.

Shortly after the stock sale, Harley's Policy Committee convened at the American Club in Kohler, Wisconsin, "to figure out what to do with our new-found wealth," according to Vaughn Beals. "A key conclusion was that we would become vulnerable to reduced sales as baby-boomers aged. This led to the idea of acquiring an RV [recreational vehicle] manufacturing company because of the similarity—'bigger toys for older boys (and girls).' Almost immediately, Deli came up with the Holiday Rambler offering."

Holiday Rambler was a profitable manufacturer of luxury motorhomes, and Harley-Davidson moved quickly to acquire the company. "It was a very quick deal," said Beals. "We closed by December (1986)."

For 1987, the Big Twin engines got an all-new crankshaft assembly that consisted of three major pieces (left and right flywheels and a crankpin) instead

of the five (left and right flywheels, crankpin, pinion shaft, and sprocket shaft) that had been used from time immemorial. Instead of being cast-iron, with pressed-in main shafts, each flywheel was forged from steel to include the mainshaft, and then machined to final shape.

Why the change, after so many years of faithful service? Several reasons, actually, including some failures under the increased torque of the Evolution engine, but the main reason was ease of manufacture. The old flywheels and shafts had to be machined with matching tapers and keyways, and then had to be assembled and trued on the production line. "We used to straighten all those crankshafts with big copper hammers," remembered Tom Gelb. "We'd take the assembly after we had the rods and the bearings on there, put the thing between centers and try to true it up by banging on it with those big hammers. Now the things barely even get touched."

Also new on the Big Twin powertrain was a new one-piece tranny main drive gear , a ball-and-ramp clutch actuating mechanism, and a stylish ribbed end cover.

During the model year, both Sportster engines got new cylinder heads. These new castings were made in a low-pressure die-casting process that gave "cleaner" looks than did the old sand-casting process. Both also got revisions to their combustion chambers, from a "bathtub" shape to a hemispherical shape, which was suddenly back in vogue. The 1100 heads were also given smaller ports and valves that, along with changes to the ignition advance and mufflers, resulted in a claimed 5 percent improvement in power.

Sportster gearboxes were gone over, too, raising the perceived gearing (lower numerical ratios) of first through third gears to get closer spacing of the gears.

In the news, on March 17, 1987, Harley-Davidson petitioned the International Trade Commission to end the tariff. On May 16, 1987, President Ronald Reagan visited the York, Pennsylvania, assembly plant and gave a speech announcing the early end to the tariff. On July 1, 1987, Harley-Davidson stock was listed on the New York Stock Exchange. On October 10, 1987, Harley-Davidson bought the manufacturing rights for the MT500 military motorcycles from Armstrong Equipment of England. Overall sales rose by about 7 percent.

THE XLH-1200 SPORTSTER ENGINE AND THE 1988 UPDATES

The big engine news was all Sportster for 1988. The 1,100-cc Sportster engine was replaced by a new 1,200-cc Sportster engine, created by increasing the bore to 3.5 inches. Harley's "small" engine wasn't anymore. It now displaced 74 cubic inches, the same as the Big Twin engines prior to the displacement increase to 1,340 cc, or 80 cubic inches, that began in 1978.

With the increased cubes came more horsepower and torque (what would be the point otherwise?)—12 percent and 10 percent more, respectively. It didn't all come from the displacement, however. Redesigned camshafts helped some, and a larger carb helped a bunch. The new 40-millimeter carb was of the CV (constant-velocity) type. Compared to the old 34-millimeter butterfly carb, the new CV gave smoother running and more top-end power. It also had

Even the Sportsters got their own version of the chrome-and-black engine treatment on the 1200C Sportster Custom, first produced for the 1996 model year. Shown is a 2001 model.

the inherent flow potential to serve on even hot-rodded Sportsters. Even the smaller 883s got the larger carb.

Big Twins got new lower rocker covers and revised gaskets. Forty-nine-state models got new camshafts with greater duration and lift. To meet the ever-tightening CARB emissions standards, California models got cams with 24 percent less intake duration, 28 percent less exhaust duration, and 14 percent less lift. All that earlier work in getting its casting suppliers to make higher quality castings and in getting its chrome plater up to speed was finally paying off, too. The black-and-chrome engines were now available in even the FLT and FLHT models.

The tough times were finally becoming good times for The Motor Company by 1988. Though the U.S. motorcycle market was down 28 percent, Harley's sales were up by nearly 14 percent, surpassing 40,000 for the first time since the crash of the U.S. motorcycle market in 1982. Celebrity converts began showing up everywhere (even in the 1988 Harley catalog) on their Harleys, turning The Motor Company's products into American icons.

Updates were few for 1989. All the Big Twins got the larger alternator from the police models, which was rated for 32 amps (rather than 22). More importantly, it was redesigned to correct some of the faults of the previous design—the stator plug would disconnect itself from the plug to the main wiring harness, and the thick insulation on the stator would cause the unit to overheat—so it gave more power and better reliability. Big Twins also got a new, more powerful "compound" starter. Softails also got revised primary cases, on which the starter mounted pointing inward toward the engine rather than forward.

The U.S. motorcycle market continued its death spin, as new bike sales fell a further 28 percent. In 1989, the market for street bikes was one-third the size it had been in 1981. The only bright spot was for Harley-Davidson. The Motor Company's sales rose 17 percent, to 55,507, the first time the company had topped 50,000 since 1976, and even more impressive when you consider that back in 1976, many of those sales were of the Aermacchi two-strokes, while in 1989 they were all Sportsters and Big Twins. Once again, Harley took the lead in sales of over-850-cc motorcycles, with 46.5 percent of the market. Another new trend: Sales figures were starting to reflect Harley-Davidson's production capacity more than the actual demand. Waiting lists began for the most popular models.

For 1990, the Big Twins caught up to the Sportsters in getting the 40-millimeter CV Keihin carburetor. As it had on the Sportsters, the new carb gave much better low-speed response and more top end, too. Lower rocker covers and gaskets were updated again, as another (and largely successful) fix for seepage at the rocker boxes.

While the old clutch had been strong enough for stock power, it slipped or broke under hot-rodding and severe use, so Harley engineers completely redesigned it for 1990 with a new hub (with steel "fingers" replacing the aluminum ones of the old), twice the plate area, and a stouter spring. This wet clutch was strong enough to handle almost twice the stock horsepower, and even pushing cars with your motorcycle. Sportsters got few updates because the whole engine was due for replacement the next year.

Harley's sales were up again, by about 7 percent, but that probably doesn't truly reflect demand because by this time, Harley-Davidson was operating at

A new Sportster model was introduced for 1996: the 1200S Sportster Sport. For 1998, the Sport engine was upgraded with dual-plug heads and single-fire ignition. Shown is a 2000 model.

capacity for many models, so the numbers reflect what it was capable of building rather than what it was capable of selling. For the year, Harley-Davidson captured a 62.3 percent share of the 850-cc-plus part of the market. Honda, Harley's closest competitor, had about 16 percent. These sales came despite the fact that Harley's best customer and perhaps most flamboyant booster, publisher Malcolm Forbes, died on February 24.

THE FIVE-SPEED SPORTSTER

Nineteen ninety-one was a really surprising year for The Motor Company and its powerplants. Most prominent and long overdue was a nearly all-new Sportster powerplant with a five-speed transmission. A new variation on the Big Twin powerplant was offered, too, in the new, limited-edition Dyna Glide Sturgis, which introduced several new features that would spread to other models in the line.

Five-Speed Sportster

In 1991 Sportster fans rejoiced when a new Sportster hit the show-room floors with—at long last—a five-speed gearbox. This was the first real upgrade to the Sportster transmission since the Sportster was created by grafting on an OHV top end onto the old side-valve Model KH. While some would argue that the Big Twins really didn't need a five-speed, almost everyone agreed that the Sportster did. Everyone also agreed that it took too damn long to get it.

Why did it take so long? And why wasn't it done when Harley did the change from the old iron engine to the Evo engine? Simply, it was a *really* big job, bigger than Harley had the resources to do at the time. The existing Sportster cases just didn't have room for the fifth gear set and were a bit on the weak side anyway, so it became a major and expensive revision from the base gasket down. Since this wasn't compatible with the goal of making the Evo engine cheap enough to produce that the 883 version could be sold (profitably) for $3,995, it was put on the back burner for the day when The Motor Company had more money, more engineers, and more time.

With the return to prosperity in the later 1980s, Harley finally had the resources to complete the job. Since new cases were necessary to get that fifth gear set, the company took the opportunity to change a bunch of other things, as well, turning the whole redesign into a bigger project than the redesign of the old iron-barrel Sporty engine into the Evo had been.

First, the tranny. Every part in it was completely redesigned and updated to modern practice, with a rotary shift drum like that of the Big Twin tranny, and all the parts reworked to mesh better and be easier to manufacture and assemble without having to shim for all the fits. Ratios were juggled for a broader spread of gearing, with a lower first, and a higher fifth (actually, fifth was "direct-drive," with a 1:1 ratio). The 1200 was given a higher primary ratio of 1.600:1 to lower engine rpm. The 883s got revised final-drive ratios.

Next, the engine. Again, it would be more accurate to say "all new" than "revised." The only major parts that weren't changed were the cylinders, pistons, and connecting rods. The redesigned cases included more internal passages to eliminate oil lines, the lifters were pinned to resist rotating in their

bores, and the breather system was revised to a new "head-breather" type that included umbrella valves in the rocker boxes.

Clutch and alternator were completely redesigned, too, to eliminate all the problems with the combined clutch and alternator that had been introduced on the iron Sportsters in mid-1984. The clutch worked fine; the problem was that the magnets of the alternator's rotor were part of the clutch basket. To work well, clearance between the alternator's rotor and stator had to be 0.060 inch or less. If any of the bearings in the clutch got a bit sloppy, or the chain was adjusted too tight or had a tight spot, or a combination of all these, the magnets of the rotor would crash into the stator and take out the charging system.

On the five-speed Sportster, clutch and alternator were separated. The clutch stayed where it had always been, but the new 32-amp, Big Twin-style alternator was moved to its new home on the left end of the crankshaft assembly, where it was spun at the higher crankshaft speed for better output at low rpm.

In the end, the results were worth all the work. The 883 and 1200 Sportster engines were stronger, the charging system was more bulletproof, the oiling and breather systems were cleaner and more effective, the shifting was far smoother, and the whole powertrain was easier and less expensive to produce.

In addition to the new engine and tranny, the 1200 and 883 Deluxe both were fitted with belt drive. Because of the Sportster's lower weight and power, Harley-Davidson was able to fit a narrower belt to the smaller twins—1.25 inches vs. 1.5 inches for the Big Twin.

"Optimum Evolution" and the Dyna Glide

In the early 1980s, work was begun on a program called "Optimum Evolution." Basically, the Optimum program was another concept by Hank Hubbard, this one to finish the job started with the Evolution. That is, it would take the new top end that was the Evo and mate it with an updated bottom end to create a really new engine. Hubbard tried many different updates on the Optimum, including a one-piece nodular iron crankshaft with side-by-side connecting rods, dual cams instead of the single four-lobe cam of the Evo, a direct mounting interface between the engine and transmission, and a single counterbalancing shaft. Ultimately, the offset-cylinder design (necessary with the side-by-side rods) was rejected because it made the engine wider and compromised the styling too much.

Some parts of Optimum were used, however. First, Hubbard's rigid interface between the engine and transmission was a feature introduced on the new Dyna Glide Sturgis of 1991 (the Dyna Glide chassis was originally started to carry the Optimum engine; see chapter 6). Second, the two-cam concept was later revived when work began on the P22 project that ultimately resulted in the Twin Cam 88 engine.

To get the rigid tranny-engine mounting (in effect creating a unit-construction powertrain), the engine and transmission cases were redesigned to include a mounting interface on each. And while they were doing that, they added other meaningful updates. Most noticeable was that a boss for the oil filter was added to the front of the engine. Most importantly, the oil tank was incorporated within a new casting underneath the transmission. This did three

Though it was a fine machine, the FLT never proved popular with Harley's customers and was finally canceled for 1997. After making subtle refinements to the fairing and front fender that totally transformed the look, Harley rereleased a new version of the FLT, the FLTR Road Glide, for 1998. Shown is a 1998 injected Road Glide.

For 1999 and 2000, Harley's Parts and Accessories Division assembled the special-edition FXR^2, FXR^3, and FXR^4. These machines were fitted with nearly every chrome and billet cover and accessory imaginable to dress up the engine and chassis. Shown is a 1999 FXR^2.

things. It eliminated the need to find space on the frame for the oil tank. It made oil routing easier and more reliable (oil lines didn't have to run between the stationary frame and the vibrating engine). It also eliminated the long-standing problem of "wet-sumping" during periods of disuse by storing the oil below the level of the oil pump so that it couldn't drain past a leaky check valve and fill the sump. Soon, these features would be passed on to other Big Twin models.

Other Big Twin Updates

In addition to the changes incorporated into the Dyna, all the Big Twins got fairly major powertrain changes in 1991. First, the crankcases were redesigned to eliminate the steel inserts for the main bearings. In the late 1980s, Harley had been replacing a lot of cases under warranty when the inserts failed or began allowing oil to transfer from within the crankcase to within the primary. This update seems to have fixed that problem for good. Big Twins also got an updated pinion gear, and transmissions got a redesigned mainshaft.

Demand outstripped production capacity by wide margins for most models. As a result, waiting lists and surcharges above retail price became the norm for Harley customers into the new century.

For 1992, the Big Twin engine got major updates. All the Big Twins got revised cases with the oil filter boss out front, as on the Dyna engines of 1991, and a breather system redesigned to vent through the cylinder heads

and then into the carburetor (as on the five-speed Sportster). Everybody loved the convenience of the new oil-filter arrangement, but some weren't so sure about the new breather system. The new breather worked well for normal highway or in-town use. Unfortunately, it became known for dumping oil into the air box under extended high-rpm use. Carburetors had recalibrated jetting for easier cold-starting. As a running change in January 1992, the factory switched to an INA-type cam bearing (from a Torrington type). This is another update that stood up well in normal service but not so well under hot-rodding.

Only one notable change was made to the Sportster engine. In April, a new oil-pump gear was introduced. The new gear was made of iron and proved to be more durable, especially in hot-rodded Sportsters driven at high rpm.

Nineteen ninety-three was the company's 90th anniversary and a cause for celebration, rather than change. In June, about 100,000 believers joined the celebration in Milwaukee. The only major powertrain changes fitted to all the Big Twin models were a new front belt pulley with 50 percent more spline area and revised cylinder studs introduced midyear. The FLHT-based models got a new transmission case and undertranny oil tank similar to those of the Dyna. The basic 883 and the 883 Hugger both (finally) got belt drive.

The Evo engine, close to bulletproof from the start, had slowly been refined to the point where it was bombproof. Changes started trickling off to almost none in the last years of the Evo Big Twin and the recent years of the Evo Sportster. That doesn't mean all those powertrain engineers were just sitting back, though. A little program dubbed "P22" was being refined in Milwaukee, and it had two parts—"alpha" and "beta." More on this later. No one else at the company was sitting back, either. Major emphasis was put on increasing production capacity to meet demand, as waiting lists stretched out to more than a year for the most popular models.

The major update for the 1994 Big Twins was a revision of the primary ratio to put the gearing more in the starter's favor in turning over the engine. Midyear, new cylinder studs and base gaskets were introduced that really helped eliminate base-gasket leaks. Sportsters got a new primary cover in 1994.

In 1995, Dynas got a new inner primary with more ribs to stiffen it. Also that year, a 30th Anniversary Electra Glide was offered, the FLHTCI, with fuel injection. The FLHTCI's sequential port fuel injection, a first for The Motor Company, gave the injected Electra Glide 10 percent more torque and easier starting. Sportsters received a revised clutch-release mechanism to work with a new quick-change clutch cable.

In 1996, stronger, quieter high-contact-ratio (HCR) gears were introduced, and fuel injection was used on three of the big FLHT models. In 1997, the fuely models got a much-more-powerful, 45-amp, ultra-high-output (UHO) alternator. Sportsters got freer breathing intakes and exhausts for a bit more power.

In 1998, the Sportster 1200S was given a hotter version of the Sportster engine, with new cams, higher compression (10:1 instead of 9:1), single-fire ignition, and dual spark plugs in each head to hold pinging at bay. These changes gave the 1200S about 10 percent more horsepower and torque than the regular 1200. All the Sportsters got a new oil pump designed for better scavenging of oil from the crankcase. Big Twins got a clutch update to lower lever effort.

The 2000 FXR^4 will likely be the very last we see of both the Evolution engine and the FXR chassis. Instead of chrome and black, the engine of the last of the Evo Big Twins is chrome and silver powdercoat.

THE TWIN CAM 88 AND BEYOND

The "alpha" part of the P22 development program became a production reality with the introduction of the Twin Cam 88 engine, which became Harley's main Big Twin engine for model year 1999, fitted to all models except the Softails.

While the Evolution was mainly an update "from the base gasket up," the Twin Cam was essentially all new, top to bottom. (By 1999, though, you could also call the Evo all new from top to bottom, too, because nearly every part of it had been updated between 1984 and 1999.)

Between the increased production capacity Harley was gaining every year and the continued increases in demand, Harley gained the U.S. sales lead during the Evolution Big Twin's last year. We're not just talking the over-850-cc category here,

either. Combined sales of the Big Twins and Sportsters surpassed the U.S. sales of the whole Honda line for the first time since we all met the nicest people on them in the early 1960s. That's a hell of a send-off for the engine that made it all possible to get to this point—the Evolution Big Twin.

Though 1999 was the end for the Evo Big Twin (except for the special-edition FXR^4 models, the only 2000-model Big Twins to the carry the Evo motor), the Evo Sportster soldiered on. For 1999, it got silver powdercoat on engine cases. For 2001, the 1200S got black ceramic exhaust pipes and mufflers. It's too soon to tell whether the Evo Sporty engine will survive another year.

But enough about engines. The real fun's in the motorcycles they power. And the many models of Evo-powered Big Twins and Sportsters are the subjects of the chapters to follow.

CHAPTER 2

The FX and Softail Models

1984 – 1999

GETTING IN TOUCH WITH HARLEY'S "SOFT SIDE"

"Our big advantage was that we understood the soft side of the business. Our friends from Japan never did."

—**Vaughn Beals, former Chairman and CEO**

The hidden rear suspension of the Softail chassis re-created the look of a hardtail frame, making it possible for Harley to build a modern version of its classic Hydra-Glide from the 1950s. With its combination of modern technology and classic styling, the 1986 1/2 Heritage Softail started a nostalgic trend that has now spread to the automotive world. A 1987 1100 Sportster and a 2000 FXR[4] rest in the background.

When the new Evo Big Twin engine made its debut for 1984, Harley was definitely strutting its technical stuff, with improvements that showed the company was back on track in mastering the "hard side" of the business—engines, chassis, and so on.

That was only half the story, however. It wasn't even the important half.

Also on hand that day was an all-new motorcycle that served notice that Harley-Davidson was also back on track when it came to mastering the "soft side." That new model (the only new Big Twin that year) was the FXST Softail, a masterful combination of the best of the new Harley-Davidson, with the best of the old. It came from Harley's collective "heart," rather than its "head."

So, what's this soft side Chairman Beals was talking about?

In the broadest terms, it's a lot of intangible stuff that some call "marketing." Really, though, it's much more than that; it's a unifying philosophy, one that drives everyone at the company. In Harley's case, that philosophy came from listening to its customers.

While the ink was still drying on the buy-back agreement, Beals and some of the other officers got serious about listening. They rode home from the signing in York to Milwaukee, visiting with dealers and riders at every stop. Then they started spending more time at motorcycle rallies and listening some more. Eventually, they formed the Harley Owner Group (HOG) and really got an earful.

Much of what they heard was encouraging. Riders and dealers alike loved the improvements in function and reliability the company was making. Everyone—even the motorcycle press—loved the reduced vibration, stiffer frames, and better handling. They all commented how the new machines were better than the old FL models in every way that's measurable on performance charts and spec sheets. As a result, the FLT (see Chapter 3) and FXR (see Chapter 4) won new respect for the company and new converts to the Harley fold at a time when both were in desperately short supply.

Success, right?

Not so fast. Sure, even the "old faithful" appreciated the reduced vibration and better handling when they took a test drive, but a large and dedicated group of them didn't buy because all that "improvement" came at the expense

Conceived in the mind of independent engineer Bill Davis and given birth in Milwaukee, the FXST Softail was an instant hit when released for model year 1984. Shown is a 1985 model, which differed from the 1984 Softail in only a few minor details.

of the one point on which these folks would not compromise: the traditional Harley look.

See, those rubber mounts that made the FLT and FXR so much smoother required room for the motor to dance around, so the frames were no longer "shrink-wrapped" around the engines. Triangles replaced teardrops as the basic form. "If that's what it takes to get rid of the vibration," these folks'd tell you, "serve my vibes straight up. And anyway, Harleys don't vibrate, they *throb*." Rubber? "Just a barrier between a man (or a woman) and a really good time." You're free to call them what you want, but we'll call them "traditionalists" here.

"We heard it from them all the time," Beals told me. "They [the FLT and FXR] don't look like a Harley should look; they look Japanese."

Ouch! "Japanese!?" Talk about a size 13 engineer boot to the 'nads!

It hurt enough that everyone from the top on down got the lesson: Improve the bikes, if you will, but in the end it's gotta look like a Harley or we're not gonna buy it. It's a soft-side lesson The Motor Company is not likely to ever forget, and all the new models designed since about 1984 are the product of it.

Which brings us back to the subject of this chapter, the FXST Softail, the first product of Harley's new soft side, and the other Evo FX models.

SOFTAIL SAGA

The standard story of the production Softail's origin started in the magazine reports of the day and has been carried through in numerous books ever since. It goes like this: At a motorcycle event he was attending, Harley chief Vaughn Beals saw a homemade prototype of the Softail that an independent engineer (whom we shall soon meet) had built. Beals liked it so much, he talked the engineer into selling the idea.

Ask Beals, though, and he'll tell you (or at least he told me), "That's a fairy tale."

So, let's dispense with the fairy tale and get on to the real story of the Softail. We don't need a fairy tale because what we've got here is a real-life "Cinderella Story" (in the *Caddyshack* sense).

Call this bike Softail One. Bill Davis' first iteration of what became the Softail rear end was built onto his customized 1972 Super Glide, shown here. Davis loved the hardtail look but liked to ride long distances, so he needed a hardtail that wasn't so hard on the tail. This bike's now part of the Harley-Davidson collection. *Bill Davis photo*

Here's how he got it. His first system used the triangular swingarm shown, along with a snowmobile shock absorber and twin springs up under the seat. *Bill Davis photo*

I'll Walk The Line

Rewind way back, to the Year of Our Hog 1936, year one of what many call "The Line" and year one of the modern Harley. That year saw the release of Harley's first real styling masterpiece, the Model E 61-cubic-inch OHV V-Twin, commonly known as the "Knucklehead," and probably the most stylistically influential motorcycle ever built.

What's "The Line"? Look closely at the photo of the 1936 Knuckle in this chapter, and your eyes will naturally pick it up. There it is, that unbroken line that extends from the top line of the teardrop-shaped tank all the way down and back to the rear axle. That line and the way it extended the teardrop of the tank were the hallmarks of the Big Twin look from 1936 until the late 1950s. Both have been carried forward to this day as an essential styling element of the best-looking customs, and mimicked around the world. You saw it on the choppers once the custom movement broke into the mainstream. You see it today on any number of Softail knock-offs from Japan.

That first Knucklehead was to motorcycle design what the Gee Bee racers were to aviation design. Both machines embody the philosophy that "the

Here are the springs and the shock. This arrangement worked well, but the shock and springs took up the room under the seat that Davis wanted for a horseshoe oil tank, and forced a higher seat height than he wanted. On this version, he used the vertical oil tank shown on the left side of the bike. *Bill Davis photo*

teardrop is the perfect form," taken to the most radical extreme. The Gee Bee consisted of a stubby teardrop fuselage with wings and tailplanes tacked on. The Knuckle was a teardrop tank superimposed on top of a teardrop profile, with a rear wheel tacked on.

The Line was first partially broken (in the name of progress) on the 1958 Duo-Glide, when a swingarm and twin shocks replaced the old hardtail rear frame. Nevertheless, an onlooker's imagination could easily fill in the missing pieces on the Duo-Glide, because all the other styling cues were still there.

That all ended in 1965. That year, The Line was discarded completely when Harley-Davidson redesigned the FLH frame to accommodate further progress—the electric starter that gave the Electra Glide its name. The sheer size of the 12-volt battery needed to run the starter meant that it would no longer fit inside the cavity of the traditional horseshoe oil tank, so that lovely link to the past was also discarded. The upper frame rails were bent almost horizontal at the rear to make room for the new battery box on the right and rectangular oil tank on the left. These new pieces so larded up the E-Glide's midriff that even the strongest imagination was strained to find The Line. Say good-bye to The Line and hello to the Hog.

Willie and the Poor Boys

By the time the Electra Glide appeared, change was happening fast in all the concentric circles of American society, but especially fast in the circles occupied by Harley-Davidson. The days of the big AMA clubs riding in formation with their squeaky-clean matching uniforms and decked-out FLHs were long past, as long past as "I Like Ike" buttons and outrageous tailfins on cars. The uniform of the era had become faded Levi's, tall leather engineer boots, and a scuffed leather jacket. And the ultimate ride was a stripped and modified Big Twin.

But these weren't the stripped "bobbers" of previous decades, either. They weren't stripped to make them lighter for racing (or to look like they'd been); these bikes were stripped purely for style—more specifically to set them apart from Dad's old "decked" Duo-Glide.

Fenders weren't just bobbed—they were sometimes thrown away altogether. Same with the other practical features Harley built into the FLH—like front brakes, sprung seats, 16-inch tires, electric starters, and shock

Before Harley bought the design, Davis began selling aftermarket versions of his frame. Here, Davis is shown with six frames he built with a revised, twin-shock design and "wishbone" downtubes for even more of the 1940s look. *Bill Davis photo*

absorbers. In their places sprouted skinny, 19- and 21-inch front tires on extended forks, tiny "peanut" and coffin tanks, stepped saddles, and hardtail frames. The bobber became the chopper, and the whole styling movement took each of these features to more decadent extremes with each passing year, until the average guy just couldn't keep up. After all, not everyone's a welder, a sheet metal bender, or a custom painter.

The predictable result? A whole new industry fired up to meet their needs, producing tanks, fenders, wheels, and even hardtail frames for the real hardcores.

One look at the Harley-Davidson accessory catalogs of the day will tell you how out of touch the company was. Want chrome trinkets, extra lights, bologna-slicer bumpers, or saddlebags? Got 'em. Lots of 'em. Want a tall sissybar or a skinny front wheel (let alone a 10-inch-over fork)? Get the hell out of my dealership, kid!

Bad as that was for the company's bottom line, the real problem the chopper movement presented for Harley-Davidson was that these guys intended to strip off so much of the FLH anyway that they saw no need to buy new, getting by quite nicely with the castoff Knuckleheads and Panheads of yesteryear.

Fortunately, at least one person at H-D Central was watching—Willie G. Davidson. He'd been watching for a while, too, first when he was in design school in California and later at events he attended after joining The Motor Company in 1963. Even more fortunate: He held the keys to the styling department.

Here was opportunity, and Willie made good on it by making the first example of what would later become known as the "factory custom," the FX Super Glide. Reportedly, Willie had refined the concept and had it all ready to go by about 1967, but those in charge (including, some say, his own father, the president of the company) thought the new model would only take away from Sportster sales. Thus, it didn't come to market until 1971, when AMF was calling the shots.

"Custom," the Super Glide really wasn't, except that it was a canny mixing of standard factory parts: the taller, skinnier front end and boat-tail seat off the Sportster grafted onto the FLH plus unique tank graphics. As we all know by now, it worked better than anyone (except maybe Willie G.) had predicted—mostly because anyone who had the money could go down to any Harley

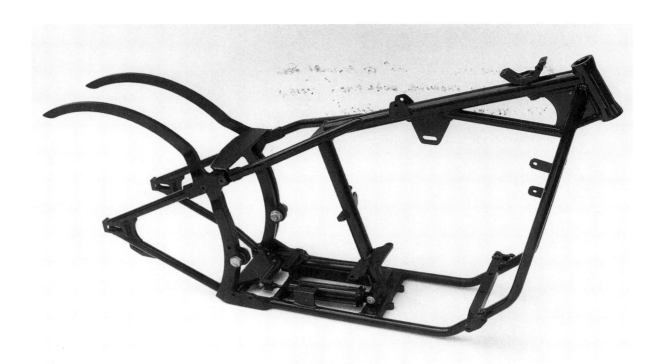

After several revisions on the basic design, Davis hit upon the idea that made the whole hardtail look possible: He put the shocks under the transmission and designed them to work in extension rather than compression. The shocks shown are actually made of urethane, which acts as both spring and damper but didn't last as long as Davis had hoped. After that, he designed more conventional hydraulically damped shocks and began advertising the frame as the "Sub Shock." *Bill Davis photo*

dealer and ride away on a factory rendition of the latest styling trend, with no cutting torch required. Best of all, the Super Glide created its own niche; its excellent sales record that first year didn't come at the expense of FLH or Sportster sales.

Customizing trends moved on, and Willie did the best he could (within a large corporate structure) to keep pace, first with electric start and a new single tank on the Super Glide, and then with a lowered, raked, and even more customized version of the FX called the Low Rider. After that came the Fat Bob, a Super Glide with the saddle tanks and speedo-and-tach dash of the Low Rider. Willie struck again in 1980 with the Wide Glide, featuring even more of the chopper look. Next, Willie took the lead with the Sturgis, a new version of the Low Rider sporting the "drag-bike" look: long, low, lean, and blacked out, and featuring rubber belts in place of both the primary and drive chains. Successes all, the FX line of "cruisers" started a whole new tradition for The Motor Company and won a whole new customer base.

To these customers, form was far more important than function. Most never intended to ride for hours on end, so vibration, too-low or too-high bars, forward controls, and minor contortions to adapt to the riding position dictated by the styling were of small concern. It's easy to scoff and dismiss these folks as "fashion victims" or some other slur, but before you do, answer me this: Is the 6-foot-4 dentist in full leathers pretzeled onto a Ducati 916 or other stubby racer replica any less a victim of fashion?

Even easier to scoff at was the "hardest core" of the custom set, for whom form dictated that even rear suspension was taboo. Why? You see, shock absorbers forced an unpardonable sin: they cluttered up the clean look of a rigid rear end and broke The Line.

Hardtails and the Hardcore

Some of these hardtailers just kept customizing the pre-1958 Big Twins, while others made their own hardtails from later Harleys (and other makes) using aftermarket frames or welded-in rear sections. But for every guy who accepted all the consequences to have that clean, uncluttered look to his bike's rear end, there were a hundred who wished they didn't have to. What they wanted was the gain without the pain.

Bill Davis, a young mechanical engineer and motorcycle enthusiast from the St. Louis, Missouri, area, was one of them. "I loved the custom hardtail look," said Davis, "but my interest was in long trips, so I couldn't live with the horrid, uncomfortable ride of the rigid."

Predictably, several small aftermarket manufacturers set themselves up to cash in on the desire for the painless hardtail. Most settled on variations of the old "plunger-style" rear suspension (in which only the axle was sprung) that had been used by Indian, BMW, and many other manufacturers in prior decades. "To me, these weren't very efficient," continued Davis, and worse yet, "they didn't look like a rigid, either." The market agreed, and plunger rear ends soon faded back into history. (As an aside, one of these ill-fated systems was even marketed as the "Softail" for a time.)

The Father of the Softail

A mechanical engineer by training and a tinkerer by temperament, Bill Davis looked at the problem and came up with a better idea—one that had actually been tried before, but for different reasons. To get the hardtail look, he designed a triangular swingarm with the pivot on a vertical member between the upper and lower arm and the springs and shocks under the seat, similar in concept to the design Vincent had used in the 1940s. Yamaha also introduced a similar idea on its dirt bikes in the 1970s and some street bikes of the early 1980s.

Function was the driving force in using the design for both Vincent and Yamaha, so both companies flaunted their rear suspension. Davis was after style, so his design was complicated somewhat by the need to hide the fact that it really *was* suspension.

Davis worked out the design for the swingarm and rear frame modifications on paper in 1974–1975 and immediately went to work building the swingarm and grafting it onto his 1972 Super Glide. To get The Line, he bent the frame rails down so they lined up with the top rails of the swingarm. For the suspenders in the new system, Davis used a shock absorber from a snowmobile, flanked by two heavy springs. These he hid under the seat and behind the seat post. The frame and undercarriage hid the swingarm pivot.

Though the modified frame and new swingarm had the hardtail look, some refining was still required to get a lower seat height and to find room for a modified version of the classic "horseshoe" oil tank under the seat. Before long, it was finished and on the road. "It performed very well," remembered Davis, "but the springs were too soft. I replaced them with heavier ones, and it was perfect." So he took it on long trips. "Everywhere I went," he said, "people who really knew Harleys told me how much they loved it." We'll call this historic machine Softail One.

Reaction was such that he began to think of building and selling copies of his frame, so he hired a patent attorney and filed patents on the design. Then, Davis got another great idea: Why not show it to Harley? Why not, indeed? Davis picked up the phone, dialed Harley's number, and asked for Willie G. "In those days, they'd put you right through," Davis remembered. "Nowadays, all you'll get is a recording." Willie G. seemed receptive, so they arranged a meeting.

"I rode the bike up to Milwaukee accompanied by a friend who had just bought a Gold Wing," Davis remembered. "It was August 1976, and it was hot!" After going inside the Juneau Avenue plant and meeting with Louie Netz (Willie G.'s right-hand man in Styling), Davis and his friend escorted Netz and some engineers outside to see Davis' faux hardtail. Later, Willie G. came down, too.

Willie G. and Louie N. looked at it from every angle. Eyebrows were raised. The engineers looked even closer. Chins were scratched.

"They were very impressed," remembered Davis, "but they didn't really make any commitments. I didn't hear from them again until about six months later. I got a letter from Willie G. that said, 'Our engineering plate's full right now, but we *are* interested.'"

"After that," Davis continued, "I figured, maybe I can make it myself. So I continued to improve the design to make it easier to manufacture." After building jigs and fixtures, Davis cranked out "6 to 10" frames for other customizers in the St. Louis area. While building the frames, he devised a way to further lower the seat height by using twin shocks (still under the seat, but parallel to the frame rails) and a new oil tank that got him closer to the look he was after. He built "about a dozen" of these frames and even designed and built a similar frame for Sportsters.

Meanwhile, a guy brought his Knucklehead to Davis for some frame work. While at Davis' shop, the Knuckle guy saw Davis' new design and fell for it—hard. He asked Davis if he wanted to form a company to make and sell the frame.

"He was a sales guy, almost mesmerizing, real good with business and people," said Davis. "Really, he was the perfect complement for my personality. When I agreed, he just took the ball and really ran with it." (Davis prefers not to give his former partner's name, so let's call him the "Business Guy," "BG" for short.)

First, the BG did marketing studies and sent out questionnaires within the industry to test the market. Then, he arranged a loan to start the business while Davis continued refining the design for production and building tooling. Before long, they'd set up a shop, and selected a company name: Road Worx.

During all this, Harley called. This time it was Jeff Bleustein (then Harley's vice president of engineering, now CEO). Bleustein liked the concept and advocated for it within the company. He told Davis that Harley was still highly interested in making an offer for the design, so Davis journeyed to Milwaukee to discuss the offer. Harley's offer seemed "lowball," so Davis talked with his lawyer and asked for more. Harley then upped the offer, but not enough to change Davis' mind.

The "Sub Shock"

Returning home disappointed once again, Davis continued working on the last real problem with the design: He kept having to raise the seat to keep the springs from scraping on the seat pan. He tried several ideas before true inspiration struck.

"In desperation, almost," remembered Davis, "I figured out a way to fit the shocks underneath the tranny. It was really tight, but that solved all my problems with seat height and using a really good-looking horseshoe oil tank." (As an aside, motorcycles with underengine springs or shocks had also been tried in the past, even by Harley-Davidson, on the 175-cc Model BH Scat of 1963.)

Unfortunately, it also created formidable challenges. "All the shocks that I knew of at that time operated in compression," he said. "But my system

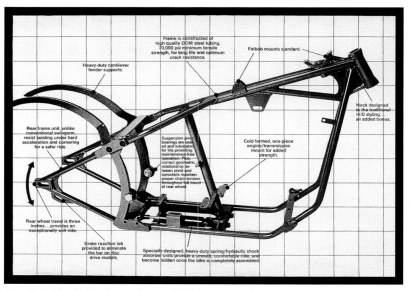

The Sub Shock brochure shows the frame and lists its many unique features. This is the design Harley used as the basis for the Softail. *Bill Davis*

required shocks to operate in tension. And I didn't have much room because if the shocks were too large, they'd bottom out on the road." He ended up making the "shocks" out of cylinders of polyurethane, a polymer that served as both spring and damper because the material is self-damping by nature.

Davis quickly built a prototype of the improved rear end, and testing began. Over many miles and subtle refinements, he modified his new design and added innovative features such as Teflon-lined spherical swingarm bearings and belt drive. Eventually, Davis and the BG settled on a name for it: "Sub Shock."

In early August, satisfied that the Sub Shock was working well, Davis and the BG headed out on Softail One and the new Sub Shock bike, hoping to create a stir among the tens of thousands of Harley faithful gathered at Sturgis, South Dakota.

It wasn't to be, however. Along the way, the polyurethane cylinders on the Sub Shock began to take a "set" and Davis' new creation began acting more and more like a real hardtail. Heat building up in the enclosed shocks was gradually breaking down the polyurethane, so the BG decided to bail, turning the Sub Shock bike back toward St. Louie, while Davis went on to South Dakota on Softail One. Further misfortune struck once Davis reached Deadwood, when a bunch of his stuff was stolen from his saddlebags. Disgusted, Davis headed for home without ever showing the bike at Sturgis.

Upon his return home, Davis finally settled on a solution for the spring and damper problems: "I realized I had to use the tried and true metal spring and oil-damper system for the shock absorber. Still, there wasn't much room for the springs, so I ended up using die springs. They're powerful and are designed to stand up to lots of cycles, but they're also expensive."

With all the bugs worked out of the Sub Shock design, Davis and the BG took on another partner, a mechanic and fabricator. "He was a real asset to

Road Worx introduces... "Sub Shock"

A truly rigid looking frame with hydraulically dampened rear suspension.

While cruisin' down the road smooth and comfortable, show off the sleek, stylish hard-tail look with a ROAD WORX "Sub Shock" frame.

This entirely new frame concept, developed by professional engineer/bike enthusiast, took seven years of design work before ultimate perfection was achieved.

The attractiveness of "Sub Shock" lies in its rigid appearance and unique location of its specially-designed spring/hydraulic shock absorber units which become hidden once the bike is completely assembled. What you see is a traditional rigid...what you ride is a much improved swingarm.

But that's not all!

Rear axle travel is three inches. Correct geometric relationship between pivot and sprockets maintain proper chain tension throughout full travel of rear wheel. Frame is constructed of high-quality steel, 70,000 psi minimum tensile strength, with inde-

pendent suspension bearings lubricated for life. Rear frame unit, unlike a conventional swingarm, resists twisting under hard acceleration and cornering.

"Sub Shock" is patented, built with stock rake and stretch, and currently accommodates most 74/80 cubic inch H-D models, kick or electric start, disc or drum brake.

Introductory Price: $695.00. Complete with serial number and title. Limited warranty information available free upon request. VISA or Mastercharge accepted.

For the ultimate experience in style and comfort, ride "Sub Shock" from Road Worx, 7606 Idaho, St. Louis, MO 63111.

ROAD WORX INDUSTRIES

To order, CALL TOLL FREE: 1-800-325-9693 or write for FREE brochure. In Missouri, call collect: 1-314-631-6701.
Dealer Inquiries Invited

"Enhancing your motorcycle through innovation"

Here's the one big ad run by Davis and his partners in Easyriders. Note that, like the Softail Harley built on the idea, the Sub Shock bike is based on a Wide Glide and even has the chromed horseshoe oil tank. The swingarm pivots even have Teflon spherical bearings, similar to those later used on production Softails. Ron Kay collection via Rob Carlson

the company," remembered Davis. He and Davis then designed and built the production tooling, while the BG sent out the final promotional flurry, including the purchase of a full-page ad in April 1981 *Easyriders* magazine. The ad showed the Sub Shock frame and a Wide Glide fitted with it. Looking at that Sub Shock Wide Glide, it's easy to see how little the styling was really changed for the production Harley Softail.

By the time the ad came out, however, everything was beginning to fall apart, as the BG began to chafe under the mundane routine of running the office. "It turned out that all the fun was over for him once the business was set up," remembered Davis. "You can't believe the pain and horror he put me through. He turned the whole thing into living hell."

As a result of the promotion the BG had already done, orders came in for 21 frames. Pulling together one last time, the Road Worx crew constructed the frames and shipped them off before parting ways.

When Road Worx dissolved, Davis was left far in debt. His lawyers advised him to find someone to take on manufacture of the design. Reluctant to "crawl back" to Harley, he approached several aftermarket builders and an investment group. "I was so naive!" he said of the experience. "I almost lost the rights to my patents to some of those sharks."

Finally, completely discouraged, his head "just swimming from all the deception," Davis gave Bleustein a call. "He was still interested and made a much, much better offer."

Davis consulted his lawyers. The deal looked good. Harley would pay Davis a royalty on each unit sold—up to a lifetime cap on total royalty earnings. Davis objected to the cap, but Bleustein wouldn't budge, insisting that Vaughn Beals was adamant that Harley would only pay that much, no matter how many units were sold. Finally, realizing that it was the only good option available for getting

Here's the Sub Shock Wide Glide from the Easyriders ad. Except for the Shovelhead motor, curved fender supports, and old ham-can air cleaner, this could pass for a 1984 production Softail. *Bill Davis*

his design on the street and a little dough in his pockets, Davis signed on January 6, 1982, selling Harley the patents to the Sub Shock design, all the tooling, and six frames, which Davis then had to construct.

Once the deal was done and the six frames were built, however, Davis didn't think much more about his design until one day about a year and a half year later, when a friend showed him a picture in a magazine of an all-new Harley model that looked an awful lot like the Sub Shock Wide Glide from the *Easyriders* ad.

Team Softail

Vaughn Beals, Jeff Bleustein, Willie G., and a few others in senior management were 100 percent committed to getting their new acquisition

to market as soon as possible, but several others were less sure, including Tom Gelb (retired vice president of operations), who recounted the scene in a Product Planning Committee meeting:

"Vaughn Beals told us all, 'That's gonna be the best-selling Harley-Davidson ever!'

"We said, 'Vaughn, you're full of shit.'

"He said, 'No, no! I'm telling you!'

"Some of us thought he was crazy, but it was one of the many things we thought he was crazy about that really sold."

Recalled Beals: "The Softail was a dynamite concept. It just takes the vehicle back a whole generation. The Japanese don't have that heritage, but we do. It gave us something we could do that was unique."

The Softail was Harley's only really new model fitted with the new V^2 Evolution for 1984. This Softail shows one of the few differences between the 1984 and 1985 models: the "winged ball" tank graphic. Softail tanks for 1984 wore a gold Harley-Davidson bar and shield.

For the Softail, Harley fitted the old dual saddle tanks and the tank-mounted speedo, a styling treatment dating back to the first of the "modern" Harley Big Twins, the 61 OHV "Knucklehead" of 1936. Shown is the 85-mile-per-hour speedometer fitted to 1984 models. Tanks on the Softail were the 5-gallon version of the Fat Bob tanks, similar to those first used on the 1965 Electra Glide.

The marketing department was hot for the Softail, too, according to now-retired vice president of engineering Mark Tuttle: "Marketing saw that motorcycle (Davis' Sub Shock, figuring it was complete) and said, 'Hey great, we can have this in six months!'

"What they didn't realize was that all we had was a very good concept that still had to be refined and validated. We said, 'No, you can't have it in six months. We've got to design all these new parts and test them; it's gonna take three years or something.'

"Of course, they said that was totally unacceptable, so we set up a focus team—hand-picked people with Ron Hutchinson in charge to launch the

product in as short a time as possible. It took about a year and a half—longer than marketing wanted but significantly shorter than engineering said it would be. That was the first product we used focus teams on, and we still jibe each other about it. Ron's view is that he got it done in spite of engineering; our view is that he got it done *because* of engineering."

Hutchinson and his engineers (including Russ Miller and Tom McGowan) were sequestered in their own separate space to foster quick work and close cooperation. For the purposes of this book, we'll call them Team Softail.

Here's the bike that really introduced what we now consider the Harley look: teardrop-shaped saddle tanks, tank-mounted speedo and gauges or idiot lights in an integrated console, horseshoe oil tank under the seat, the plunging line from the top of the speedo console all the way back to the rear axle ("The Line"), and the overall profile of a teardrop with a back wheel tacked on. The 1936 Knucklehead is probably the most stylistically influential motorcycle in history.

Despite the time pressures, Team Softail spent considerable effort to refine Davis' Sub Shock, using computer modeling and working closely with Styling to get what one team member called "the whole hardtail look." Before long, it was ready for testing and further refinement, both of which progressed rapidly because of team coordination.

For Bill Davis—a one-man show—the laid-down, under-tranny shocks had provided the most vexing problems. For Harley-Davidson, they were no big deal. Said Mark Tuttle, "We were able to go to our shock manufacturer with an envelope of load curves and say, 'We need a shock that fits in this space, with these spring and damping rates,' and we let them do the rest."

That someone was the Japanese suspension manufacturer Showa, which had started building XL and FX forks for Harley-Davidson in the 1970s and had gradually been taking over all of Harley's suspension business. "Showa jumped into the Softail project and came up with gas-charged shocks that worked pretty well," said Rit Booth, an engineer in Harley's Applied Mechanics/Design Analysis Department.

The classic horseshoe oil tank, with the battery nestled in the "U" was an essential part of the look they were after, but team engineers worried that the heat from the oil tank would damage the battery. In the end, though, there was no other

With the Softail, Harley brought back "The Line," and the whole look of the custom Harley built on the old hardtail frames of 1936–1957.

good place for the battery, so they designed a tank with the right look and developed a battery that could take the heat and do the job. The Line was back.

The 1984 FXST Softail

For the rest of the styling, Willie and Louie did what Davis had done in building the bike shown in the *Easyriders* ad: they grabbed nearly everything but the frame, swingarm, and shocks from their most audacious styling statement to date, the FXWG Wide Glide. The result was a styling masterpiece that made its debut along with the new Evo engine in June 1983, for the 1984 model year.

The Wide Glide was another great idea plucked from the aftermarket. The Wide Glide look originally came from stripping the headlight and fork covers off

As on Bill Davis' "Sub Shock," the production Softail uses a revised and chromed version of the old horseshoe oil tank that was a key styling cue of all the OHV Big Twins from the Knucklehead of 1936 until it was replaced by a rectangular oil tank on the Electra Glide of 1965.

Like most Evo-era Harleys, this one's been modified a bit, with an aftermarket seat, exhaust, saddlebags, small windshield, and some extra chrome, including a version of the old teardrop-shaped tool box.

of the standard Hydra-Glide front end, substituting longer fork tubes and a smaller headlight, and lathe-turning the sliders for a slimmer look. Substitute a slim, 21-inch front wheel and a "bikini" fender, and the whole front end has that slim, wide-spaced look, "Wide Glide" in chopper lingo.

Chopper guys had been doing it for themselves for years, but according to Vaughn Beals, a Southern California dealer also got in on the act. He began building and selling them as "Wide Glides" several years before Harley did it. "These were high-mileage California police bikes," said Beals, "and he was selling the damn things for about the same price as a brand-new Harley. I figured people must want one badly to pay that. We decided that the Wide Glide would be a hell of a good bike to produce. The head of Marketing and I were the only guys, I think, that believed it, though. We had to beat the rest of them up to do it."

To emphasize the slim, wide-spaced look of the Wide Glide front end, Willie and Louie graced the Softail with the Wide Glide's 5-gallon "Mega Bob" tanks first used on the 1965 Electra Glide, rather than the narrower 3.5-gallon tanks (nicknamed "Fat Bob" by the customizers and later trademarked as such by Harley) used on most of the earlier and later FL-based Harleys.

At the rear they fitted the Wide Glide's bobbed fender, with taillight and strut-mounted license-plate bracket underneath. Atop that fender they bolted a seat unique to the Softail, though very similar to that of the 1977 Low Rider. Deeply stepped and thinly padded, the seat that soon earned the "clamshell" moniker gave the lowest seat height of any big bike: 25.3 inches, according to H-D specs. Quipped *Cycle* magazine (in the February 1985 issue), "If seats get much lower than this one, tall riders will be able to plant both knees firmly on the ground at stoplights."

The original Softail package included forward-mounted foot controls and pegs, as well as old-style long primary cases with starter motor facing into the wind.

Powering the Softail was the new Evo engine, of course. Defining difference here, though: No rubber engine mounts. Just that familiar throb transferred in all its glory straight from motor mounts to frame to rider. Same with the drive—chains for both primary and final, just like on granddad's Knuckle. And the tranny? Gramps would recognize it, too. Four speeds, kickstarter and all. Oh yeah, the air cleaner. It was round again! After years of that huge, hideous ham-can, courtesy of the EPA and AMF, the air-cleaner housing reverted to its "natural" shape. Exhaust consisted of the stylish shorty duals, with a blacked-out crossover spanning the two headers.

As on all the rest of the models, the paint was a standout. For 1984, the Softail came in your choice of Vivid Black or Candy Red, each with gold pinstripes on the tank and the grand old Harley bar-and-shield tank emblem, also in gold.

From far or near, from front or rear, and from either side, the new Softy was a looker. Predictably the "biker" press (*Easyriders*, *Supercycle*, and all) loved it. So did their readers. Better yet for a company that was looking to break out of the mold, the more mainstream press gave it their begrudging admiration, too.

Style was clearly what Softy was about, but it worked well enough that even editors who month after month fawned over the latest Interceptors and

Softails were built for those who would not compromise on the traditional Harley look. The four-speed Softails, built for model years 1984 and 1985, even retained the kickstarter. The new Evolution motor looked new and old at the same time. New for 1984 was a return to the classic round air cleaner used from 1937 until it was abandoned in the 1970s in favor of the larger, quieter "ham-can" air cleaner.

From the engine forward, the Softail was basically a Wide Glide. The FXWG Wide Glide had been introduced in 1980 as the first real factory chopper. Its spindly looking, wide-spaced forks emulated the look customizers had been creating for decades by stripping the shrouds off the Hydra-Glide fork, turning down the sliders on a lathe, extending the fork tubes, lacing up a skinny 21-inch rim, adding a small bullet light, and chroming everything. Bill Davis' original Sub Shock was based on a Wide Glide, too.

Combining the classic looks of an old hardtail custom with the modern functionality of the Evolution motor, the Softail became Harley's best seller in 1984, then split and split again into a whole range of new models that topped the sales charts. Said Harley CEO Vaughn Beals, "Once we had the Softail, we could do all kinds of wondrous things with it."

You're looking at the end of an evolutionary line, here, a 1985 Low Rider. Model year 1985 was the first year that the FXWG Wide Glide, FXSB Low Rider, and FXEF Fat Bob were fitted with the Evolution motor, and the last year for both Low Rider and Fat Bob in four-speed FX form.

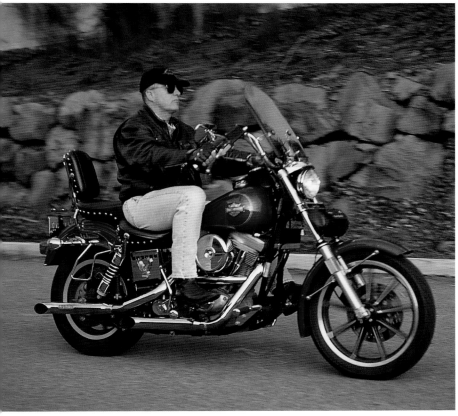

Owner Peter Bratz on his 1985 FXSB Low Rider, which he has owned since it was new.

The FX rear end, with forward-mounted shocks, dates to the first Duo-Glide of 1958 and was used last on the FXWG of 1986. That look was what Harley then re-created on the Dyna Glide in 1991.

Ninjas and imitation Harleys from Japan couldn't fault it too much. "At 55 miles per hour the vibes are pretty tolerable," wrote the editors of *Cycle* (January 1984). Of course, they couldn't resist a clever cut that, because of those vibes, "The four-speed 80-incher is one of the most effective speed-limitation devices known to mankind." Nevertheless, those same editors acknowledged the FXST's essential appeal, calling it "a rolling picture frame for the individual rider." And who among Harley's traditional fans couldn't picture themselves sitting there?

Better yet, Harley's new "rolling picture frame" was so gilded that scads of nontraditionalists could also imagine themselves sitting there, as well—vibes or no. That this rolling frame was more handsome than most of its riders was the point entirely and a sincere tribute to the skill of Willie and Louie. That it also felt and sounded right was testament to the fact that everyone at Harley pulled together to get the "soft side" right. At $7,999, it was more expensive than any other nonbagger Harley. Despite that, the Softail went on to outsell everything else in the Harley Big Twin line in its first year. Even better for the cash-strapped Motor Company, the Softail's success was won without cutting notably into sales of the other Big Twins. Best of all, according to Vaughn Beals was "Once we had the Softail, we could do all kinds of wondrous things with it." And before long, they did.

Seen It in a Magazine

All that success aside, what did the father of the Softail, Bill Davis, think of Harley's new machine?

After acquiring the design, Harley had worked its magic on it almost entirely without input from Davis. "The first time I saw it was when a friend showed me a picture in a magazine," he remembered.

So was he exhilarated that his hard-fought battle to get the hardtail look to market had succeeded on such a grand scale? Not at all. The pain was still too fresh, you might say. "I'd gone through such horror with that guy [the BG], that I wasn't excited about anything. I didn't love it anymore; I just didn't care."

All the Harley Big Twins came with the Evo motor for 1985, and 1985 was the only year the FXSB Low Rider and FXEF Fat Bob were Evo-powered.

This look made its debut in 1977, on the FXS Low Rider. Basically, it was a Super Glide, with the smaller Fat Bob dual tanks (3.5 gallons or 4.2 gallons, depending on the year), an all-new tank-mounted dash featuring both a speedo and a tach (one behind the other), and longer forks with more rake. It was a look that was popular then and is still popular now, on the Dyna Low Riders that are still in production.

The 1985 Low Rider came with the bar-and-shield emblem and pinstripes on the tank and belt drive. The lower-priced Fat Bob that year was basically the same, except it came with chain drive, shorter forks, and a bald-eagle tank graphic.

That all began to change when he finally saw a Softail for real. With a creative engineer's singular brand of insecurity, he'd long wondered how good his basic design really was. What would need changing for mass production and to please everyone at a big company like Harley? Would they validate all the choices and trade-offs he had made or would they scrap much of it and make different choices? To his delight, Harley hadn't made fundamental changes to the design. "I felt it confirmed my engineering ability," he said.

With that validation, he probably would have been happy, but the really gratifying part came along a short time later: The royalties started coming in. "Remember, I was out of a job [when Road Worx folded] and in debt," he emphasized. "Mr. Bleustein had promised me more projects, and after working for a medical company for a few years, I did get a full-time consulting job with Harley."

So, with his creation thundering down roads all across the fruited plain, did Davis take some of his royalties and buy a new Softail?

No, and he still hasn't.

At the time, he still had Softail One (based on a 1972 Super Glide, which he subsequently donated to Harley-Davidson for the company's upcoming museum), as well as a special, stretched version of the Sub Shock frame on which he always intended to build his next ride (but still

ties will never get there.'" Regrettable last words.

Nevertheless, Davis is anything but bitter. "Of course, if that cap wasn't there, I wouldn't have to work today," he said, "but Harley's treatment of me was the only shining part of the story."

1985 FX MODELS

Of course, the Softail was back for 1985, from here on after with belt final drive. Back, too, were the traditionalist's three remaining old friends from the 1984 Harley line-up—FXWG Wide Glide, FXSB Low Rider, and FXEF Super Glide Fat Bob. For 1985, they came with one big difference: All were Evo-powered.

Except for the engine, the Low Rider and Wide Glide changed little from the previous year. The Super Glide Fat Bob was now the "stripper" of the line for 1985 (no pinstripes, no sissybar, less stylish seat, chain instead of belt, no kickstarter, and less chrome, but with the twin, 4.2-gallon Fat Bob tanks this year).

The whole FX line was updated with the powertrain changes listed in chapter 1, a more ergonomic locking screw for the throttle, and a 120-mile-per-hour speedometer to replace the 85-mile-per-hour joke foisted on us in the 1970s. That none of these bikes could really push the limits of a 120-mile-per-hour speedo is not the point. The point is we won one from the safety-crats.

The Softail and Wide Glide came

Not quite the classic that the Softail's horseshoe tank is, the side-mounted tank on the FX machines dates back to the Electra Glide of 1965. Thought by many to be ugly at the time, in comparison to the horseshoe it replaced, it became a part of the classic FX look in the 1970s and early 1980s. That oil tank died with the last of the four-speed FXs in 1986, but the look of it was revived on the Dyna in 1991.

hasn't). As before, his main interest was in long-distance rides, so when he finally did forgo some of his royalties to buy a new machine, it was a 1985 FLHT. He still has it, and still has no regrets. "It suits my needs perfectly and has given me no trouble in the 84,000 miles since I bought it."

As the original Softail eventually branched out into a whole new Harley family tree, those royalties kept coming and coming until, against all odds, the amount reached the lifetime cap. "I didn't like the idea of the cap when we were negotiating the agreement," remembered Davis, "but my patent attorney told me, 'I've never seen that much money for a cap. Take it; the royal-

with beautiful eagle-wing tank transfers for 1985, encircled by a double pinstripe. The Low Rider got the same bar-and-shield badge the Softail had in 1984, with the pinstripes. Harley had to save money somewhere, so the loss-leader Fat Bob got a unique bald eagle transfer and no pinstripes. The gas tanks of Softies and Wide Glides were up-rated to 5.2 gallons (from 5 gallons). As for paint, all were available in Vivid Black and Candy Red. Both Softy and Bob were also available in Candy Blue. For extra cost, Low Riders, Wide Glides, and Softies were available in Candy Burgundy with Slate Gray panels. For those not satisfied with Willie G.'s choice of colors, Harley offered its custom paint program that

allowed a customer to order any new machine painted in the color combinations featured for that month, so mention of color for regular production models will be omitted from this point on.

All those updates came at a cost. The stripper Fat Bob was up to $6,999, $500 more than the FXE Super Glide of 1984. The Softy's price was up $400 to $8,399, while the Wide Glide's increased $600, also to $8,399. Despite the price increases, all increased in sales, most notably the Wide Glide, sales of which nearly doubled.

SOFTAIL CUSTOM AND HERITAGE SOFTAIL

Model year 1986 brought good news and bad news for the traditionalist. First the bad: Old favorites Fat Bob and Low Rider were dropped from the FX line-up (though they were reincarnated in FXR form; we'll meet them again in chapter 4), leaving Wide Glide as the last of the exposed-shock FX breed. The good news: Softail reemerged in five-speed form and multiplied, with two versions available at the start of the year, and an exciting newcomer that was introed at Daytona, in March.

Along with the rest of the Harley-Davidson line-up, all the Softails were given the following updates: turn signals that double as running lights, locking turn signal switches, revised starter relay, new exhausts, tuned intakes, and powdercoated frames (except on the FXSTC Softail Custom). In addition, all the Softails got new shocks with revised spring and damping rates, and new shift levers.

Starting in 1984, most Harleys got a single 11.5-inch front brake rotor to replace the dual 10-inch rotors previously used. Despite one less disc, the new system actually stopped better than the old, though it still wasn't up to the standards of the day. All the 1985 models featured the new clutch introduced midway through 1984. It was a wet-type clutch with a diaphragm spring.

The FXWG Wide Glide was built in Evo-powered form for 1985 and 1986. To the very end, it was fitted with the four-speed transmission and the kickstarter. When the last of them were built in 1986, the kickstart died as a feature on new Harleys. Shown is a 1985 model that has been repainted, without the pinstripes that the factory had applied.

FXWG Wide Glide

The Harley-Davidson sales brochure nailed the appeal of the Wide Glide in its model brochures: "In 1986, [the Wide Glide] retains what only a select group of motorcyclists would demand on their new Harley. Like kickstart. And a rigid-mount, four-speed engine. Features that can't be found on any other Harley-Davidson. And [hinting at the future?] may never be found again on any motorcycle."

If you were one of "the few among millions" who wanted your new Harley with a four-speed tranny and a kicker, the Wide Glide was your only choice among the 1986 line. Last of the old-frame Big Twins, the Wide Glide was clearly reaching an evolutionary dead end, but sales had doubled during its first year in Evo form, so the Evo Wide Glide was certainly deserving of another year.

Nevertheless, it just wasn't economically feasible to forever make the old frame and four-speed tranny (which required a lot of hand shimming during manufacture) for just one model, so Harley gave the old Wide Glide one last limited run. In a final and fond nod to all the Wide Glide had contributed to Harley's heritage, the final-edition Wide Glide was available once again with (and without) "scorching" tank graphics—the flamed tank that had made the original so striking. The new Fog Candy Red flames blazed over the Candy Burgundy of the rest of the bodywork.

For 1986, the FXWG cost $8,699, $300 more than the previous year and just $50 less than the Softail. Once the 1,000 or so Harley built were all sold, that was it. Goodbye, Electra Glide frame. So long, four-speed. And hope to see you again, kickstarter. As for the Wide Glide as a model, it would rise once again like a Phoenix out of the metallic flames on the final edition's tanks. That story, however, is in chapter 6.

Five-Speed FXST Softail

For 1986, the Softail gave up a bit of its character to gain some meaningful improvement, when it was fitted with the fine five-speed transmission used by the rest of the line. To fit the five-speed, some revision of the frame was required, so Rit Booth and the other FX chassis engineers took the opportunity to make it stiffer, easier to manufacture, and better looking, all at the same time. The major change was to design a stout new forging to replace the flame-cut curved piece on each side that bridges the upper and lower frame rails at

The Wide Glide died out as a Harley model after 1986, until its classic looks were revived on the FXDWG Dyna Wide Glide in the 1990s.

the rear. "It was a beautiful piece," said Booth, "if you like sculptured steel."

Gone with the old four-speed was the kicker. Many mourned (and still do) the loss of this macho link to the past. "We had a major insurrection over that," remembered Beals, but the company decided "the hell with it" and just ignored the noise. All the vibes were still there, though, because even though the 1986 Softail got the five-speed and a revised frame, rubber wasn't part of the formula.

The five-speed Softail sold even better than the four-speed, even though the price for the basic Softail was up to $8,749. By the end of the year, there was a waiting list in many parts of the country for the Softail—another look into Harley's future. Tank emblems were updated versions of the "winged ball" emblems of 1985.

FXSTC Softail Custom

I ask you this: Has Harley ever gone wrong by adding more chrome and polish to its motorcycles, and charging more? Of course not! In fact, it became one of the keys to Harley's resurgence in the 1980s and dominance of the U.S. big-bike market in the 1990s.

On the Evo-powered bikes, this practice all began with the limited-edition FXRDG Disc Glide of 1984, which featured special paint on the bodywork, and chrome on the engine covers. With the Disc Glide, Harley started perfecting the difficult process of chroming aluminum castings and building disc wheels on a mass-production basis. That story is part of chapter 4, but mention of it is pertinent here because by 1986, Harley was confident enough in its processes to release the FXSTC Softail Custom. This was the first of what would soon be a long line of chrome-encrusted, regular-production "Custom" models.

The most notable features of the Softail Custom were its disc-type rear wheel, a custom styling treatment on the engine (crinkle-black finish on the crankcases, cylinders, cylinder heads, and transmission case, all highlighted with polished cooling-fin ends, chrome rocker-box covers), chrome outer primary, and chrome transmission covers, and a frame painted (all the others were powdercoated) to match the Candy Burgundy paint on the tanks and fenders. Striking it was, especially combined with the disc wheel and the overall Softail styling. Add on the new "pillowy" seat, sissybar, and special tank graphics with "curlicues" behind the vintage script of the company name, and this off-the-rack Harley showed more style than the majority of one-off customs. All that for

The Softail chassis was redesigned for 1986 to make room for the five-speed transmission and to strengthen the rear suspension. The line also split into two at the start of the year—the regular Softail and the new FXSTC Softail Custom, which featured a disc rear wheel and a chromed and blacked engine treatment. Midway through the model year, this machine made its appearance, the FLST Heritage Softail.

The Heritage took the Harley look even further back, to the look of the Hydra-Glides of the mid-1950s.

$9,299, only $500 more than for the standard Softail. Despite the higher price, the Softail Custom outsold not only its less expensive and plainer brother, but every other Harley Big Twin, as well.

FLST Heritage Softail

"Only Harley-Davidson could get away with this," proclaimed *Cycle* in its March 1986 review of Harley's most important new model for 1986—the FLST Heritage Softail. What did Willie G. and company get away with? Well, an even more audacious future-from-the-past trick than they'd pulled off with the original Softail, creating a new styling masterpiece that looked for all the world like a hardtail Panhead from the 1950s. Truth is, only Harley could get way with it because only Harley had the heritage to actually pull it off!

Better yet, Willie G. and the styling department gave us a hint of the company's future in the *way* they'd mined the company's past. How's that, you might ask?

Instead of the 5-gallon Fat Bobs of the regular Softail and Custom, the Heritage was fitted with the slimmer 3.5-gallon version, but with the same tank-top dash and speedo.

While most of the rest of the Heritage was plain old Softail, the front end was a special new piece, designed to recapture the look of the fat front end of the old Hydra-Glides. In an attempt to improve the handling, Harley's engineers put a lot of effort into reducing the moment of inertia of the front end, even narrowing the tube spread and lightening the fender and its trim pieces.

Think back now to the first factory custom, the FX Super Glide. How had Willie done it? He'd put the front end from the Sportster on the big FLH tourer, transforming the old "standard" to the new "custom." Same with the FXR a decade later, grafting the same front end on a revised FLT frame. For the FLST Heritage Softail, however, Willie G. and Louie N. did the opposite, recreating the look of the 1950s standard from the modern custom by reinstalling a polished version of the heavy, shrouded Hydra-Glide front end. Clever, no?

In doing so, the Harley design team revived the simple, bold lines of the old FL Hydra-Glide hardtails made from 1949 to 1957. All the really important styling cues were there. The "fat" front look was courtesy of the shrouded fork, valanced front fender, and 16-inch front wheel, just like in 1949. For the top shroud of that fork, Willie G. revived the more stylish design first seen in 1955, with three chevrons standing proud on each side of the gleaming chrome headlight. Fattening up the rear was a version of the old FLH valanced rear fender. Also blasting back from the past to help complete the 1950s look were the wide buckhorn bars, footboards, and slimmer, 3.5-gallon version of the Fat Bob saddle tanks used on all the Knuckles and pre-1965 Pans, rather than the 5-gallon tanks of the regular Softails. The rest was pure Softail—chrome horseshoe oil tank, rigid-rear look, five-speed tranny, and so on.

The illusion of age was carried through by the only paint option offered: Signal Red with Creme tank panels, highlighted by pinstriping. Add a tractor seat and replace the shorty duals with the proper 1950s two-into-one and you'd fool even the old-Harley mavens—from a distance anyway. Hey, the frame tube to mount the seat post's still there, so why not include that? Alas, modern tastes demanded low seat heights, at the expense of comfort.

The Heritage was another masterpiece from the styling department, and one that got noticed everywhere, most notably on the sales floor. *Cycle* called it a "machine of arresting simplicity" and "the most elegant Harley-Davidson of its generation."

Getting that look required far more than just a raid on the obsolete parts bin, however. "The biggest challenge was that we were going backward from a low-inertia front end to a high-inertia front end," said Mark Tuttle. "The biggest issues were getting the high-speed stability and handling right. We put a fair amount of effort into making that combination of frame and front end functional."

Initially, Harley engineers put an old front end on the Softail to see how it would do. The results weren't encouraging: "It went around corners kind of like an old FL," remembered Rit Booth (then product manager for the FX line), "and that wasn't good enough anymore."

From all the work done on refining the FLHT's handling (see chapter 3), Harley's engineers knew that the key to improving the handling of the Heritage

Softail front end was to center as much of the mass as close as possible to the steering axis. To get it right, Booth and company reengineered every part, lightening everything possible, paying special attention to the heavy fender. To lighten the front and rear of the fender (the parts farthest from the steering axis), Booth and company designed a lighter front fender tip and bobbed the rear of the fender, replacing a big chunk of steel with a lighter aluminum trim strip. Side-to-side mass was tucked in closer by decreasing the spacing between the fork legs as much as styling would allow.

All that work to refine the handling forced changes to the triple clamps, so they took the opportunity to redesign the clamps to allow even more of the 1950s character: "The last version of the FL had this cast-aluminum housing for the headlight," said Rit Booth. Its triple clamps wouldn't work for the Heritage

project, so we decided to go way back to a stand-alone bullet headlight and two-piece stamping that went around the triple clamp. I was working with Bill [Willie G.] Davidson at the time, so I went back to him. Turns out that older look was really what he wanted anyway, but everyone had said that that would be the hard way to go. Turned out it was the easiest way to go." That older look, with the stand-alone headlight, had been a signature feature of all the Hydra-Glides and of the Duo-Glides of 1958 and 1959. As noted earlier, though, they chose the best-looking version of the tinwork for that fork, the triple-chevron style used from 1955 to 1959.

To help get the overall look even more right—"We wanted the lower frame rails horizontal, like on the old FLs, not sloping uphill toward the front like on the regular Softail," Booth remembered—he used fork tubes about an inch and a half longer than those on the old Hydra-Glide front end.

So, how did it all work? Perfectly for the Heritage's target audience. This machine was all about looks, and those looks came with compromises. The Heritage was a great ride, so long as you didn't wick it up too much (the vibration at 85 miles per hour is not bearable for long), tilt the horizon too far (unless you love the sound of footboards scraping across asphalt), or stay in the saddle too long (unless you love that tingling feeling in your fingers). But for oozing along at 60 to 70 for a few hours or for a night on the town, it was 650 pounds of rolling grace.

In its ads, the company called it "a legacy fulfilled." Truly, it was, and the Heritage was a resounding success in its first year. All 2,510 sold as fast as they could be built. Like the original Softail before it, the Heritage would go on to spawn its own distinct model line—and its own imitators, for Willie G.'s shadow disciples in Japan took notice.

For 1987, the Softails were Harley's only offering for the traditionalist. Fortunately, the Softail came in all three flavors from the year before (regular, Custom, and Heritage) and two new ones (FLST-S Heritage Softail Special and the FXST-S Softail Special).

Echoing the theme from the Softail Custom of the year before, the new Heritage Special was the basic package with a blacked-out and polished engine, more chrome, custom two-tone paint on tanks and fenders, a Lexan windshield, passing lamps, leather saddlebags, and a special two-piece seat

Of course, the fat 16-inch wheel and skirted fender were important parts of the Hydra-Glide look, too, as was the two-tone paint on the tank. This 1986 1/2 Heritage sports its original paint, Signal Red and Cream.

The teardrop-shaped tool box wasn't standard on the first Heritage, but it certainly looks as if it belongs. It was standard on the Knuckles and Pans built from 1940 to 1957. This view shows how well hidden the rear suspension really is on the Softails.

Though the look of the front end was fat, the rest of the bike was trim, despite the larger rear fender used on the Heritage.

Softails first got belt drive in 1985. In 1986, the frame and swingarm were revised to stiffen the assembly and to fit the five-speed transmission. One of the most visible parts of the redesign is the new frame forging shown here just ahead of the passenger peg. On 1984 and 1985 Softails, a less-sculptured flame-cut piece was used instead of the forging.

and backrest with studs and conchos. It was the soul of the 1950s tourer and was offered in only one color combination: Metallic Blue with Creme tank and fender panels and red and gold pinstripes.

The Softail Special was a very limited edition of the basic Softail brought out late in the season. It differed from the basic Softail mainly in that it was painted Candy Brandywine with Brilliant Silver tank panels. Harley's figures show that only 398 were built.

Tanks on the Heritage models were uprated to 4.2 gallons (from 3.5 gallons). Little else was changed, except for the color options. The Softail Custom was available in new colors, as well, and the frames were still color matched for all, but now in powdercoat rather than the paint used in 1986.

Once again, the Softails were the sales leaders of the Harley line-up. First among them was the Softail Custom, outselling the standard Softail almost three to one, and even outselling the 883 Sportster for the first time.

SPRINGER

Great ideas always have one thing in common: They seem all too obvious in retrospect. The original FXST Softail of 1984 was one. The FLST Heritage Softail was another. For model year 1988, Harley-Davidson introduced the third in what would later become an even longer string of great ideas: The FXSTS Springer Softail, created by bolting up to the Softail a modernized version of the Harley's old springer front end. And like all great ideas, it was seemingly simple in concept, but a great deal of work in the actual execution.

Befitting its 1950s Hydra-Glide looks, the Heritage was fitted with footboards for the rider. In later years, the Heritage spawned its own line. First came the Heritage Special in 1987, with the chrome-and-black engine, special seat, and leather saddlebags. The Special became the Heritage Custom in 1988. In 1990 came the Fat Boy, and even more later.

Opinions differ about who first voiced the idea of building a modern Springer front end. Many of those interviewed for this book say it was from Styling, but others said the idea came from within Engineering. Nevertheless, one thing is clear: Within the company, the idea was immediately recognized for its greatness. Remembered Vaughn Beals: "I don't recall the genesis of the idea, but there was no discussion about do we want to do it or not. There was total unanimity that it made sense for the company. I loved the idea because it gave us a way to attract new customers and screw the Japanese, because they didn't have anything like it in their heritage to go back to. The only problem was that making it happen took longer than any of us would like to have seen."

Team Springer

"We all knew that there were major problems with the old springer, with stiffness, ride quality, and so forth," remembered Mark Tuttle, "so we put a group together to look at the feasibility." We'll call that group "Team Springer," an extension of the team (headed by Ron Hutchinson) that had worked its magic in getting the Softail to market so quickly.

In the 1950s, the Hydra-Glides had the 3.5-gallon twin tanks, so that's what the Heritage was given, even though the other Softails had the wider 5-gallon tanks. The owner has replaced the stock bar and risers with this integrated piece.

Jerry Sanden on the first-year Heritage, which he has owned since it was new.

72

In midyear 1988, Harley released a bike the likes of which many thought would never roll out the factory gates again, the FXSTS Springer Softail. It flaunted an updated and chromed version of the old Springer front fork, last used on a few sidecar-equipped Big Twins in 1949, the year the Hydra-Glide fork made its debut on the solo Harleys. This Springer is a 1991 model. Those in 1988 wore special winged 85th Anniversary tank graphics.

As in all the other updates it had done, Harley-Davidson's standards for this one were high: The new springer had to look like the old springer, give adequate fork travel, allow for a disc brake, and have modern durability. The team quickly began studying how to bring the old spring fork up to date.

The first problem, according to team member Rit Booth, was that they didn't just have an old springer front end laying on the shelf. "We had to buy one from somebody that had old stuff," he remembered.

You may not be able to guess it from a quick look, but that old-looking fork is pretty high-tech. Harley engineers tried for years to make one with modern reliability before finding just the bearings they needed to take the place of the wear-prone bushings in the original fork.

After studying the old parts, all the challenges seemed manageable except one: How to get modern durability out of the bearings on the fork's rockers. "Remember," said chief engineer Don Valentine, "the old rockers at the bottom of the forks had bushings and grease fittings. No matter what you did, those bushings would wear out and get sloppy real fast."

So, that's where the team stalled for a while. "That was a very tough engineering process," recalled Vaughn Beals. "Jeff [Bleustein] will tell you that I chewed his ass lots of times on that one because it seemed to me that it wasn't beyond our abilities to do it. As was often the case, in our conservative approach we would conclude that something wasn't practical and the next thing you knew, you could go to a dealership and you could ride one. Somebody who hadn't been to MIT would figure out how to do it. [That's as much a cut on himself as on anyone—Beals has a master's degree in aeronautical engineering from MIT.] That put some pressure on."

Finally, engineer Tom McGowan worked with Aurora to develop a half-spherical version of the company's spherical Teflon bearings. "The unique part was in splitting the bearing so we could preload and adjust it," said Mark Tuttle. "When Tom came up with those bearings, we went back to Styling and said we had a concept that would allow us to do a modern springer."

Bearing problem solved, it was simple enough for the team engineers to employ their well-proven computer techniques to optimize pivot and link geometry, to increase its stiffness, and to increase wheel travel to 4 inches. Similarly straightforward were the tasks of designing the clever links that allow use of a modern disc brake and pivoting fender with the redesigned Springer. (On the original springer, with about 2 inches of travel, the fender was fixed in place; the new springer was to have twice as much travel, so it was decided to make the fender move with the wheel to avoid the "motocross" look.)

After prototypes were built with the new bearings, testing proved that the new Springer was durable enough for the modern world, requiring adjustment at about 10,000-mile intervals. Better yet, it actually provided a more compliant ride than modern telescopic forks. Shock-absorber technology had come a long way in the 40 years since the springer fork had been out of production, so the new dampers units developed with shock manufacturer Monroe actually did a reasonable job of controlling the Springer's 21-inch wheel.

Just when the team thought the challenges were licked, new ones surfaced during pilot production. "It was a very significant manufacturing challenge," said Tuttle. "In the forgings and oval shapes on the legs, you'd get stress risers and cracking if you didn't do it right. We spent as much time solving the manufacturing problems as the engineering problems." In solving those problems, the Harley team finally resorted to complex forgings and investment castings.

"It was a real bitch to make!" affirmed Tom Gelb, then vice president of operations. "With that mechanical setup, there were a million parts, and I mean they were all polished and chromed. It was a very labor-intensive process." All that chrome was subject to cracking on the more stressed parts of the fork, so H-D was forced to use the more expensive triple-plating process. "At the time," joked Gelb, "we [Manufacturing] were just hoping we wouldn't sell too many of them. I think at one time we told them we couldn't make more than 10 springer front ends a day."

To get the slimmer look of the pre-1965 Big Twins, Harley stylists went with the slimmer Fat Bob tanks then in use. Originally rated for 3.5 gallons, starting in 1987, these tanks were rated for 4.2 gallons. Except for the tanks and fork, the rest of the bike was pure Softail.

Using computer modeling, Harley engineers modernized the old fork by optimizing the locations of the pivots, redesigning it for almost twice the travel as on the old version, and devising linkages to allow use of a disc brake. To reduce maintenance, they fitted aircraft-quality half-spherical Teflon bearings that need adjustment at about 10,000-mile intervals, versus the weekly greasing necessary on the old Springer. To get a custom look, they fitted a 21-inch laced front rim and severely bobbed front fender.

The FXSTS Springer Softail made its debut midyear in the 1988 line-up, to derisive snorts from the racer crowd and admiring whistles from just about everyone else. Even the mainstream motorcycling testers loved it, despite all their instincts, commenting that the new fork was not only stiffer and more comfortable than the old telescopic unit (except over really harsh bumps), but that it worked so well that it accentuated the weaknesses in the Softail rear suspension.

On top of all that function, Harley dished up high-test (as in high testosterone) good looks, featuring the slimmer (3.5-gallon) Fat Bob tanks, black paint with red-and-yellow pinstripes, the blacked-out and chromed engine from the Softail Custom, 85th Anniversary tank graphics, and all that chrome on the front end. Needless to say, the 1,300 numbered copies of this limited-edition classic sold out almost instantly, despite being priced at nearly $11,000, almost $1,400 more than for the regular Softail.

The Others

Clearly, the Springer was the star of the 1988 Softail line, but the regular Softail, the Softail Custom, Heritage Softail, and the "baggerized" version of the Heritage (now called the FXSTC Heritage Softail Classic) were all back with revised paint choices and graphics. All were updated with the engine changes listed in chapter 1, a new eyelet-end clutch cable, American-made Hayes brake calipers and master cylinders, wide-angle convex mirrors with ball-and-socket joint, and turn signals mounted to the lower end of the mirror stalk.

Compared to the previous four years, which had seen the Softail line branch out from one to five, all was quiet on the Softail front for 1989. In fact, not much changed except that the shocks on all were redesigned to offer adjustable preload for the springs and a very welcome 0.75 inch more travel. For even more of a 1950s touring look, the FLSTC got fishtail muffler tips.

For 1989, Softail sales were up substantially, and the more-expensive Custom and Classic versions outsold the plain ones by three- or four-to-one margins. The lesson illustrated is one Harley-Davidson has taken to heart:

Blacked-out engines and more chrome result in increased sales, despite the higher prices.

FAT BOY

After a year's rest, the Softail group made a bold, new mark with a new version of the Softail for the new decade: the FLSTF Fat Boy, a production replica of the custom Heritage Softail ridden to Daytona by Willie G. in 1988.

This 1991 Springer has classic bar-and-shield tank graphics because it was ordered with them through Harley's custom paint program. Standard that year were graphics with the company name on one line, with the outline of an eagle's head leading the way.

Springers retained the classic Softail rear, with a laced wheel, rather than the Softail Custom's disc wheel.

Fat Boy featured a futuristic industrial look, courtesy of the Fine Silver Metallic paint slathered onto not only the gas tanks and fenders, but also the frame, swingarm, oil tank, fork sliders, and fender supports.

What's in this name? Well, the second atomic bomb dropped on Japan was code-named "Fat Boy." And rumor has it that the FLSTF Fat Boy's silver-on-silver look was inspired by the sleek silver B-29 Superfortress that carried the atomic bombs to Japan. One Fat Boy was even customized by a dealership to look even more like the B-29 *Enola Gay*, the bomber that dropped the first atomic bomb (which was code-named "Little Boy"). Was the Fat Boy named after The Bomb? "As competitors, we didn't like the Japanese much, but we're not that insensitive," said Vaughn Beals.

As the Harley ads for it pointed out, Fat Boy was "sweating with custom details." Highlighting the silver monochrome look were atomic yellow "hot spots" on the center valve-cover spacers, timing cover, "derby" clutch cover, and tank console, and the all-new Fat Boy tank emblem. A new over-under shotgun-style dual exhaust made Fat Boy look even longer and lower. The turn signals were moved to the fender supports, and the tip light on the rear fender was left off to give a cleaner look to the rear. The front fender was bobbed and flared at the rear and stripped of lights and trim, and twin 16-inch disc wheels with polished rims and rough-cast centers and an unpainted engine completed the silver-on-silver look.

By design, Fat Boy had the tough look of bolts and rivets and plate steel. In fact, the only parts soft and humanistic about it were the pigskin seat with

hand-laced detailing on the seat valance and the hand-laced leather tank trim. It was, as the ad said, "a heavy-duty hunk of style," but if the Heritage was a rolling Elvis tune, Fat Boy was Nine Inch Nails forced to play in the triplet cadence of a Harley V-Twin. Fat Boy was also the natural choice as Arnie's ride in the movie *Terminator 2*, which was filmed the next year.

Fat Boy made it six Softail models for 1990, including all five from 1989, with few changes. The basic Softail and Heritage were available only in solid colors. Springer and Custom Softails were available in solids or two-tones, and

Just about every piece on the Springer front end is polished and chromed. That's really what limited its availability so much in the model's early years. Polishing and chroming so much sculptured steel takes time and personnel away from other tasks, and it's expensive, too.

Forty-five years after the original "Fat Boy" atomic bomb exploded over Nagasaki, Japan, Willie G. Davidson dropped his own "bomb" on his Japanese emulators for model year 1990: the FLSTF Fat Boy.

Heritage Classic only in two-tones. New graphics appeared on each: FX Softails got a new tank transfer featuring the outline of an eagle's head in front of the company name; FL Softails (except Fat Boy) got a new transfer featuring a "deco diamond" overlaid by the company name. In addition, Heritage Classic models got redesigned leather bags with new mounts that made doffing the bags easier.

For 1990, the Softy Custom and Heritage Classic were Numbers 1 and 2 in sales, at 6,795 and 5,483 (respectively), trouncing even the cheap 883 Sportster. Coming in at Number 4 was the Fat Boy on the block, with 4,440 sold, followed closely by Mr. Springer, with 4,252. Once again, the plain Her-

itage and Softail trailed their more expensive brothers, with 1,567 and 1,601 (respectively), so both were dropped from the line-up at the end of the year.

The Softail line for 1991 was down to the four best sellers from 1990: Softail Custom, Springer Softail, Heritage Classic, and Fat Boy. Except for engine and tranny changes listed in chapter 1, changes to the remaining Softails were limited to cosmetics and prices (up, naturally). Fat Boy lost his silver-on-silver Superfortress look, in favor of bright new color combinations, a blacked-out engine, and a lot more chrome. With all those changes, Fat Boy took on a new character. It was a Heritage that didn't look old.

Like that of the B-29 Superfortress that dropped the original Fat Boy plutonium bomb, the Harley Fat Boy's look was all silver and rivets. Frame and sheet metal were painted silver, and the silver version of the Evolution engine was fitted. Disc wheels on both ends added to that look, as did the sleeker, bobbed front fender.

Fortunately, sales didn't suffer for all this lack of improvement. For the first time, the Heritage Classic took the sales lead, with 8,950 sales, relegating the Softy Custom to Number 2, with 7,525 sales. In Number 3 was the XLH-1200 Sportster. The bright new Fat Boy came in Number 4, with 5,581 sales, and the Springer was Number 6, with 4,265 sales.

The four old-reliable Softails were back for 1992, again with the engine updates listed in chapter 1. New paint options were available for all, as well as new tank emblems for the Springer and Custom Softies. Harking back to the colorful U.S. Army Air Force unit emblems of World War II, the new tank transfer featured a star being dive-bombed by an eagle, talons brandished. "Softail One to Heritage Leader—Viragos at 12 o'clock." "Fire at will, Softail One." *Rat-tat-tat-tat-tat!*

It wasn't just the colors that were new, however; the process was, too. Harley had long (and justifiably) been famous for the quality of its paint work, but the paint on Harley-Davidsons reached whole new heights of quality in 1992 when the company turned the key on its new paint facility, which gave the company the capability to do what many had tried but few had actually pulled off: Apply a powder clearcoat as smooth and glossy as the best sprayed-on paint. In the new process, a two-step corrosion-control process is applied, followed by sprayed-on base and color coats, followed by the powder clear and a trip through the oven. The result is the best-looking and toughest paint in the industry.

"Brighter than a thousand suns" was how one observer described the flash of a nuclear bomb. Willie G. added nuclear yellow "hot spots" to accent the silver-on-silver look of the Fat Boy. Even the Air Force–inspired Fat Boy tank graphics got a splash of nuclear yellow. The pinstriping shown on this machine was added by its owner, as was a two-into-one exhaust, in place of the stock "shotgun" duals.

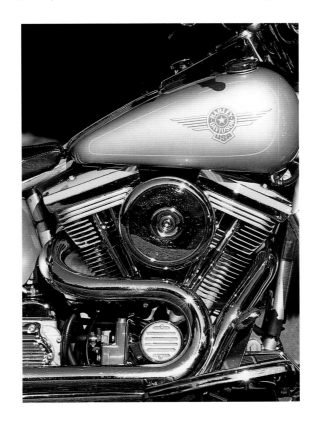

HERITAGE NOSTALGIA

Four became five for Harley's 90th anniversary season with the introduction of a new cut on the Softail chassis, the FLSTN Heritage Softail Nostalgia. Oddly, none of the Softails were offered in the special 90th Anniversary trim that was offered on many of the other lines.

The FLSTN was a stunning new machine created by Willie and Louie as a clever mix-and-match job, with a few new parts, that gave a whole new look to the old Heritage. Starting with a Heritage Classic, they added the shotgun exhaust, leather seat, wide FLH bars, tank emblem, and leather tank trim from the Fat Boy, but with a few important differences: fishtail mufflers replaced the Fat Boy's straight ones, the tank emblem was chrome and fired enamel, and hair-on, black-and-white Holstein hide was stitched in place of the textured inserts on the seat. From the Softail Custom came the 5.2-gallon *uber*-Fat Bob tanks. New to the line were the "fat gangster whitewalls" on the laced wheels and the Pony Express-sized Fat Boy saddlebags, also with Holstein inserts. Paint work carried through the Holstein theme—Birch White with Vivid Black panels on both tanks and fenders, with red-and-gray pinstriping.

Nostalgic it was. Dressed but not decked, in the fashion of the late 1950s. Said Harley of the new machine, "Who would have thought black and white could be so colorful?" Who, indeed! Naturally enough, the Nostalgia took on several appropriate nicknames: Moo Glide, Cow Glide, or Heritage Holstein, depending on who's talking. And naturally enough, all 2,700 numbered copies sold out quicker than you can tip a cow.

The whole Softail line got higher gearing to lower engine rpm at cruise and new "low-profile" brake and clutch levers. In addition, the Springer got a new "low-profile bullet-shaped" headlight that looked a lot more like the headlights of the 1940s, and the Heritage Classic got larger leather bags.

The fab five Softails were back again for 1994, except that the FLSTN was called the Heritage Softail Special instead of Nostalgia. (Why not FLSTS for Heritage Softail Special? Well, Harley was saving that serving of alphabet soup for 1997.) The Special retained the hairy inserts (only all black this time) but got a stunning Birch White and silver two-tone paint scheme.

After its first year, the Fat Boy lost its Superfortress looks when it became available in a variety of bright paint schemes to become a factory custom version of the Heritage Softail.

BAD BOY

Like nearly every "movement," motorcycle customizing marches along to the rhythms of human taste. When standard is paint, custom is chrome, right? Well, several years later, when chrome's standard, what then does it take to be custom? Go back to paint, right? So that's just what Willie and Louie did to create their boldest styling statement for the year, the FXSTB Bad Boy of 1995.

Paint replaced chrome on the fork legs (but not the springs), oil tank, triple clamps, bar risers, rear-fender supports, and tank-mounted speedo console. New custom touches included a slotted disc rear wheel, floating brake rotors, wider and flatter handlebar, cloisonné emblem for the tank, and a deeply stepped and studded new seat. All the black gave it a sleek look that really set it apart. Setting it even further apart were the scallop graphics on the tank, one of which even rocketed back along the bobtail rear fender. All that for only $13,850, only $475 more than the Springer. As Harley said, the Bad Boy had a "dark beauty all its own."

Little was changed on the rest of the Softails (Custom, Springer, Heritage Classic, Heritage Special, and Fat Boy), other than paint options and power-train updates listed in chapter 1, except that the FXSTC and FXSTS were given a new tank transfer that featured "Harley-Davidson" over a diamond shape over a stylized eagle in flight. Bigger changes were slated for the years ahead.

For 1996, the same six Softails were available as in 1995: Custom, Springer, Bad Boy, Heritage Custom, Heritage Special, and Fat Boy. All were fitted with an electronic speedometer (like that of the Road King) and revised handlebar switches, and were offered in new paint schemes for the year.

HERITAGE SPRINGER

Ever see an idea put to metal and think, "Yeah; 'bout damn time"?

Well, that's what thousands of us thought in late 1996 when Willie G. and Louie N. unveiled their latest rendition of a Harley idea whose time had never really gone: the FLSTS Heritage Softail Springer.

Start with the Heritage Softail. Modify a springer front end to fit a fat 16-inch front wheel and top it off with a chrome horn just like the original. Revive and update the old springer front fender (but this one's mounted so it swings upward with the tire, unlike those of the 1940s) with running lamp. Resurrect the tombstone taillight first used in 1947. Throw on whitewall tires and a big saddle with outsized tooled-leather skirts, long leather fringe, red trim, chromed grab rail, and removable passenger section. Bolt up chromed dual exhaust with fishtail mufflers and fringed, tooled-leather bags. What you've got is the Heritage Springer, and an almost spot-on re-creation of the pimped-up bikes the bobber guys of the 1940s and 1950s derided as "garbage wagons," but let's not go there, all right? Truth is, all it needed to get rid of the "almost" was a tank-shift, the old post-mounted tractor seat, half-moon footboards, and a front fender mounted to the rigid leg of the fork and showing more of the tire, but we won't go there either. After all, even Harley has to make concessions to modern tastes.

The Harley literature will tell you that the new model re-creates the look of the 1948 Panhead, and in general terms, it really does. Willie G. and Louie N.

In 1995 Harley introduced a new version of the Springer Softail with (in Harley's words) a "dark beauty all its own": the FXSTB Bad Boy. Single disc brakes front and rear were full-floaters, and the rear wheel was a special slotted disc-type. It remained in production through the 1997 model year.

The Bad Boy featured black in place of much of the chrome and wild scalloped graphics. Shown is a 1996 model with a sprinkle of added chrome. Bad Boy's fork was mostly black, but it featured the revised front fender and linkage introduced in 1993, which lowered the fender to reduce the dreaded "motocross" look.

know better (or at least I hope they do). If you want to see where that dynamic duo really got their inspiration for the tank cloisonné emblem and tank stripes, you have to look back just a little further, to the Knucklehead of 1940 (emblem) and the 1936 flathead models (stripes).

As with the regular Springer Softail, the old look came at very little price in function. The spring fork is stiction-free, and its 4 inches of travel will absorb a hefty jolt before bottoming hard. For those who like to tilt the horizon, though, this isn't the bike. Just as with the regular Heritage, the Springer version grounds its footboards and other bits with gusto just when things are *starting* to get fun. No matter, though. Ridden the way it was intended to be, it's quite possibly the most satisfying Big Twin in the Harley line.

Birch White was the only color offered, but you could get it with your choice of blue or red trim. Both were stunners and will go down in future books as classics of their time.

Just as on the Springers of the past, the Bad Boy's fork damper was fitted with a sticker listing the patents on the front-end design. Low handlebars mounted to black "dogbone" risers.

The slotted disc rear wheel of the Bad Boy was a first for Harley. Later, the slotted disc would be used on other models.

Just as the Springer followed the Softail, the Heritage Springer followed the Heritage, though it took a while. Before the new machine made its debut for model year 1997, few saw it coming, but we all should have, and then we wondered, "What took them so long?" When it did arrive, it was an instant sensation.

The Rest of the Line

With the new Heritage Springer, the Softail line was up to six. Returning almost without change were the Custom, Springer, Bad Boy, Heritage Classic, and Fat Boy.

For 1998, the Bad Boy was cut out of the line-up, leaving just five Softails, all of which returned with just minor cosmetic updates and a clutch that had been reworked for lower lever effort to disengage it. Fat Boy and Heritage Springer were also available with a special Midnite Red and Champagne Pearl paint job, and a new fired-enamel cloisonné emblem commemorating the company's 95th anniversary.

NIGHT TRAIN AND SOFTAIL STANDARD

For 1999, the "alpha" part of the P22 program mentioned in chapter 1 made its debut as the thumping, new Twin Cam 88 motor, which was put in all non-Softail Big Twins (except the special edition FXR[2] and FXR[3]) for 1999. Once again, the FX line (now along with its other branch, the solid-mount FL Softails) was cast in the dual roles of providing a "fall-back" position for H-D in case of troubles with its new engine, while at the same time easing the pain of transition for Harley traditionalists. Once again, the Softail line-up played its role with grace.

Considering all the effort necessary to get the new Twin Cam motor into production, you'd expect the "fall-back" Softail line to be back without change. And you'd be wrong. In fact, two new Softail models thundered out of York to carry the Evo motor through its final year of regular series production.

The Night Train: "Softail Stealth"

For 1999, Willie and Louie let out of the hangar the ultimate factory Harley for the "stealth pilots" of the counterchrome movement. The new "bad boy" in the line-up was the FXSTB Night Train, based on the Softail Custom, with con-

Once again, the fork was the star of the show. Unlike the original springer on Knuckles and Pans, the fender on the new Springer mounts to the movable legs of the fork and moves up and down with the suspension. That fender is the one piece on the bike that looks conspicuously different than on the originals, looking more like the "wheel pants" on an old biplane than the high and rigidly mounted fender on the old Knuckles. While we're at it, where are the half-moon footboards and tractor seat?

Heritage Springer was available only in white for its first year, but two trim options were available: red or blue. Both are shown here. Harley-Davidson literature called the FLSTS Heritage Springer a re-creation of the look of the 1948 Panhead, the last year before the Hydra-Glide fork. In reality, it's a mix and match of styling cues off a number of old Harleys.

If you look closely (and know your Knuckles, Pans, and flatheads), you'll know where the trim and details came from. Tank badges and stripes are most similar to those of 1940. Stripes alone? Straight off the 1936 flatheads.

ventional fork and disc rear wheel. Even blacker than the Bad Boy had been, the Night Train wasn't just black, it was matte black, like a Stealth fighter, with black crinkle on the oil tank, the entire engine (except the pushrod tubes and fasteners), the tranny cases and covers, and the rear fender supports. Just about everything else was shiny black, save the fork assembly.

Lean, ever so black, and with a performance edge courtesy of the 6-inch straight (no pull-back) chrome risers topped with flat drag bars, the Night Train was easily the best looking blacked-out Harley yet, proving that juicy styling treats could still be wrung out of the old Evo Softail.

The Softail Standard: "Softail Subtle"

Making a surprise reprise was a new version of the plain old FXST (which had been axed at the end of 1990), now officially dubbed the Softail Standard.

With so many versions of the Softail already available, and waiting lists for every one built, why the Standard? Well, the easy answer is to provide a less expensive option in the Softail line, but I really don't believe that was it. After all, why tie up the production line with a cheap stripper when you can sell all the expensive deluxe models you can build? I think it all comes down to another Willie-and-Louie counterchrome styling statement. If the Night Train was "Softail Stealth," the Standard was "Softail Subtle," with the matte silver of its powdercoated engine castings glowing softly against the Vivid Black paint.

Here's where we see how much had changed in the decade and a half that the Evo had powered Harley's world. In 1984 the "plain" Softail was the swankest, most "custom" bike in the whole Harley line-up—in any company's line-up, for that matter. Just 15 model years later, the original Softail would look as much of a stripper compared to the 1999 Softails as the 883 Sportster does compared to the Sportster 1200 Custom. Well, the Softail Subtle was even less primped than the original, showing how far Willie and Louie pushed to make their statement.

In the name of subtlety and price, the dynamic duo took back all the extras that had been added in 1986 to create the Softail Custom—disc wheel, blacked and polished engine and tranny, sissybar, and so on. But they went even further, replacing the chrome on the oil tank with gloss black and foregoing even the polish on the primary cover. In fact, except for the polish on the rocker covers, the whole motor wore its silver finish as a proud mark of distinction. Though the masses clearly preferred the blacked-out and polished motor of the other Softails, for a certain group, the matte-silver motor of the Softail Subtle really scratched an itch—and left a few bucks in their pockets that they could spend on the custom touches that mattered most to them.

The rest of the Softail line was back with little change, except for the usual paint and trim changes. Oh, and one part restyled like that of the new Twin Cam 88: a gleaming new derby cover with five mounting screws (instead of three).

Trim and light on the front fender are similar to pieces from the past, too. For the Heritage Springer, Harley even brought back a new version of the old fork-mounted horn.

With the Springer Heritage, Harley has gone back into its Heritage about as far as it can on the Big Twin line. Perhaps it's time for some Heritage Sportsters? Like a re-creation of the old high-pipe XLCH?

Taking the blacked-out theme of the discontinued Bad Boy to the next extreme, new-for-1999 FXSTB Night Train roared into the Harley line-up like a Stealth Fighter. The Night Train was based on the Softail Custom, with a disc rear wheel and the larger, 5-gallon Fat Bob tanks but the theme here was black.

REQUIEM EVO

Since the day of its introduction, the Softail had been the most visible link between the Harley's future and its past. By midsummer 1999, for the 2000 model year, however, even the Softail line was stripped of the Evo engine and delivered into the Twin Cam era, with the release of the final product of the P22 program: the Twin Cam 88B ("beta") motor, featuring counterbalancers to take the edge off the vibes. The first new model to carry the Evo engine, the Softail was also the last (save for a few special production FXR^{2}s, FXR^{3}s, and FXR^{4}s). It also proved to be the most important new Harley model since the Super Glide of 1971, and perhaps since the Knucklehead of 1936.

Evo and Softail. Together, they bridged the gap between Harley-Davidson's "hard" and "soft" sides, having all the functional benefits of the new motor with the "good vibrations" and (most importantly) the classic looks of the old

The whole engine (except for a few bits) was coated in wrinkle black—even the rocker boxes—and no polished fin ends, either. For 1999, only the Softail models and the two special-edition FXR models were fitted with the Evolution engine. For 2000, the Evolution would be gone even on the Softails, replaced by the Twin Cam 88B engine, with twin counterbalancers.

Harleys. Together, they became Harley's best seller, at a time when every single sale was a small step away from bankruptcy. Together, they helped return Harley-Davidson to profitability and provide the funds to start a whole new era for The Motor Company. Would either one have succeeded as it did, without the other? We'll never know. What we can say for sure is that the spirit in which both the engine and the motorcycle were created lives on in Milwaukee, and that's the most fitting epitaph for the Evo-powered Softails.

Even the primary cases were wrinkle black. If you're fed up with the "chrome-everything" movement, here's a bike for you.

Instead of tall bars, the Night Train was fitted with short bars on 6-inch chrome risers, for more of the drag-bike look of past Harleys, such as the original and Dyna Sturgis models.

CHAPTER 3

The FLT and FLHT Series

1984 – 1998

The FLT and FLHT taught us that Harley customers want improvements and modernization, but those have to come with the classic look.

—Tom Gelb, former senior vice president of operations

In an effort to offer a more traditional Harley look with the rubber mounts and five-speed of the FLT, Harley reworked the old FLH fairing and put it on the FLT chassis to create a new model, the FLHT Electra Glide, introduced in 1983. It quickly proved the most popular of Harley's big baggers and is still in production with the Twin Cam 88 engine introduced for 1999.

arley's baggers were still the "Kings of the Highway" and the machines that defined the marque when the Evo engine made its debut for the 1984 model year. The new Kings weren't granddad's old Electra Glide, however, because the solid-mounted FLH-80 was given last rites, along with the Shovelhead engine. Only the recently introduced FLTC Tour Glide Classic and FLHTC Electra Glide Classic were given the new engine and anointed to carry Harley's baggers into the future. But since neither the FLTC or FLHTC was a new model for 1984, we need to look back at how they came to be to understand where the Evo engine would take them.

TALE OF THE TOUR GLIDE

If Hank Hubbard could be called "father of the Evo" (see chapter 1) and Bill Davis "father of the Softail" (see chapter 2), then former Harley engineer Ray Miennert could be called "father of the Tour Glide," the person whose skill and sweat laid the foundations for the whole design.

"Dirty-Hands" Engineering

Miennert joined The Motor Company in 1960, right after graduating from the Milwaukee School of Engineering. By the late 1960s, Miennert was a key member of Department 43, Harley's experimental wing. "That's where *all* the action was," he explained. "Department 43 was virtually all experimental. Virtually everything we needed as a one- or two-of-a-kind was built there because we had complete machine-shop facilities and the best mechanics. I functioned as what they call a 'dirty-hands' engineer, because I was building things, as well as testing and designing."

His most momentous work resulted from an assignment given him in the late 1960s by Harley's legendary chief engineer, Chris Spexarth (who reportedly did most of the design work on the original Knucklehead of 1936). According to Miennert, "Spexarth basically said, 'We want a new motorcycle with three things: a rubber mounting system for the engine, a reduced-cost frame, and less sensitivity to chassis maintenance. You design it!'

"In other words," continued Miennert, "he wanted a frame that wasn't built from forgings and castings anymore because they were very expensive to

When it was introduced for 1980, the FLT was really the first all-new Harley Big Twin in nearly a generation. It featured a frame-mounted fairing, an innovative "balanced" fork, integrated bags and trunk, a new frame, a five-speed transmission, and rubber mounts for the engine. When the FLT was fitted with the new V^2 Evolution engine for 1984, it finally had a powerplant the equal of the rest of the machine. Shown is owner Steve Acord.

build and machine, a frame with rubber mounts to isolate the engine vibration, and one you could run the shit out of without having to do anything to it, which is what most people do. They'll put $10,000 worth of chrome on it, but won't change the rear tire 'til the cords are hanging out of it. The initial program was set up to be five years, and that's about what it took to get the bike where we wanted it to be."

Until it reached its near-final form for production, the machine that resulted from this assignment was referred to as the "Rubber Mount."

Let the Testing Begin

Miennert's first task was to research how good or bad the Harleys and other motorcycles of the time were. Miennert remembers:

"Basically, first we sort of laid baselines by going through all the bikes of the equivalent size on the market to see how their frames were built, and then full-scale testing of them at a high-speed track near San Antonio [Texas]. We tested a whole bunch of them—Triumphs, Nortons, the big Kawasakis, and Hondas. We had BMWs, Moto Guzzis, Laverdas—all the Italian jobs. We even got a couple racers from the race department and tested them, too.

"We wanted to create a worst-case scenario for the tests, with heavily loaded motorcycles, to simulate police use, so we outfitted these bikes with a Tour-Pak full of instrumentation and added weight to the saddlebags or hung on weight in that area if there were no bags.

"We'd check them all by riding at 70, 80, and 90 miles per hour on the straightaway, taking your hands off the bars, and moving your butt real hard to induce a weave. We wanted to know how big it was when you induced it and how many cycles it took before it decayed down to where we could no longer feel it.

"In the Tour-Pak, we had a light-beam strip-chart recorder, so all we'd have to do is take the strip out, develop it in sunlight, and look at it. Five minutes after the run, you had everything laid out in front of you. It recorded speed, steering angle, and left-to-right acceleration at the Tour-Pak. If things had gotten good enough that we couldn't discern the differences by feel, it gave us final resolution."

Pity the fool who drops this sucker—not just because its owner will kill you, but because it weighs the best part of 800 pounds when all gassed up. On the move, however, it's 800 pounds of rolling grace, courtesy of its balanced front end and well-engineered chassis. For 1980–1984, the FLT came with an enclosed rear-drive chain. In 1985, it was given belt drive, as announced by the graphic on the front fender.

Miennert did his own test riding, assisted by a Harley test rider, Charles Zieglar. "We'd go down for two to three weeks at a shot and work 12 to 15 hours a day," he remembered. The conclusion of this round of testing? "Each one had its own little handling flukes," he said, "but some of them were really bad." Also, they found that a properly maintained and adjusted Harley FLH was about as good as most of the competition.

Crushing the Competition

"It took a while to get through all the vehicles," Miennert continued. "After we were done riding them, we'd tear them down to see how they were made and what kind of wear, if any, was happening to certain items. Sometimes we'd reassemble them and sell them, but often, we'd scrap them out. If you've done something to change a bike, you're legally liable for it. During testing we sometimes would change rake and trail to see if we could improve them, and they were run fairly hard. Just to save trouble, we'd take it to the dump and run over it with a Caterpillar tractor.

The Evo-powered FLTs and FLHTs of 1984 and 1985 were fitted with the large ham-can air cleaners. They allowed the engine to produce more power than the more stylish round cleaners used on the smaller Big Twins. You don't see many bikes wearing these anymore.

Hidden by that twin-headlight fairing is an innovative fork, designed by Ray Miennert of Department 43, Harley's experimental department. Called the "balanced fork," its steering head was actually forward of the fork tubes, the opposite of the arrangement normally used. By using this arrangement and putting the fork tubes at a less steep angle than that of the steering head, Miennert was able to design it so that the weight of the fork was balanced around the steering axis, for lighter steering on the heavy machine.

The FLT's tank and instruments were new, too. The tank was a one-piece, 5-gallon design, with the filler front and center. Speedo, tach, and idiot lights were clustered in a plastic "breadbox" unit attached atop the steering stem. For 1985, all the Harleys were fitted with a 120-mile-per-hour speedo, replacing the government-mandated 85-mile-per-hour units fitted through 1984. In its first year, the FLT sold well, but sales plummeted thereafter because traditional Harley customers never accepted the look of its frame-mounted fairing. At the end of the 1996 model year, the FLT was axed from the line-up. For 1998 it was back, however, in modified form as the Road Glide.

Shown is a 1986 Liberty Edition of the FLHT. The Liberty Editions were numbered special editions to commemorate the 100th anniversary of the Statue of Liberty. According to Harley's figures, 810 Liberty FLHTCs were built.

"That's what Harley did with a lot of overstock parts, too. The parts department would fill a big dumpster, take it out to the landfill. They'd dump the parts and run over them with a Caterpillar a dozen times to smash the parts to smithereens."

Lord, Help Me

In between trips to San Antonio for high-speed testing, Miennert began sketching out the improvements he would make to the new motorcycle. Although years of testing and refinement were necessary before he was done, the first few Rubber Mount prototypes had most of the features that would later set the FLT apart from the old FLH: rubber mounts for the engine, new frame and rear suspension, and the innovative "balanced" fork. "Things happened very fast," explained Miennert. "We put in the improvements as a lump, and within a month or two, we had bikes on the track. I normally had one or two mechanics working with me, so we could crank them out quickly."

Inspiration for the rubber mounting system came from the Norton Commando, with Isolastic mounts that he'd tested and then torn down for inspection. "We looked at the Norton system very extensively," said Miennert. "It had some flaws, but it gave us a starting point for where we wanted to go."

One huge problem involved figuring out how to allow the engine to move in the mounts without having it be twisted around by the tremendous loads from the primary and secondary chains. Miennert's solution was identical, in concept, to Norton's. "First, we welded some mounting lugs on the motor and transmission," he explained. "We used those lugs to bolt the engine and transmission together to resist the primary loads, and we mounted the swingarm to the transmission lugs because if we didn't, the secondary chain loads would have pulled the whole engine sideways in the mounts." Without this the bike would need

The "C" in FLHTC stood for "Classic," as the fender graphic proclaims.

such stiff mounts that there would have been little reduction in vibration.

With this system, the whole driveline—engine, transmission, swingarm, and rear wheel—was essentially a separate system attached to the frame only by the rubber mounts. That meant that the rubber mounts would have to be pliable enough in the vertical plane to isolate the shaking of the engine but stiff enough laterally to keep the driveline assembly from squirming around independently of the frame.

Optimum placement of the mounts was one of the keys to making the design work. "We looked at the center of gravity of the motor," he explained, "and we tried to get the mounts spaced at equal distance from the center of gravity of the motor and transmission." He placed two at the rear (on each side of the swingarm pivots), two at the front of the engine, and another at the top of the engine, in the V. It also meant that the engine and transmission no longer contributed their strength to the chassis, so the frame would have to be stiffer to compensate.

Mounts with great lateral stiffness were another key. For help in designing the rubber mounts, Miennert turned to a familiar source. "We had used Lord rubber mounts on Harley handlebars for many years," he recalled. "Knowing we weren't going to get off-the-shelf mounts, we brought their engineers in when the whole thing was still on paper and asked, 'What can you do and what can you tell us?' We came up with a pretty good system that sandwiched three or four steel plates in the rubber to make them flexible one way and stiff the other."

A BETTER BACKBONE

Miennert designed the frame meant to carry the rubber-mounted driveline around the mounting system. He used box-section steel tubing for the frame's backbone and round steel tubes and stampings for everything else, eliminating all the expensive forgings and designing in stiffness with gussets and triangulation.

For the rear suspension, he knew what he wanted right away. "On the FLH," he explained, "the shocks had been basically grafted on to the old rigid frame. The shocks were mounted forward, which meant they had to be shorter and the swingarm would flex behind the lower shock mount. We moved the shocks to the rear, with the lower shock mount over the axle because it's an easier suspension to work with and is more rigid."

BALANCING ACT, PART I

The "balanced" front fork was probably the most innovative part of Miennert's Rubber Mount. What's meant by "balanced"? Miennert explained: "Basically, our idea was we could reduce the motorcycle's sensitivity to maladjustment of the steering-head bearings by making the moment of inertia of the whole front end as

low as possible, while keeping the same trail, for stability. The FLH front end was very heavy, so the object was to drive that steering axis right through the center of gravity, which made that moment of inertia as low as it could possibly get, no matter what else you tried."

That's far easier to say than to accomplish without throwing all the other related (and conflicting) factors of rake, fork angle, and trail out of whack. Miennert's solution was to reverse the status quo.

In a conventional front end, the fork tubes mount to the triple clamps forward of the steering axis or alongside the axis; on most, the tubes are also parallel to that axis. "With a standard fork, the whole doggone fork was in front of the point you were steering," Miennert explained. To get the steering axis near the center of gravity, Miennert tried putting the steering axis and tubes at an angle to each other. Even that wasn't enough.

Fortunately, work Miennert had done years ago supplied the solution. "Back in 1962 or 1963 we took one of the smaller motorcycles, the BT, and tried a balanced front end on it," he remembered. Through experimentation, he found that by designing an extended steering head into the frame and new triple clamps that placed the fork tubes *behind* the steering axis and at a less steep angle than that of the steering head, he could keep the front wheel in the same place, relative to the frame, while getting the low moment of inertia and trail he wanted.

When Miennert tried a Big Twin–sized version of the balanced fork on the Rubber Mount, it gave incredibly light steering to what was in fact a very heavy machine. "It was almost like having power steering," he said.

Operation Paper Boy

At the start of the Rubber Mount program, Harley-Davidson was still very much doing things the old way. Miennert and his colleagues still relied on "seat of the pants" more than on instruments and computers. By the time the Rubber Mount was being polished for production as the FLT in the late 1970s, computer modeling, finite-element analysis, and sophisticated testing instruments were becoming an indispensable part of the design process. Such technical capabilities don't get developed overnight.

For Harley, it all began as part of the Rubber Mount program. Harley-Davidson began working with CALSPAN (a for-profit research organization that was spun off of Cornell University's Aeronautics Lab) to develop a computer program to model the chassis dynamics of a motorcycle. "CALSPAN had developed a handling program for bicycles," remembered Miennert. "They figured they could adapt the program for motorcycles." Unfortunately, it wasn't as easy as CALSPAN thought.

"My understanding of the history," added Mark Tuttle, "is that Schwinn bicycle started the work because paper boys would load their bicycles up full of newspapers and get going too fast down a hill, and the bicycle would get unstable and they would crash. Schwinn wanted to understand what was going on and hired CALSPAN to study the problem."

Starting in 1986, the Classic package included a standard AM/FM/cassette stereo with channel-19 CB monitor, and extra gauges.

Miennert and others at Harley worked with CALSPAN for several years, supplying test data and even taking motorcycles to CALSPAN for testing. "In the end," he recalled, "the computer told us, 'If you want a good high-speed handling motorcycle, you should have a rake of 90 degrees, and the trail should be infinite.' You can't design a bike that way. The whole effort just proved to us that the computer and program weren't yet good enough for what we wanted."

For 1986, the old ham-can air cleaner was replaced by a more-classic round air cleaner, replaced here by an aftermarket unit. More-luxurious passenger accommodations were now standard on the Classic, too, including footboards, a better back rest, hand rails, and an improved seat.

Texas Rangers

With all the basics for his new Rubber Mount touring machine in place, Miennert began building and testing a long string of experimental machines at the track outside San Antonio. It was an exhaustive process that involved dozens of trips back to the track and the assistance of many outside vendors, including tire manufacturers.

Said Miennert:

"It was just a matter of getting the machines made up and getting enough of them that we felt secure in what we were doing, because sometimes you can build one machine and it's great. Build another one and the doggone thing's all over the road!

"We'd usually build four or five of each variety. We would run them, and if there was some change indicated, we'd cut the frame apart down at the track and reweld it in the position where we wanted it. I did some of that work, too. If it was an improvement, we'd put it on a couple of them, and if it still felt good we'd put it on the rest of them, and then move on to more changes. Altogether, by the time I was off the project, we probably had built 20 or 25 motorcycles. In the end, we were sort of zeroing down, so each change might be just a slight one.

"We experimented a lot with rubber mounting, using softer and stiffer mounts. There was one that was optimum, and that's the one that we chose, and we chose it based on rider's feel, or seat of the pants. Same with the weave decay. We had all the instruments, but in the end we stopped when it felt right to the rider."

As refinement of the Rubber Mount neared its end, other engineers (including Mark Tuttle) and test riders (including racer Roger Reiman) were brought into the test program to give a wider base of opinion on how well it all worked.

Two things were obvious to all of them. First, the rubber mounts were very effective. A typical comment was, "I can look in the rear-view mirror and actually see something!" Second, the steering was very light for such a huge machine.

Bodywork on the Liberty Editions was painted Blackberry with silver panels.

Even the fairing was given a Liberty graphic.

Onto the Shelf

After Miennert was done testing the Rubber Mount and the last test report was written, in 1975, he moved on to a new job in a new department. What happened to his Rubber Mount? "The whole thing was put into mothballs," he remembered. "Our illustrious management didn't think there was a need for a rubber-mounted motorcycle. They said, 'The Japanese have that kind of stuff. We don't want to go that way.'"

That assessment may be a bit harsh, however, according to Mark Tuttle, who was then chief test engineer. "Ray did a hardware development program," Tuttle said. "It was a feasibility study to see what could be done, and whether or not we could accomplish the goals that had been set for the program. He completed that work. Then, the program moved from Department 43 up to the design area, and there may have been a period where there wasn't a lot going on with it, because at that time we had a very limited capacity to do multiple programs. It may have had to wait in line until some other programs got done."

Fortunately, the Rubber Mount's time was soon to come.

Retreat? Hell No, Advance!

One of the concepts that crystallized at Harley's momentous management retreat in April 1976 (see chapter 1) was to design a new flagship touring machine that would at once trump all of Harley's competitors, and the aftermarket, as well? See, by 1976, Harley's hold on the touring market was under full frontal assault from both.

Most worrisome, Honda had turned the whole touring world on its ear the previous year with its innovative GL-1000 Gold Wing. Though the Wing had no factory-mounted bags or fairing, it was almost carlike in the other conveniences it offered, including a water-cooled four-cylinder engine, slick-shifting five-speed transmission, and shaft drive. Its reliability soon became legend, and before long it was the best-selling touring bike in America.

The aftermarket had been ramping up for a while, too. By the time the Gold Wing came along, the market was awash in high-quality fairings and bags that made it easy for anyone to turn their Wing or any of the other large

The FLHT combined the best of old and new. Its fairing looked like the old "bat-wing" fairing of the FLH, but it was mounted to the better handling, rubber-mounted chassis of the FLT.

Japanese or European bike into a full-on bagger that was faster, smoother, more comfortable, and more reliable than Harley's old FLH.

A bad situation, obviously, but after the retreat, Harley-Davidson at least had a plan. "We knew if we were going to compete with what we were starting to see from the Japanese, we needed to update our bikes," Vaughn Beals said. "Honda came out with the Gold Wing, which at that time was a plain-vanilla motorcycle—it didn't have any touring gear at all. We thought we had value in the uniqueness of our touring equipment, but we had to have a motorcycle that worked and didn't shake. The whole concept was one of let's make it a much more rider-friendly vehicle."

Fortunately, Ray Miennert's prototypes included most of what Beals envisioned as the new rider-friendly Harley, so when AMF gave the green light to

Creating the FLHT wasn't as easy as just bolting the old fairing onto the new fork. Harley tried that, but putting all the weight of the fairing back on the fork made the machine handle like an old FLH, and that was no longer good enough in the 1980s. By cutting as much weight off the fairing and fender as possible and moving what weight they couldn't eliminate in closer to the steering axis, the FLHT engineers were able to get the handling up to modern standards and the looks back to classic standards.

Owner Chuck Myers on his FLHT.

proceed with the new long-range product plan in mid-1977, the heat was at last turned up under the long-simmering Rubber Mount program.

Team Tour Glide

A group of engineers was assigned to pick up Miennert's rubber ball, dust it off, and run with it. For the purposes of this book, we'll call the group Team Tour Glide. Among them were designer Dick Donaj and project engineer Bruce Fiorani.

"At the time," said former Harley engineer Rit Booth, " Harley was seen as losing the battle to the Japanese motorcycle manufacturers. A lot of it had to do with handling and cornering, so the FLT project started off with the idea that we needed to upgrade the FLH with rubber mounts. Well, a rubber mount system requires a new frame and a new transmission case. Since we're designing a new frame and transmission case, why don't we design a new suspension with more ground clearance and make the transmission a five-speed? As long as we're doing all that, why don't we do a new frame-mount fairing? As long as we're doing a new fairing, why don't we design new saddlebags? This just went on until everything was new. It ended up being a pretty big project."

From Booth's vantage point in the trenches, the FLT program may have seemed that haphazard, but the view from higher up was a bit different. "The FLT was done as a program," explained Mark Tuttle. "While a whole litany of things wound up on the FLT that had started out as separate conceptual projects, the motorcycle was developed with some very specific objectives in mind concerning operator comfort from a vibration standpoint, vehicle dynamics from a high-speed handling standpoint, and chassis stiffness."

Norton Rumblings

As work began on refining the Rubber Mount for production, concern grew that the rubber mounting system on the prototypes was too similar to the one Norton had patented. It's one thing to build and test a few prototypes, but quite another to start building thousands and selling them in the marketplace, so Harley engineers substantially revised the system to differentiate it from Norton's.

With its knife-and-fork connecting rods, the Harley Big Twin motor vibrates primarily in the vertical plane, so team engineers were able to reduce the number of rubber mounts from five to three. The "donut" mount on each side of the swingarm pivot and one block-type mount up front were kept, which combined to take care of the vertical shakes. The other two mounts were replaced by aircraft-type, Heim-jointed stabilizer rods, one at the front from the frame to the engine, and the other from the frame to a bracket bolted between the cylinder heads. With this system, the motor-tranny-swingarm unit was free to pogo up and down, and even fore and aft, while the ball-jointed rods kept it from squirming side to side.

In the process of refining the mounts themselves, Harley engineers coordinated efforts with the two vendors in competition to manufacture them: Lord

and Barry Controls. Through that process, Barry suggested a substantial improvement to the design. "The front mount was flat on our original design," explained Rit Booth. "Barry suggested rotating it 30 degrees, and that change made the whole isolation system much smoother. Because of that and because Barry adapted their mounts to give us the exact stiffnesses we needed, we bought our mounts from them."

The revised mounting system—called "Tri-Mount" in the early ads—substantially quelled the quaking of the Harley engine. At idle, the vibes remained strong, but the whole machine went eerily smooth as the revs climbed. Not as smooth as a Gold Wing, perhaps, but smoother than any Harley-Davidson Big Twin had ever been before, and smooth enough to improve rider comfort substantially.

Here's an historically significant FLHT and the historically significant couple who owns it—former Harley CEO Vaughn Beals and his wife, Eleanore. This bike is one that Vaughn and Eleanore rode from Los Angeles to New York to raise money for the restoration of the Statue of Liberty. Once they got the bike to New York, they auctioned it off to raise even more money. The top three bidders eventually backed out of the deal, so Beals later bought the machine and still rides it. *Nolan Woodbury photo*

Mainframe Frame

In the half-dozen years that had passed since Ray Miennert had worked with CALSPAN on modeling motorcycle frame design with computers, a lot had changed. Computers and software had advanced remarkably. Motorcycle frames had gotten much stiffer. And AMF had kicked loose a little money for Harley-Davidson to invest in all three—and in bringing in a new crop of young engineers who were eager to mix motorcycling and mainframes.

One of those guys was Rit Booth. Not long after earning a degree in mechanical engineering from MIT, Booth joined Harley-Davidson in 1977 as the third member of the company's new Design Analysis Department. "Harley had just started up a department to do computer-aided analysis and was really interested in growing the department," said Booth. "When I started, it was just Bruce Dennert and I [both supervised by Richard Herman]. We handled more than just the

The aft end of the Beals' FLHT. *Nolan Woodbury photo*

computer-aided stuff. We would assist in anything that was more than just a simple computation."

Harley-Davidson put the Design Analysis staff to good use in designing the FLT frame. "Historically, the engine and transmission had played a structural role in the chassis," Mark Tuttle explained. "With the rubber mounts, we took that structural role out, so the chassis had to be significantly stiffer." Booth and Dennert made use of the relatively new science of finite-element analysis to help the project engineers predict the stresses on the frame. "In our first go-around, the goal was to make the new frame by itself, without the engine, as stiff as the old frame with the engine and transmission bolted in place." Team Tour Glide refined Miennert's Rubber Mount frame to make it both stiffer and easier to produce—and they hit the stiffness goal on the first try. Unfortunately, meeting the stiffness goal didn't mean it was stiff enough, as later testing revealed.

Give Me Five

"The need for a totally unique transmission case was driven by the need to add the swingarm pivot to the case, because of the rubber mounts," said Mark Tuttle. "But while we were doing a new transmission case, it only made sense to add the fifth speed."

Simple rationale, that, but the need for a new transmission case wasn't the only impetus behind the tranny redesign. "We were under pressure because everybody had five-speeds, while we had a four-speed," said retired Chief Engineer Don Valentine. "Of course, with the torque we had, there were those of us who felt a five-speed was superfluous, but that's what Marketing wanted."

Another even-more-practical consideration—manufacturing cost—came into play.

Another FLHTC, this one a 1988 model. New for 1988, the Classics were given the chrome-and-black engine and 10-spoke mag wheels, though this one has been retrofitted with a laced front wheel.

The cockpit of the 1988 FLHTC Classic, with a new stereo featuring an integral clock and weather-channel monitor.

Also new for 1988, the position of the Tour-Pak was adjustable to create more or less room for the passenger. Another change was more subtle: The air nipple at the end of the hand grip is there to add air into the sealed handlebar that now served as the reservoir for the antidive system for the front fork.

Though it looks less imposing than the FLT, the FLHT is still a massive machine. Ponderous at parking-lot speeds, it feels better the faster you go.

"We had to hand-shim the old four-speed," continued Valentine. "It was very labor-intensive, so one of the main goals in the five-speed design was that manufacturing be able to just assemble it with parts off the shelf, without having to shim everything. That was just a matter of tightening up on tolerance control."

Engineering got to work on the design and eventually came up with a tranny that was a vast improvement over the old four-speed in every way. Its gear ratios and gear profiles were optimized by computer modeling for the 80-cubic-inch version of the Shovelhead engine that was released in 1978. In addition, many of the parts were lighter, so shifting was improved over that of the old four-speed.

Then, it was manufacturing's turn. "On all the old designs, both the engines and transmissions, there was lots of hand work," said Tom Gelb, the retired vice president of operations. "This was part of the design, but it was made worse because manufacturing couldn't hold real close specifications. Our old four-speed case was put in something like 23 different fixtures to machine it. The tolerance stack-up was unbelievable with all those separate operations. We needed something better if we were to meet our goals for the five-speed. This was before CNC and numerically controlled machine tools

Sidecars have always been popular accessories for Harley's Big Twins. This aftermarket Liberty sidecar is attached to a 1988 FLTC that was stripped of its fairing and fitted with the headlight and fork shrouds from the FLHS Electra Glide Sport, a model introduced for 1987.

New versions of the classic Harley-Davidson bar-and-shield emblem were fitted New versions of the classic bar-and-shield emblem were fitted for 1988. The words "Motor" and "Cycles" were now in H-D racing orange. Nineteen eighty-eight was the last year for the gas tank pictured here.

could really do what their manufacturers claimed, so I decided in my infinite wisdom that we were going to get a pallet-transfer machine for that. At the time it cost, I think, six million and change for that tool. That was the largest single capital investment in a machine that AMF had ever made.

"It was also about the biggest goof of my life! Well, the second biggest anyway. It was a straight-through machine that moves the part from station to station to perform all the various operations. It did the job better than what we had before, but it was very inflexible. To make any change, you had to shut the whole thing down. We finally got rid of it. When I retired they gave me the big brass plate off the machine as a millstone around my neck because we had nothing but trouble with it."

I Pronounce You Engine and Transmission

Because the swingarm would now pivot on the transmission case, the FLT's engine and transmission had to be fastened together in a manner stiff enough to carry all the lateral loads from the rear suspension to the frame. The ideal setup to get maximum rigidity between the two would have been to redesign both so they shared the same case or so that the two cases could be bolted rigidly together. In the late 1970s, however, Harley-Davidson didn't have the money for such a massive rework, so the company's engineers designed a "T-bracket" adapter to link the engine and transmission into a more rigid whole. It wasn't ideal, but you can only spend what the boss gives you.

Another thing about this union of engine and transmission: With no seat post on the frame to keep the two apart, Harley's engineers could move them closer together, to make them even more rigid as a pair. This, of course, meant designing shorter primary cases.

Balancing Act, Part II

Miennert's balanced forks demonstrated that an 800-pound touring bike didn't have to steer like one. At low or high speeds, it gave the feel of power steering. Unfortunately, not everyone liked that feel. Mark Tuttle explained: "We determined through testing with a larger audience of people that we still needed to make minor adjustments to the front-end geometry. It had too light a feel, almost like power steering, and so we moved a little bit away from Ray's theoretically ideal configuration to one that gave a little more feedback to the rider through the handlebars."

What they did was fiddle with the geometry to get a little more trail, which reduced the power steering feel and felt a little more like conventional steering. That work paid off, too. Its light but reassuring steering feel became one of the FLT's most dearly loved features.

Turn Your Head and Cough

Harley's 80-cubic-inch engine was slipped into the FLT in the same basic state of tune as in all the other models. It did, however, cough out burned hydrocarbons through an all-new dual exhaust system that was as odd as many of the others Harley came up with during the era.

The FLT's front pipe came down out of the head, bent back to the left side of the engine, and flowed back over the primary case to its own muffler below the left saddlebag. The rear pipe bent forward to loop around the timing cone on the right side of the engine and then back to its own muffler below the right saddlebag.

Road Gear

Though Harley had been offering windshields and saddlebags since at least the 1920s, the company didn't release its first fully "decked" machine until almost 50 years later, with the release of the fiberglass "bat-wing" fairing that was available as part of the King of the Highway option group on the FLH in 1969. In the modern sense, with that FLH package, Willie G. had invented the American-style touring bike.

Thanks to the efforts of Craig Vetter, Bates, and dozens of other aftermarket suppliers, frame-mounted fairings were *de rigueur* on home-rolled touring rigs of the late 1970s. Thus the goal for the new Harley tourer was that it come from the factory with a frame-mount fairing. Willie G. and the team combined

To improve handling with the sidecar attached, this FLTC/FLHS was fitted with raked triple clamps.

efforts to create an innovative fairing to trump all the aftermarket fairing manufacturers. Unfortunately, the new FLT fairing also picked up a bit of the "ugly" of the era, at least when compared to the batwing. Nevertheless, when compared to some of the styling monstrosities of the day such as the Bates Clipper (the true Quasimodo of fairings, with a pig-snouted front section and lowers mounted to the frame *and* a bar-mounted windshield section), the FLT fairing was actually a paragon of beauty.

Rider comfort and convenience have a beauty all their own, however, and the FLT fairing offered vast improvements in both. Its aerodynamics made the whole machine feel more stable at speed and gave much better weather protection to rider and passenger. Also, its twin, car-size headlamps really lit up the night. And its new "breadbox" cluster put all the instruments and idiot lights atop the steering head, where they were easy to see while riding.

As for the bags and Tour-Pak, they definitely looked a large and handsome part of the package from the outside. From the inside, however, the bags were definitely a disappointment because the shocks and battery intruded on carrying space. Still, the FLT had more luggage space than most tourers, and the bags had quick-release mounts. The Tour-Pak was trend-setting, in that its

hinges were on the side, allowing access to the trunk without forcing the passenger from the pillion.

Don't Shaft Me

It wasn't just the comparative reliability and smoothness of the other touring bikes that was wooing the late-1970s touring rider over to the dark side. Partly, it was shafts. Moto Guzzi and BMW had had them for decades. Honda and a bunch of other makers had them, too. Clean, they were. Less needy of day-to-day maintenance, too, so a lot of riders quickly got spoiled by the convenience. Here was a new front on which Harley-Davidson was forced to compete.

Harley had even flirted with the idea of shaft drive, for about, oh, a nanosecond before conceding that it probably wasn't a good idea and settling on a fully enclosed chain drive. "Unfortunately, a shaft drive isn't as efficient as a chain, and we didn't have the horsepower to burn," Vaughn Beals quipped. "We concluded that, to compete, we had to have something that you didn't have to oil or adjust, that didn't spray oil all over you. Ultimately, that's what we got in the belt drive, but the enclosed chain was a pretty good first step."

For police departments who wanted an FLHT-based cop bike (rather than the FXR-based FXRP), Harley offered the FLHTP, starting in 1983. Starting in 1986, two versions were available—one with the fairing and one without but with the windshield. Shown is the fairing-less version, a 1993 model. In 1987, a civilian version of the fairing-free FLHT was offered, the FLHS Electra Glide Sport. In 1989, the gas tank shown was first fitted to all the FLT- and FLHT-based machines. The new, slimmer console and chrome filler cover were a welcome change from the old plastic console. The speedo, tach, and other indicators were housed in a version of the old FLT breadbox console. Functional it was, classic looking it wasn't.

Beals was right; it was a pretty good first step. As used on the production FLT and the later FLHT and FXRT, the system completely enclosed the drive chain and its lubricating oil supply inside metal shrouds that kept the oil in and the grit out. This extended service and replacement intervals on the chain to unheard-of extremes.

Back to San Antone

As the whole bike continued down the funnel of refinement, Team Tour Glide would haul the prototypes to San Antonio or to another track outside South Bend, Indiana, to test each new refinement, and then the whole package.

Much had changed since Miennert's tests in the early 1970s, however. For example, instrumentation was more sophisticated. No longer was all the data recorded on photographic strip charts. Instead, a radio telemetry device sent the data to be recorded in the support van and later to be fed into a computer.

All the FLT- and FLHT-based models were substantially revised with Dyna-type cases for 1993. The oil tank was moved to an undertransmission casting, the oil filter was moved to the front of the engine, and the battery was repositioned. All these changes allowed a redesign of the bags to make them roomier inside, without being much larger on the outside.

Without the fairing, Harley had to fashion some covers to make the headlight area presentable on the naked FLHTP and civilian FLHS. Though they were presentable, they weren't terribly attractive, having a "punched-in" look.

Still, some things had not changed.

First, even though America was still the land of the 55-mile-per-hour speed limit, Harley's engineers were still preparing for a more high-speed future. "The concern was always, 'How does it handle at higher speeds?'," Rit Booth explained. "We were going 85, 90, even 100 miles per hour for most of the testing."

Second, while the FLT hacks were outfitted with instruments to detect steering motions and frame deflection, the subjective impressions of the riders were still more important than the instrument readings.

Like the police model shown, the FLHS came with bags and a windshield but no Tour-Pak.

Third, while at the track, a welding torch was still a useful thing. "We were working to make the frame stiffer and had finished most of a day's testing, before we realized we weren't where we wanted to be. I had brought some gussets I wanted to try. We cut a hole in the stamped-steel plates on either side of the steering head and welded those gussets right in at the test track. We went out there the next day, and it was 100 percent better. The rider said, 'This is what I was after.' With that change, we went from just a little too little to just a little bit more than was required."

By the time the new machine was ready for production in the early spring of 1979, it had been in design and development for over 10 years and had been ridden hundreds of thousands of miles. Even more convenience features had been added, including a spin-on oil filter, electronic ignition, and new one-piece gas tank with locking fill cover on a plastic console. One test yet remained, however . . .

An "Intimate Road Test"

"Before we put the FLT into production," said Vaughn Beals, "we wanted to give it a good, intimate road test, so we shipped a half-dozen of the advanced prototypes down to my in-laws' place in St. Petersburg [Florida]. A bunch of us and our wives flew down and rode them down to Key West and back up to Daytona. The FLT was an excellent improvement, so we put it into production."

That task turned out to be a little more difficult than they thought, however. "I remember when we first got it into production," said Tom Gelb, laughing as he spoke. "Jeff Bleustein was the vice president of engineering then, and he spent a long time down at York working on that frame himself. There were a lot of start-up problems, but you gotta remember, this was really the first new motorcycle Harley-Davidson had tried to build in a long, long time."

THE 1980 FLT TOUR GLIDE

By the time the FLT hit the streets in the fall of 1979, competition in the touring category was even hotter than when the effort began. All the Japanese companies were rushing to market with new fully decked tourers, led by the all-new GL 1100 Gold Wing Interstate, which also debuted for the 1980 model year, complete with integral fairing and lowers, bags, and trunk.

As a result, the FLT was just one among the full-dress herd and had to succeed or fail on its other merits. Fortunately, it had some merit, because from the standpoint of real-world function, the FLT was a stunning leap forward, and the first real sign since 1965 that Harley-Davidson's engineering department might actually be coming into its own. Harley was pretty damn proud of the new Tour Glide, announcing it with four-page color ads that touted the FLT as "The first touring bike built to handle like a sport bike."

Hyperbole like that aside, the FLT gave the copywriters something substantive to talk about, really, for the first time since Harleys got disc brakes in the early 1970s. They took full advantage, too, breathlessly touting each feature: balanced front end ("Even in the showroom, you can turn 700 pounds of static motorcycle with your little finger!"), five-speed gearbox ("it clicks in smoothly . . . effortlessly"), rubber mounts ("The ride is incomparably improved. Look in the mirror—there is no ghosting!"), oil-bath chain ("So now, the most power-efficient drive system in motorcycling is virtually maintenance free and long lasting"), and sport-bike-like cornering clearance ("Lean through an S-curve at a 35-degree lean angle without fear of scraping").

Did the FLT live up to the hype? Sort of. Tour Glide's handling abilities, ride quality, and vibration isolation were all vast improvements over those of any other Harley. The new enclosed, oil-bath chain kept the rear end clean and more than doubled chain life, helping make the FLT less maintenance intensive than other Harleys. And the new electronic ignition helped in that regard, too. The Achilles' heel was that it was still powered by the old Shovelhead motor.

Still, as a functional, rideable *motorcycle*, it was the best *Harley* yet built. Unfortunately, it still was far from being what Harley-Davidson really wanted it to be, and that was the best *touring motorcycle* yet built.

Nevertheless, the mainstream motorcycle magazines took notice. *Motorcyclist* (in the June 1980 issue) deigned to include the Tour Glide in its long-distance test against the competing big-bore tourers, after years of ignoring the FLH.

How'd it do? Not as well as Harley would have liked, but certainly not as badly as the FLH would have. The editors pronounced it expensive at over $6,000 (over $2,000 more than a Gold Wing, but surprisingly $1,000 *less* than the BMW R100RT), the handling "imprecise," the footboards too high, the seat "poor," the oil consumption too high (4.8 quarts in under 4,000 miles), and the brakes "awkward." Worst of all, the Harley was the only bike that broke on the test.

Overall, the editors placed the FLT in the "also-ran" category but acknowledged how far Harley had come with the Tour Glide: "But although it loses against this crowd, the Tour Glide is still a breakthrough machine, because last year Harley didn't even have a machine that could play in the same league."

By 1993, Harley and the companies that supplied the castings and chrome had gotten so good at their jobs that the chrome-and-black deluxe engine was even available on police bikes. In fact, only a few basic stripper models were available with the plain silver engine.

Better yet, some of them got the feeling that Harley was demonstrating that it was a company on the mend. Said tester Art Friedman: "I'm not ready to buy a Harley now, but if they keep making advances in areas like comfort and handling which they made on the Tour Glide, I may be ready in a few years."

An even more gratifying critique was the sales results that first year. Harley sold 4,480 FLTs in 1980, making the model a strong seller in a very strong sales year for Harley. Most important of all, the FLT brought in new customers more than it took away sales of the FLH or FX models.

No question, then, that the FLT had a success that first year. Even so, disquieting feedback from the dealers indicated that things might not be so rosy in the future. Traditional Harley customers loved the way it worked but were not at all pleased with the way it looked. Remember that quote from chapter 2 about some of the newer Harleys looking too "Japanese"? Well, the Tour Glide was one of those models that had to bite its lip and endure that slur.

"PRETTY COVERS," LESSON TWO

While the FLT was in the final stages of its design, Harley was in the first stages of learning a hard lesson. Unfortunately, it hadn't sunk in in time to help shape the FLT or even the later FXR machines, because the learning started on the disastrous Sportster restyle for 1979. That story's in chapter 5, but here're the basics: Harley-Davidson thought that its customers wanted modernized machines (which they really did) and that they wanted the changes

While the FLHS and naked FLHTP suggested the more elemental look of the 1960s FLH, the headlight shrouds and instrument housing stood out as being from a later time.

enough that they'd tolerate compromises in traditional Harley styling to get the updates (which most of them wouldn't).

On the old FLH, the battery and oil tank were right out there (on the right and left sides, respectively), with no attempt to hide either or make both sides of the machine look the same. Battery and oil tank became part of the character of the machine.

Because of the triangulation necessary to add stiffness to the FLT frame, these components had to be placed where they would fit. That left them hanging off the right side of the frame, so a set of odd-shaped covers (can you really call the covers on the FLT pretty?) were designed to cover the oil tank and front of the battery on the right and the electrics on the left. In looks, they said, "modern," not "Harley-Davidson," and that proved to be a big problem in later years.

"The FLT was done with the philosophy that you could make things pretty with covers," said Rit Booth. "Through the school of hard knocks—the FLT not really selling well after the first year—we found out that, no, it isn't covers. What we learned was that what the Harley customer wanted in a motorcycle was good-looking machinery, not good-looking covers."

In the following years Harley made steady improvements to the FLT. In 1981, a fancier version was added, the FLTC Tour Glide Classic. Unfortunately, sales began a steep downward slide that year for all Harley models, but for the FLT models in particular, down to 1,157 FLTCs and 1,636 FLTs, not much more than half the sales of the first year.

What happened? For one, the economy was going ever deeper into recession. For another, pent-up demand by riders who wanted rubber mounts more than they wanted the traditional Harley looks may have been satisfied. For yet another, while the FLT was improved enough to bring in some new customers, it was still powered by the old Shovelhead motor, and many potential customers had heard too many bad stories about the old Shovel.

The primary reason for the poor sales was that traditional Harley customers continued to reject the new model because it didn't look the way they thought a Harley should look. "No question," said Tom Gelb, "our traditional customers didn't like the styling of that frame-mounted fairing and the sidecovers as well. The FLT and FLHT taught us that Harley customers want improvements and modernization, but those have to come with the classic look. That is a real design challenge, but it's also what makes our motorcycles unique."

Harley-Davidson learned from the misstep, though, and learned fast. Some of those who remained were hard at work on a means of combining the best of the new FLT with the best of the old FLH.

THE NEW ELECTRA GLIDE

"What the customers and dealers said they wanted was a bike that rode like the FLT but looked like the FLH," said Tom Gelb. Harley studied the problem, but engineering had real doubts about whether it could deliver on both the ride and the look because "what we found," said Rit Booth, "was that if we bolted an old FL fairing on an FLT, sure enough, it handled like an old FLH again. That wasn't good enough any more."

Still, people wanted that look, and heavier steering wasn't going to hold them back. "What we said we couldn't do from an engineering standpoint," remembered Vaughn Beals, "our dealers did for their customers, and pretty soon, you could go down to the dealership and ride one." What Beals alluded to is that some dealers began outfitting used FLTs with the FLH fairing and putting them on the showroom floor, to compete with brand-new FLTs.

While sales of these used, FLH-ized FLTs were good for the dealer's bottom line, they were bad for Harley-Davidson's. And it came at the worst possible time, during the "crash" and layoffs of early 1982. Harley's production had been cut below the minimums specified in the asset-based loans Beals and his cohorts had gotten when they bought the company. The banks were free to foreclose any time. Harley-Davidson simply *had* to find a way to get the old look with the new function because every additional sale they could get was a small step away from writing a new chapter in the company history that no one wanted to write—Chapter 11 bankruptcy.

Most of the work in forging the new model was done to the front end. And once again, lowering weight and moment of inertia was the key to success.

"A lot of the reasons that the FLT went around corners better than the FL was due to the fact that it didn't have the fairing mounted on the fork," explained Rit Booth. "When designing what became the FLHT, we were stuck with the fairing, so the challenge was looking at every other component to get its weight as close to the steering axis as possible and as light as possible. One of the ways we did that was by cutting off the last 2 or 3 inches at the back of the front fender. That section already had a lightweight trim piece covering it, so we just cut away the steel underneath it. We also lightened the brackets and the bumper at the front. It may not seem like much weight at all, but it's all weight that's carried far from the steering axis, so it made a noticeable difference."

Track testing showed there was really no way to get the new front end with fork-mounted fairing to steer like the FLT. Nevertheless, steering on the new machine was a vast improvement over the old FLH. Also, the old-look fairing on the new machine came along with all the other niceties of the FLT—rubber mounts, five-speed transmission,

The 1960s FLH look was revived the next year, 1994, with the introduction of the FLHR Road King.

stiffer frame, oil-bath chain, integrated bags and trunk, and excellent cornering clearance—so it was deemed good enough and put into production.

In Harley's sometimes-logical alphabet-soup nomenclature, the new bike was tagged FLHT. Why FLHT? An explanation overheard long ago in Sturgis is as good as I've heard: On testing the prototypes, the old FLH riders complained that they had too much FLT in them, while the pampered FLT riders complained that they had too much FLH in them. So they split the difference and called it FLHT.

Harley's ads touted it as "a motorcycle of the future that comes complete with a glorious past" when the FLHT was released for sale in spring of 1983. Highlighting that theme, Harley's new rubber-mounted tourer for the traditionalist was given the grand old name of Electra Glide, though the rightful heir to the name was still in production, but now called the FLH 80.

How did it work as a motorcycle? For all practical purposes, it was just as good as the FLT—even better, some would say, because the FLHT's fork-mounted fairing was positioned closer to the rider and thus gave better wind protection. The major problem was the same as that of the FLT: the Shovelhead engine was the weak point of the machine.

Available in basic (for a full-on bagger) FLHT, deluxe FLHTC Classic, and FLHTP Police forms, the new Electra Glide quickly outsold the FLT by more than three to one, despite having only a half year in which to do it. The people had spoken, and to Harley's credit, the company had listened.

1984 EVO TOUR AND ELECTRA GLIDES

For 1984, Harley's two rubber-mounted heavyweight touring bikes were both fitted with the then-new V^2 Evolution engine, which finally brings us back to where we started this chapter.

Smoother, more powerful, 20 pounds lighter, and much more oil-tight, the Evolution engine complemented the rubber mounts and enclosed chain and the many new improvements for 1984 to change the Tour Glide and Electra Glide into truly world-class touring machines. The contrast between the rubber-mount machines with the new engine and the final editions of the

The other key was in moving the speedo back to where God and Bill Harley intended it to be—front and center on the tank-mounted console.

old Shovelhead-powered FLH that were still in the line-up showed the great leaps forward The Motor Company had made in just four years.

As the flagships of the fleet, both Tour Glide and Electra Glide were offered only in deluxe FLTC and FLHTC Classic forms to civilians, and with or without sidecars. Police and Shriner versions were also offered to those in uniform or in fez. Both civilian models cost $8,599 without sidecar, or a then-breathtaking $12,229 with sidecar.

Both got some real functional improvements, in addition to the new engine. Suspension on both ends was air-adjustable, and the front end of each was fitted with the antidive system introduced on the FXRT of 1983 (see chapter 4 for more information). Brakes were made more powerful by fitting larger (11.5-inch) discs, new master cylinders, and new calipers. Overall weight was down by over 20 pounds (because of the Evo engine). Seat heights were lowered, to 28

One key to getting back the old look was to redesign the headlight and shrouds to recapture the look that began on the 1960 FLH.

inches for the FLHTC and 29.7 inches for the FLTC. In midyear, a new diaphragm-spring clutch was introduced (see chapter 1).

Cosmetically, the FLTC was given "deco-marquee" tank emblems and the FLHTC was given bald-eagle tank emblems.

Harley's sales rose an astonishing 31 percent for the year. Sales of the FLTC rose with the rest of the tide, but sales of the FLHTC were actually down slightly, perhaps affected by the FLHT's record sales in the last half of 1983.

RUBBER BELTS

Again, the big baggers were only offered in deluxe Classic form to civilians, but police and Shriner versions of the FLHT were also offered.

The big news for the FLTC and FLHTC was that, at last, they came with belt rear drives, adding a truly meaningful level of convenience, and a great new look. By 1985 belts were a proven and well-loved feature on Harley-Davidsons, and their use on the five-speed models was long overdue.

Also for 1985, saddlebags and Tour-Pak got improved locks, and the Tour-Pak was repositioned back farther for more passenger room. Both got the classic Harley bar-and-shield emblem on the tanks, new color options, and air suspension at the rear. Along with all the other bikes in the fleet, the 1985 baggers got 120-mile-per-hour speedometers (replacing 1970s-vestige, 85-mile-per-hour units), easier-to-use throttle locking screw, and AIW/AIM union decals.

As Harley-Davidson slowly developed the processes for applying chrome to aluminum castings on a production basis, the company began to release tarted-up special editions. Partway through the year, and with no real fanfare, 205 chromed-up FLTCs and another 598 chromed-up FLHTCs in a really beautiful two-tone maroon paint scheme were released and quickly sold. Bill Davis, inventor of the Softail, bought one of these special FLHTs. "I was going to get a black one," he remembered. "Then, I saw that maroon one [the special] and thought, 'Oh my God, that's pretty,' so I got it instead." He still has it, too.

Though Harley's overall sales were down for the year (largely because of a drastic reduction in Sportster production to clear the showrooms in preparation for an early introduction of the Evolution 883 Sportster), sales of both bagger models were up substantially.

Once again, the big Tour Glide was only offered in deluxe Classic form to civilians. The Electra Glide was available in both Classic and regular forms. Police departments could order the FLHT in two forms: with just a windshield or with the whole fairing. A Shriner FLHT was also offered.

In addition, special Liberty Edition versions of the FLTC and FLHTC were made to commemorate the 100th anniversary of the Statue of Liberty, and $100 for each one sold was donated to the fund to refurbish the old gal. Liberty Models were painted Blackberry and silver and fitted with special Statue of Liberty and "Ride Free" graphics. Harley built just 202 Liberty FLTCs and another 810 Liberty FLHTCs.

Harley executives participated in a ride to the unveiling of the statue, and donated the bikes they rode to an auction to benefit the statue foundation. Vaughn Beals still has the FLHTC Liberty he rode from Los Angeles to New York. "It was auctioned off when we arrived," he explained. "A year or two afterward, I found out the bike was still there because the top three bidders all welshed, so I bought it from the company, and I've had it ever since."

For 1986, the Classic models were made even more luxurious. Standard was an AM/FM/cassette/CB radio with Dolby noise reduction for the cassette and automatic volume control to adjust volume up or down as the motorcycle speeds up or slows down. Controls for the stereo were also conveniently located on the handlebars. Inner fairings were redesigned to include the stereo and speakers, a clock, a voltmeter, and oil-pressure and temperature gauges. On all, frames were powdercoated and passenger accommodations were upgraded with footboards and handrails, a larger backrest, and a new seat.

Looks were improved, too, because the old ham-can air cleaner was swapped for a new tuned intake with the classic round air cleaner and revised exhaust systems to allow them to pass the more restrictive noise limits that took effect on January 1, 1986. In addition, the whole line got turn-signal switches that stayed on once pressed.

Though it retained the "balanced" fork design begun on the FLT, the Road King's forks looked just like the 1960s through mid-1980s Hydra-Glide fork of the FLH.

Prices were up, too. The FLHTC and FLTC were up to $9,974. Even so, some of the big Japanese tourers cost more. The Gold Wing Aspencade SE-i, for example, cost an astronomical $10,598! And don't let anyone whine to you that it was because of the Harley-requested tariff, either. The American-assembled Gold Wing was exempt.

ELECTRA GLIDE SPORT

For 1987, all the old (nonspecial) baggers were back, plus a new version, the FLHS Electra Glide Sport.

The Sport was a civilian model based on the windshield-equipped version of the FLHTP that had been introduced the year before for the police market. It featured a spiffed-up headlight shroud on the fork and a revised version of the old fork-mounted windshield that had defined the Harley tourers of the 1960s.

Stripped of the fairing and Tour-Pak and fitted with spotlights and a luggage rack, the Sport was aimed at the rider who craved a more elemental touring bike, or a less expensive way to get a new Harley bagger. At nearly 50 pounds lighter than the Classic, the Sport was much easier to handle in town or in stop-and-go traffic.

Nevertheless, many felt that Willie G. hadn't spent enough time in getting the look right on the instruments and in the headlight area. The headlight looked "punched in" compared to that of the old FLH, and the gigantic instrument box looked a bit obtrusive without the fairing to mask its bulk.

As on all the other Harleys that year, the baggers got the engine changes listed in chapter 1. Nonlocking turn-signal switches were again standard.

For 1988, the regular FLHT was dropped from the line-up, leaving the FLTC Tour Glide Classic, the FLHTC Electra Glide Classic, and the FLHS Sport, plus Shriner and police versions and special 85th Anniversary versions of the Classics, with special paint and graphics. Harley was finally mastering the processes of mass-producing plated engine covers and wrinkle-black engine paint, so the two Classics were available for the first time with the black-and-chrome engine treatment. The Sport got by with plain aluminum.

All the baggers (except the Anniversary models) got new versions of the bar-and-shield tank emblem, with the words "Motor" and "Cycles" in orange. They also got a new seat with a mount for a rider backrest, 10-spoke cast wheels, and the handlebars were sealed and fitted with an air valve to become the reservoir for the front antidive system. The Classics got a new Tour-Pak that was adjustable for passenger room and 1 inch deeper to better accommodate two full-face helmets. A new stereo was fitted, with an integral clock and weather-channel monitor. On FLTCs, the turn signals were taken out of the fairing and mounted separately above the crashbars.

Like all the rest of the Big Twins, the baggers got the engine changes listed in chapter 1, a new eyelet-end clutch cable, American-made Hayes brake calipers and master cylinders, and wide-angle convex mirrors.

Responding to Honda's maximum tourer of the previous year, the six-cylinder GL-1500 Gold Wing, Harley upped the ante with its own maximum tourers for 1989, the Ultra Classic versions of the FLTC and FLHTC, both offering a way to "find luxury without losing your soul."

Replacing the FLHS Sport, the FLHR Road King was similarly outfitted for minimalist touring: just bags and windshield.

For 1989, Harley added fairing lowers (not shown), wind deflectors on the fairing, electronic cruise control, intercom, digitally tuned 40-channel CB radio, 80-watt four-speaker stereo and tape deck with separate controls for passenger, and more, to create the FLHT Ultra Classic. For 1995, Harley added fuel injection as an option on the Ultra. Shown is a 1998 FLHTCUI, the last year for the combination of Evolution engine and FLHT chassis.

The Ultra was as plush for the passenger as for the pilot.

The old FLT was dropped from the Harley lineup at the end of the 1996 model year, but the model was given a facelift and reintroduced for 1998 as the FLTR and FLTRI (injected) Road Glide. Subtle changes to the fairing and front fender gave the Road Glide the custom bagger look that was so popular in the late 1990s. Shown is 1998 FLTRI.

The Ultra Classics came with special two-tone black-and-silver paint, black-and-chrome engine, "speeding-ball" tank emblems, "Ultra Classic" badges for the front fender and saddlebags, fairing lowers with glove compartments, wind deflectors on the fairing, electronic cruise control, carpeted liner and wraparound corner lights (both stop and running) for the Tour-Pak, liner bags for saddlebags and Tour-Pak, intercom and digitally tuned 40-channel CB radio, 80-watt four-speaker stereo and tape deck with separate controls for passenger, the 32-amp alternator from the police bikes, and even a tool kit (now that it truly wasn't needed). With all these features—plus a dry weight of over 800 pounds and a suggested retail price of $12,995—the Ultras reclaimed the old "King of the Highway" crown.

All the big baggers got a handsome new tank and chrome-plated center console that looked much more like the old dual Fat Bobs and dash of the FLH, along with microprocessor-controlled turn signals. The FLHTC, FLTC, and FLHS got new tank graphics (the words "Harley" and "Davidson" in two lines, split by a long line).

The Ultra version of the Electra Glide was also a truly great seller. Despite the high price, Harley sold over 2,800 of them, plus over 4,000 of the regular FLHTC. Tour Glide sales even increased because of the Ultra version, though overall, the Electra Glide models were now outselling the Tour Glide models by more than four to one.

For the start of the new decade, all five bagger models (FLHS Sport, FLHTC Classic, FLTC Classic, FLHTC Ultra, and FLTC Ultra) were back, with new colors, three-position adjustable footboards, the engine updates listed in chapter 1, and new brake rotors and pads (to reduce cracking).

The Road Glide's front fender was stripped of trim, giving the whole front end a clean look that helped make the FLTR more popular than the FLT had ever been.

The Ultras got improvements to the cruise control and the option of a helmet-mounted or hand-held microphone for the CB radio and intercom. The Sport and the Classics got new tank graphics ("Harley-Davidson" in two lines, but without last year's line). Also, Peace Officer Special Edition models were offered for sale only to current or retired police officers. These specials were painted Night Watch Blue and Cadet Blue.

Sales were up again, by about 7 percent, but that probably does not reflect demand. By this time, Harley-Davidson was operating at capacity for many models, so the numbers reflect what it was capable of building, rather than what it was capable of selling.

For 1991, all five bagger models from the previous year were back, with new color options, new Dunlop Touring Elite II tires, and the detail changes to the engine and tranny listed in chapter 1. Sales were up 9.8 percent, again, limited by capacity.

With sales of the Tour Glide slipping further, the FLTC Tour Glide Classic was dropped from the line-up at the end of the 1991 model year, leaving just the premium-priced FLTC Ultra Classic, along with three versions of the Electra Glide (FLHS, FLHTC, and FLHTC Ultra).

All received updates to the engine listed in chapter 1, along with barrel-type locks on the bags and Tour-Pak (except on the FLHS, because it has no trunk) and new brake rotors (with refined metallurgy to prevent cracking). And as the new $24 million paint facility at York slowly got up to speed, the whole line-up benefited from improved paint with a hard layer of clear powdercoat over the top.

It was another four-bagger year in 1993, plus special 90th Anniversary editions of the FLHTC Classic and the FLTC and FLHTC Ultra Classics. The 90th Anniversary models featured commemorative tank emblems described as "forged brass, color-filled, ground, polished and plated for a jewel-like finish," special paint, and a serialized nameplate.

All were vastly improved for the year by the reworking of the engine and transmission along Dyna Glide lines, putting the oil tank in a sump underneath the transmission. The change also allowed room for the battery to be repositioned so that it no longer intruded into luggage space on the right saddlebag. Harley took advantage of this by making the bags longer and roomier, and fixing lids to the bags with sturdier locks and latches.

All the baggers got a new ignition switch with the barrel-type "Coke-machine" key that also operated all the locks for the bags and trunk, new low-profile clutch and brake levers, and (starting midyear) a new front belt pulley with 50 percent more spline area. Ultras got dual antennas, improved "tap-up, tap-down" controls for the cruise control, and redesigned wraparound lights on the Tour-Paks.

THE FLHR ROAD KING

After seven years of moderate success, the stripper FLHS Sport was dropped at the end of 1993 production, in favor of an all-new model that both recaptured the look of the 1960s FLH (at last) and became a smashing sales success: the FLHR Electra Glide Road King.

The centerpieces of the Road King's new (old) look were the new chromed headlight shrouds and a new one-piece 5-gallon Fat Bob gas tank, with dual filler caps and an electronic speedometer put back on a chromed center console. Completing the package were a black-and-chrome engine, quickly detachable windshield, lighter and simpler front fender tips and Road King fender badges, unique V tank emblem, studded seat with removable passenger section, and chrome spotlights.

The other three bagger models from the previous year (FLHTC Classic and FLHTC and FLTC Ultra Classics) were also back for 1994, with minor updates and new paint combinations. All the bagger models got the drivetrain changes listed in chapter 1 and an accessory electrical plug. The FLHTC got a new "comet" tank emblem.

THE ELECTRA GLIDE STANDARD

For 1995, all four baggers (FLHR Road King, FLHTC Classic, and the Ultra Classics, now designated FLHTCU and FLTC U) were back again for 1995, along with two new ones: the FLHT Electra Glide Standard and a fuel-injected version of the FLHTC Ultra, the FLHTCI, which was released to celebrate the 30th anniversary of the Electra Glide.

The FLHTCI's sequential port fuel injection was a first for The Motor Company and gave the injected Electra Glide 10 percent more torque and even easier starting. It also featured a unique two-tone (Vivid Black and Burgundy Pearl) paint scheme with 30th anniversary graphics, a 38-amp alternator with its plug outside the primary case (this plug had long been a source of problems), and a number plate telling where the bike fell in the sequence of the 2,000 built.

The FLHT Electra Glide Standard was the new budget model, with the bare-aluminum engine, chrome luggage rack instead of Tour-Pak, the same "comet" tank emblems as the FLHTC Classic, fewer gauges, no cruise control, no sound system (but still with cigarette lighter), and no bumper rail on the front fender. With less weight and a lower center of gravity and a price nearly $2,000 less than the Classic, it was just what a lot of folks wanted.

All these models got handier quick-release mounts for the saddlebags and vacuum-operated petcocks for 1995.

For 1996, all four basic Electra Glide models (FLHT Standard, FLHTC Classic, FLHTCU Ultra Classic, and FLHR Road King) were back, along fuel-injected versions of the Classic (FLHTCI), Ultra (FLHTCUI), and Road King (FLHRI).

The Tour Glide came only in FLTC UI Ultra Classic fuel-injected form. At the end of the model year, this last Tour Glide was dropped from the line-up because the steadily dropping sales of the model no longer justified production. Thus (temporarily) ended a 17-year run.

All those with fairings got redesigned fairing interiors with the speedo and tach housed in separate holes, revised gauges, resonance chambers for the speakers (except on the Standard, which has no stereo). All got updated handlebar switches.

With the demise of the Tour Glide (for one year), the Harley touring line-up consisted entirely of Electra Glides (FLHT Standard, FLHTC Classic, FLHTCU

Ultra Classic, and FLHR Road King, along the fuel-injected FLHTCI Classic, FLHTCUI Ultra, and FLHRI Road King).

Except for some new colors and the new cloisonné emblem on the Ultra, they all looked the same as in previous years, but important changes were made underneath. Improvements included a new frame (revised to lower the seat height about an inch and increase wheelbase), new suspension front and rear, a passive antidive system for the front, improved cruise control on Ultras, a bigger battery, and refined fuel injection and ultra-high-output alternators for fuel-injected models.

FLTR ROAD GLIDE

By the late 1990s, fashion in the custom circles had gone from the tall, slim chopper to the long, fat, and low "lead sled" look. For 1998, Willie G. presented his own rendition of that look—the FLTR Road Glide—simultaneously creating the factory "custom bagger" and a successful new model.

The Road Glide's frame-mounted fairing was based on that of the FLT, but it was chopped and lowered and given some attitude, and a very low windscreen. Twin oval-reflector headlamps gave a more modern look out front. New gauges and stereo did the same inside. A very trim, embossed seat gave it the lowest seat height in the FL line. And the front fender was stripped of all lights and trim and lengthened at the rear for a clean, "taildragger" look. The engine was the black-and-chrome centerpiece used on all the Big Twins but the stripper models. Saddlebags and luggage rack were standard.

For its first year, the Road Glide came in carbureted (FLTR) and injected (FLTRI) forms, in regular or 95th anniversary trim. Anniversary models featured Midnight Red and Champagne Pearl paint, Champagne Pearl wheels, anniversary cloisonné emblem, and numbered plate.

Road King was available in carbureted FLHR or new (injected) FLHRCI Classic trim. The Classic featured laced wheels, whitewall tires, leather-covered hard bags, slant-cut mufflers, and unique metal emblems on the front fender tip, gas tank, and fender valance. The Road King Classic was also available in anniversary trim.

The Electra Glide Standard, Classic (carbureted or with fuel injection), and Ultra Classic (only with fuel injection) returned for 1998. The Standard was available only in Vivid Black, with a new tank emblem. Classics and Ultras were available with standard or anniversary paint and trim.

All the FL models got an improved clutch (for lower lever effort). All but the Standard (which had no stereo) got new stereos and controls.

REQUIEM EVO

The Electra Glides, Road Kings, and Road Glides would be back for model year 1999, all powered by the new Twin Cam 88 motor. Even though the last Evolution motors were about as refined and reliable as any motorcycle engine on the market, reliability was now taken for granted. What everyone wanted now was more power to go along with their reliability. And that's mainly what the Twin Cam engine brought to the table.

CHAPTER 4

The FXR Series

1984–1994
1999–2000

HARLEY'S HI-PO ENGINEERS BUILD ONE FOR THEMSELVES

"There are still a lot of people out there who have a love affair with their old FXRs . . ."

—Mark Tuttle, retired vice presidents of engineering

Surprising nearly everyone outside the company, Harley-Davidson reintroduced the FXR chassis in special models built by Harley's Parts & Accessories division in 1999 and 2000. Shown here is a 2000 FXR⁴.

Some motorcycles reflect the personality of their designers. Others reflect some marketeer's interpretation of then-current fashion. Neither is the case here. Harley's original FXR models actually reflect the *alter egos* of some very special people at The Motor Company who made them a reality.

When asked about the FXRS, their voices rise in pitch, and the old enthusiasm still comes through, along with some surprising admissions. Most surprising was how many of them waxed on about the performance of some favored motorcycle from a foreign land, and then countered with "but you can't print that!" The braver among them even bought these foreign machines and rode them, most often when nobody was looking. The bravest not only bought these machines but actually rode them to work.

Who are these folks?

They're a surprisingly large group at The Motor Company, one you might never guess existed if your only basis for judging that was the motorcycles that came out the gates at York, PA, especially the motorcycles built in the 1970s, through about 1981.

They're part of engineering, testing, manufacturing, and even senior management.

They're guys who got into the business because they loved motorcycles, not just because it was a job.

Some, including Tom Gelb (retired vice president of operations) and Ray Miennert (formerly an engineer in the Experimental Department, among other positions), had been with the original Motor Company (both starting about 1960), when the descendants of the founders owned the company and the Sportster was still the meanest thing on the streets. Others, including Mark Tuttle (at the time, chief engineer of motorcycles), Erik Buell (engineer), and Rit Booth (engineer) came on under the AMF regime but had been racers before they'd been engineers, and they sought to make a career out of combining the two.

Still others, like then leader-of-the-pack Vaughn Beals, learned to ride after joining the company, but soon came to recognize the difference between a fine handling motorcycle and what Harley was producing in the 1970s.

What they all wanted was a "no-apologies" Harley, one that worked as well as it looked. One that handled like no Harley ever had. One that didn't try to shake itself and its rider apart. One that was as good from Milwaukee to Los Angeles as it was from stoplight to stoplight. One that feared no curve.

So, for once—but also most definitely within limits—these guys designed and built a bike for themselves. That bike was, of course, the FXR (in the Harley alphabet, "F" for Big Twin, "X" for XL front end, "R" for rubber engine mounts) Super Glide II, introduced for model year 1982, and lauded for the excellence of its chassis. Piece One was in place. In 1984, Piece Two *"potato-potato-potato-ed"* onto the scene: the Evolution engine. The combination of FXR chassis and Evo motor was a classic case of the whole being greater than the sum of its parts. With the Evo, the FXR came alive.

Naturally, it's the Evo-powered FXR models we'll be most concerned with here. And there were many, as the line split in later years to include as many as six different models before they were each canceled or replaced by a Dyna Glide–based equivalent. Before we get to all that, though, let's look at how the chassis got to where it was when the Evo engine was first bolted into the FXR's rubber mounts.

When the FXRS Super Glide II made its debut for model year 1982, it looked much like the one shown here, except that the 1982 had the old Shovelhead engine. Dual discs up front and tall suspension were standard.

ROOTS OF THE FXR

"Until it was done, our total focus was on the FLT," said Vaughn Beals, "but we also realized we needed a vibration-isolated sport bike, as well, to draw new riders into the Harley camp."

Sport bike, huh? That's a term that needs some context.

First, this was in the late 1970s, when the best-handling sport machinery didn't go by the name "Ninja" or "Katana" or anything else with oriental overtones. Instead, the best-handling sporting iron came from Europe and carried names such as "Commando," "Le Mans," "Jota," and "Super Sport."

Second, if "motorcycle" to you means "Harley" and only "Harley," you'll understand what Beals meant; if you're into other makes, you may not. Beals meant "sport bike" in the context of the Harley Big Twin, which meant "FX," as in Super Glide, Fat Bob, Low Rider, and even Wide Glide. Sporty the FXs were, but only by comparison to Harley's big FLH and FLT. By sport bike, Beals meant what many would call a "cruiser."

Management and marketeers envisioned the new bike as an updated, rubber-mounted Super Glide, not necessarily as a peg-scratcher. So, once the FLT was done, a new team of Harley engineers was turned loose to build that new sport bike. We'll call them "Team FXR." Steve Pertsch led the team, assisted by design engineer Bill Brown, and engineers Erik Buell, Rit Booth, and

For its first year in Evo-powered form, the FXRS's suspension was lowered, only one front disc was fitted, and it was given the new name Low Glide. Low Glide was back for 1985, and was even offered with a Performance/Suspension Package, which gave back the taller suspension and second front disc. In 1986, the FXRS was renamed Low Rider, because the FX-based model of that name had been canceled at the end of the 1985 model year. Shown is a 1986 Liberty Edition FXRS Low Rider.

many others. As we'll see, some of the engineers had a little bit different idea of what a sport bike should be.

For the new bike, Harley's engineers began in a traditional place. "It's a pattern with Harley to take a touring model and turn it into a sport machine," explained Mark Tuttle. "The FX was the sport model of the FL. The FXR is the sport model of the FLT, if you will."

That approach is, in fact, what they tried at first, but there was one big problem: "If you ever want to see an ugly motorcycle," explained Rit Booth, "put an XL front end on an FLT. It was really *unbelievable*!"

Even though the FLT frame was too "aesthetically challenged" for the planned sporting machine, some parts of the FLT were recyclable, both

because they worked well enough and because Team FXR didn't have the money or time to design anything better. As a result, "the FXR really became a chassis program to utilize the FLT powertrain in an FX-type motorcycle," said Mark Tuttle. That meant they'd use the FLT's rigid engine-transmission unit with the swingarm bolted to the back of the tranny and design for it a new frame.

A MORE SPORTING FRAME

The need for a prettier frame turned into a blessing for those engineers and, ultimately, for lovers of performance Harleys. Here's how: Since members of the team had to create a new chassis anyway, they decided to create it in their own image. Performance image that is. Stiffer than before. High lean angles. Lots of ground clearance.

"There was a group of us who were really performance-oriented," explained Booth (who at the time rode one of the premier sporting machines of the day, a Moto Guzzi 850 Le Mans—and even had the guts to ride it to work at Juneau Avenue), "so we wanted the new bike to be even stiffer and to have even more of that 'on-rails' feel than the FLT. Basically, we started with a clean sheet of paper and then decided we'd keep the FLT mounts and build into the new frame all that we'd learned about making a bike go through corners."

Fortunately, the performance-orientation went far up the chain of command, all the way up to Chief Engineer of Motorcycles Mark Tuttle. "At a personal level," said Tuttle (who had raced a BSA Gold Star before being recruited

The Liberty models were painted Blackberry overall with silver panels on the tank and fenders, and maroon and silver pinstripes. Special Liberty graphics were used on the gas tank. Only 744 Liberty Low Riders were built, and $100 from the sale of each was donated to the Statue of Liberty-Ellis Island Foundation to help finance the restoration of the statue.

In 1986, the sportier version of the FXRS was given the "Sport Edition" name, and in 1988 its own letter designation, FXRS-SP. This 1985 FXRS Low Glide with the Performance/Suspension Package wears paint and tank graphics from Harley's custom paint program. Standard FXRS models that year had bar-and-shield tank emblems.

by Harley in 1970 because of his stress-analysis expertise), "I had ridden Sportsters a lot, so I didn't particularly like the FX motorcycles because of the fact that they didn't have much ground clearance. You couldn't ride them as aggressively as I wanted to ride. With the FXR, we solved that problem. The goal became to build a performance motorcycle, but we had to work within the Harley-Davidson structure. It wasn't ever meant to be a crotch rocket or anything like that." In other words, the new machine would have to look like a Harley-Davidson. Nevertheless, some decisions *would* require choosing performance *or* traditional looks. In deciding these details, Team FXR took the path of modern performance whenever practical. "We pushed it wherever we could to make it stiffer and give it more precise steering," affirmed Rit Booth.

Using stress analysis and computer modeling, Team FXR designed the new frame for maximum stiffness. Like the FLT frame, the new frame's backbone was a large box-section that linked the steering head to a triangulated rear section, and used round tubing at all points where the frame showed. To make the new frame even stiffer than the FLT's, Team FXR added more gusseting

between the steering head and both the backbone and down tubes. In the end, it was claimed to be five times stiffer than the old FX frame. All this was fine with the boys from Styling.

What wasn't OK with Styling was the engineers' insistence on using rear-mounted shocks on the FXR, as they had on the FLT, which made the rear suspension work better and allowed for longer shock travel. "Lou [Netz] and Bill [Willie G. Davidson] had always wanted the FXR shocks laid down and forward-mounted," explained Rit Booth, "but they were told absolutely no by the engineers, myself included."

"HOW MANY MILLION DO YOU WANT?"

Having designed the frame for optimum shock geometry, the task was then to find the best shocks. To get what they wanted, Team FXR engineers worked with engineers from three different manufacturers (Showa, Monroe, and Gabriel).

At the time, and to this day, H-D was highly committed to building the company's motorcycles with as many American–made (or at least North American-made) parts as possible. Thus, Gabriel was the favorite, at first, because that company already supplied shocks for the FX and XL lines.

Monroe had other ideas, though, and put out a special effort to win Harley over. The Harley-Monroe team eventually came up with what they all thought was the perfect set of shocks for the new machine, and everyone was happy, until it came time to place the production order. "The guy from their [Monroe's] sales department asked us, 'How many million do you want?'," remembered Rit Booth. "This was the first year of production of the FXR, and I think we said we wanted about 5,000 pairs. They said, 'That's below our minimum order. We can't do that.' As far as I know, that's the last time we worked with an American shock-absorber company." Showa had no problem supplying its version of the FXR shocks in such small quantities, so it got the business.

This was another bitter blow for Harley-Davidson, because it gave the company's critics another non-American part to jeer about. Worse yet, Harley's most ardent fans were its worst critics on that issue. "I was at a HOG rally when a man-mountain, about 6 foot 5 and 280 pounds found out I was from The Motor Company," said Mark Tuttle. "He took me over to his bike and said, 'I want you to touch every part that's from Japan and tell me why it's on my motorcycle.'"

"PRETTY COVERS," LESSON THREE

History repeated itself in the design of the central and aft part of the new machine, providing the stylists, engineers, and marketeers in Milwaukee with Lesson Three of why the "pretty covers" philosophy wasn't going to work for Harley-Davidson. As part of making the new chassis as stiff as possible, the new frame was triangulated and given odd-shaped covers to hide the battery and oil tank, as on the 1979 Sportster and FLT. (For Lesson One in "pretty covers," see chapter 5, and for Lesson Two, see chapter 3.)

The FXR's clever new 3.5-quart oil tank was completely out of sight except for a rounded lobe extending forward to fill some of the space behind the rear cylinder. Its underseat filler cap had it own dipstick.

The FXRS wore its instruments Sportster-style, with tach and speedo and idiot lights mounted between the bars. The FXR Super Glide introduced for 1986 was given a different tank-top console featuring the speedo mounted in front of the filler cap, for a "clean-bars" look.

The battery was placed crossways behind the oil tank, also hidden from view by the seat and new sidecovers, but also easily accessible by pivoting the seat up and to the right on its hinges. Team FXR even included a capture cord to keep the seat from flopping all the way over on its hinge.

As for the covers themselves, they really didn't have to hide much, so they were slim and as unobtrusive as they could be, nestled within the triangular side tubes of the frame. Even so, the new "triangulated" look was ultimately the FXR's least popular feature.

To get as much of the traditional FX look as was possible with the new frame, the new machine got its own version of the Harley teardrop tank, a fat 16-inch rear tire, a Sportster-type rear fender attached to the frame by an alloy support on each side, and the complete XL front end. The new tank was a one-piece unit of 4.2 gallons designed to look like the traditional saddle-type Fat Bob tanks. Before long, it became known as the "turtle tank." Its new center console housed the filler opening and a gas gauge. Speedo and tach were mounted between the bars. Though the seat was higher than that of most of the FX models, because the new machine was given longer shocks and forks to gain more ground clearance, the riding position was still laid-back, courtesy of the buckhorn bars, stepped seat, and slightly forward peg position.

By the time the new chassis was ready for a model-year 1982 introduction, the Shovelhead engine that was to power it was also vastly improved. Less finicky and more oil-tight than previous Shovelheads it was, but it was definitely the weak point of the whole FXR package.

Nevertheless, the forthcoming FXR looked like a winner, and it handled like no Harley ever had. "We all loved it," remembered Mark Tuttle. "You could run it into a corner and tip it over to oblivion and it just all worked." Harley's performance-oriented engineers were sure the bike they'd built for themselves would soon meet the same reaction in the marketplace.

DEBUT OF THE FXR AND FXRS SUPER GLIDE II

Before you can really understand the impact the FXR had, you need a little background in what was happening in the months before the FXR made its debut.

Harley had been in the news a lot. First, Vaughn Beals led a group of executives to buy the company from AMF, and then led those executives on a triumphant ride back to Milwaukee. Ads trumpeting "The Eagle Soars Alone" had barely made it into the magazines before Beals began accusing the Japanese of dumping excess inventory in the United States. Those who were sympathetic to Harley's cause rejoiced that at last the old eagle was showing some life, while those who were hostile felt AMF had been smart to unload the company and that Beals' complaints were just the desperate last gasps of a company that was simply too feeble to compete.

Then, came the FXR in early fall 1981.

It was offered in two states of trim, regular (FXR) and deluxe (FXRS). The FXR and FXRS differed only in that the latter came with a second front brake disc, two-tone paint on the gas tank, a sissybar, and highway pegs. With the new frame and suspension, and with all the updates made to the Shovelhead engine for that year, Harley at last had a bike that was "ready for prime time." It got noticed—and outside the sphere where new Harleys were normally noticed, too.

Old-timers who run only in Harley circles (and new-timers who came on board later, as well) may not understand this, but these were the times when if you liked Harleys, those who rode other makes thought you were narrow-minded, jingoistic, or stupid. Harleys were slow, leaky, ill-handling—something other riders made fun of, and didn't buy.

Liberty Editions also were fitted with laced wheels instead of the cast wheels the other FXRS models had.

The FXRS changed all that. Your friends would still think you a bit odd if you bought an FXRS, but they'd probably understand. Even if they didn't at first, they soon would as you left them behind on a tight road. Quite simply, it was a rider's bike, and one that worked too well to be ignored.

As a result, the new Milwaukee sport bike got Harley the kind of good press it hadn't seen since the Super Glide of 1971. *Cycle* magazine, then the biggest and most influential, hadn't even bothered to test a Harley in over five years, ignoring even the FLT of 1980. Surprising everyone who'd been paying attention to Harley's reviews, *Cycle* loved the FXRS, calling it the "the most important Harley-Davidson built in a generation."

Of course, most of the praise was reserved for the sporting new chassis. Said the editors, "Our resident racer, for crying out loud, finds the FXRS entertaining; you can grind your way onto the pegs and muffler and feather the Dunlops right to their edges," and "The machine isn't a Superbike performer, but

sure as hell the FXRS has more in common with its contemporaries than with its predecessors." Still, it was powered by the old Shovelhead, so there were a few of the old faults, which of course drew this comment: "When parked, the bike left a small oil puddle the size of a silver dollar."

Not a bad start, though. In fact, until it was finally superseded by the Dyna Glide models in the 1990s, the FXRS would remain Harley's true darling among the motorcycle press. It was the first of the modern "no-apologies" Harleys, and it was the first Harley to get many of us in the showroom with a fistful of dollars.

Perhaps that's why the Super Glide II sold so well that first year: 3,065 FXR models and another 3,190 FXRS models. These excellent sales figures came at the best-possible time because the whole motorcycle market was in the midst of a crash during 1982. By spring, Harley's sales were off by 50 percent, so the company laid off much of its work force. By the time the model-year figures were tallied, Harley had had its worst sales year since 1970. Despite that, Team FXR and the marketeers were both happy because the FXRS and FXR were the Number 1 and Number 2 best-selling Big Twins that year. Happy ending, right?

To everyone at Harley's regret, FXR sales really weren't so rosy for 1983. Both FXR models were back, better than ever, thanks to a few improvements to the engine and chassis, but sales fell off drastically—by more than 50 percent.

What happened?

Basically, the Super Glide II became another victim of the same syndrome that befell the FLT. That is, it brought some new customers in, folks who'd been looking for an excuse to buy a Harley and had just been waiting until a model came along that really tickled them. Rubber mounts, sporty handling, and improved Shovel motor were enough to get the job done, but these people were fewer in number than Harley had hoped, and the bikes were good enough that they didn't feel they had to buy a new one every year.

Worse, for every Harley newcomer turned on by the FXR, several traditional FX customers were turned off because they didn't think it looked like a Harley. Once again, I refer you back to that quote in chapter 2 about how some of the hardcore thought the newer Harleys looked too Japanese. Fairly or unfairly, the FXR was tarred with that brush.

In the coming years, those feelings just got more intense as the Japanese brought out new V-twin cruisers by the dozens following the success of the

Yamaha Virago. Reason was, more of those copies became modeled after the FXR than any other, until the 1990s when copies of the more full-figured Harleys became fashionable. And why not? The Japanese are practical folk, so when they finally got really serious about copying the Harley, they started by copying the first Harley that really worked as a modern motorcycle.

Motorcyclists are practical, too. Those who wanted the uncut Harley-look more than rubber mounts or better handling could only get it from Milwaukee, while those who would compromise a little traditional style to get modern function could either buy an FXR, or they could turn to all those other suppliers and save a bunch of money, too. The latter is what happened all too often.

Revenge of the Nerds?

This brings us to the crux of the matter. Harley-Davidson is most successful when it builds a bike that could only come from Milwaukee—like a Softail. Motor and most of the styling aside, the FXR could have come from someplace else. Does that mean the FXR is less than a real Harley? Them's fightin' words, to me, and if you've read this far, them's probably fightin' words to you, too.

What was it then? Was the FXR a "Revenge of the Nerds" failure, as some have characterized it? Fightin' words again, to those who created it. "Sure, we were criticized by marketing and sales," remembered Mark Tuttle. "We got a lot of negative response to the triangular area under the seat, and we gave it a very stiff chassis, very neutral handling, and a really good lean angle, which resulted in a fair amount of ground clearance and a higher seat height, but it was probably the best-handling Harley ever built. Unfortunately, it just wasn't selling as well as the rigid mounts were."

"Best handling" it was (and still is), but the original FXR was a whole lot more. First, it was the best *motorcycle* Harley's engineers knew how to (or were allowed to) build. It brought positive press and new customers in when they were most desperately needed.

Most telling of all, though, the FXR provided a lesson, one that helped Harley find its place in the modern era by forcing the company to get to know its customers more intimately. "We found that other than a handful of riders, nobody was using that capability," Tuttle continued. "They would rather have had lower seats and more of a low cruiser look than all that handling capability." That lesson helped shape everything the company did in the following years.

Partway through the 1983 model year, before that lesson had fully sunk in, Harley shuffled its cards once more and introduced another model based on the excellent FXR chassis—which is where we're going next.

The 1982–1983 and 1985–1986 Sport versions of the FXRS were fitted with the longer 35-millimeter forks shown. In 1987, Sport Editions (and the new FXLR Custom) were upgraded to a new 39-millimeter fork. In 1988, the rest of the FXR line was given the stiffer fork. A version of the slim fender shown was first used on the XLCR.

Model year 1986 was the last for the old Sportster fender shown. Starting in 1987, all the FXR models except the FXRT got the smaller, slimmer fender from the XLCR of 1977, and later used on the XR-1000, FXRC, and the 1986 XLH 883 Sportsters.

SAGA OF THE SPORT GLIDE

My apologies, but we've got to jump back in time again. During the late 1970s, Harley gazed longingly at a niche market that didn't then have a name, but it's what we now call the "sport-tourer"—bikes lighter and better handling than the heavyweight baggers, yet with enough wind protection and luggage space for serious touring. At the time, there were really only two dedicated sport-tourers on the market, the BMW R100RS/RT and the Moto Guzzi 1000SP.

Harley did more than gaze, however. It developed a bike you've most likely never seen and aren't likely to ever see, unless Harley decides to put one in its forthcoming museum. "We were looking for something with better handling than an FLH and something that wasn't as large and intimidating as the FLT and something aerodynamically desirable," Vaughn Beals explained. "Before we ran out of money to build it, the Nova was going to be that motorcycle for us."

At least three Nova versions were planned: a naked sport version (looking just like the later Yamaha V-Max), a sport-tourer with a frame-mounted fairing, and a full bagger (with the FLT fairing).

Porsche Design developed the Nova's V-4 engine (it was planned as a modular design, so Harley-Davidson could build it in two-, four-, and six-cylinder versions), and Harley engineers under the direction of Mike Hillman concentrated on developing the basic chassis and fairing. Nova's induction system was under a false gas tank, and its radiator was under the seat. Air scoops on the sides of the false tank collected air and ducted it to both systems on the naked version. On the sport-touring version, the Nova engineers used a wind tunnel to design "cheek" openings on the fairing to duct air to the tank scoops.

With money in such short supply in the early 1980s, though, the Nova was shelved. But that doesn't mean Harley's hopes for a sport-tourer were shelved. After all, the company's then-new FXRS was a near-perfect platform on which to build a sport-tourer. All it needed to qualify was hard saddlebags and a fairing. Bags would be easy enough. But what about the fairing?

Breaking Wind

In another bout of good fortune, the fairing, too, was on the shelf. "At one point," said Tom Gelb, "we looked at the FXR and we looked at that [Nova] fairing and said, 'Hmmm . . . . the result was the RT.'"

It wasn't quite that easy, but the FXRS chassis with a modified Nova fairing grafted on was the foundation on which project leader Erik Buell built Harley's new sport-tourer. The most notable modification Buell made was to turn the cheek scoops (for the Nova's induction and cooling systems) into an adjustable venting system on the Big Twin sport-tourer.

Air Suspension and Antidive Forks

Buell also designed and added other features to help the new bike compete against the latest tourers, sport and otherwise. Air-adjustable suspension was then the latest fad, so Buell designed that feature into the front and rear suspension. Buell's system featured one fitting for the front and one for the rear, so both shocks could be filled from one, and both fork legs from the other.

Then, Buell went one better, anticipating a fad-to-be: antidive mechanisms to reduce fork compression during hard braking. Over the next five years, many manufacturers attempted many different antidive approaches, but the system Buell developed is perhaps the simplest and most effective of them all. As a bonus, it also improved the ride.

Since this new bike was to be a tourer, it was also given its own version of the enclosed, oil-bath chain system used on the FLT.

Debut of the Sport Glide

The new machine was given the designation FXRT (T for touring,

The FXRT, introduced midway through the 1983 model year, still used the Shovelhead engine. Like the other FXR models, the RT was finally complete when Harley gave it the Evo engine.

The RT was created by grafting the frame-mounted fairing from the ill-fated Nova project onto the FXR chassis. Shown is a 1984 FXRT that was continually upgraded over the years by its then-owner, the late, great Seattle-area tuner Mike McKeown. Upgrades include the police (FXRP) fairing, forks, front fender, and instruments. The spotlights on the police fairing replace the cheek scoops on the RT fairing. Those scoops were a leftover from the Nova, where they ducted air to the intake and radiator systems.

presumably) and the name Sport Glide, which is probably the name Harley should have used for the original FXR but didn't. As we've said, one market for the RT was the sport-touring crowd who rode BMWs and Guzzis, but Harley-Davidson had other specific customers in mind, as well. Vaughn Beals explained: "We introduced the RT specifically because we were trying to get Japanese riders into our camp. Later, when we got a decent engine and belt drive we had some luck at this. When we decided we would use the aerodynamic fairing from the Nova on a new V-twin, we also thought that might attract a guy to Harley who didn't 'Want to look like a bad guy.'"

When it hit the market partway through the 1983 model year, dealers were enthusiastic, at first. Harley was, too, spending very scarce cash on ads to reach riders of Japanese machines and those people who may have wanted a Harley but didn't want any part of the bad-guy image. The focus of the ads was just to get these people into the Harley dealers for a test ride. Harley-Davidson was confident that the RT would do the rest.

Originally, the FXRT was scheduled to make its debut with the Evolution engine, but the engine was delayed until the start of the 1984 model year, so the FXRT made its debut with the Shovel motor. Improved though the 1983 Shovel was, it was still the weak point of the FXRT package.

Like the FXRS on which it was based, the FXRT just plain worked. The fairing did look a little peculiar, but it did its job very well. It was stable and comfortable from a dead stop all the way up to its top speed of about 100 miles per hour, which was actually higher than that of the FXRS. It was another "no-apologies" Harley—in function anyway. Even the folks at Harley weren't so sure about its looks. While that fairing looked like it belonged on the Nova, many thought it looked "tacked on" to the FXRT.

Even with the Shovel motor, the magazines were impressed. Typical was the assessment by *Rider* (March 1983): "The FXRT is a Harley so improved that

it can go head-to-head with its competition and come out on top in many categories of performance. It handles better than most touring bikes and as well as the best, while being stable at any speed its 80-inch engine can drive it."

Despite the excellence of the Sport Glide and all the ads, sales of the new model were underwhelming, even in its first year: just 1,458. Let's put this in context, though. Nineteen eighty-three was an even worse sales year than the disastrous 1981 and 1982 model years had been. Production was below the levels specified in the asset-based agreements with Harley's lenders, so the banks could have foreclosed at any time. In that context, those 1,458 sales were critical for the company.

The FXRT also made an exceedingly important contribution to Harley-Davidson's future. "I kind of think, and others do too, that the FXRT served the purpose," Vaughn Beals said. "It got competitive riders to our stores. They looked at the RT and they rode it and then they said, 'What the hell. If I'm gonna buy a Harley, I'm gonna ride a real 'Harley like an FLHT.'"

"That RT may not have looked as good as some of the others, but it sure did all the things you wanted a motorcycle to do. It was clearly the favorite motorcycle of the Harley employees, too, which I think says a lot."

Built for Nice Guys but Bad Guys Like It, Too

Remember what Beals said about designing the FXRT for people who didn't want to look like a "bad guy"? Well, Beals learned another lesson one day at HOG rally about how you can't always outguess the customer.

"The RT hadn't been out very long," he remembered. "I went there and was parking my bike when one of the district managers came up to me and pointed out a guy who had just shown up at the rally on an RT. He said it was Sonny Barger, the leader of the Hell's Angels, and that the RT was his motorcycle of choice. I thought, 'Holy Mackerel, we brought out the RT for guys who didn't want the tough-guy image, and here's the toughest guy screwing up our whole strategy!'

"The district manager said, 'Hey, he's 45 years old and wants a little comfort, and that's comfort.'"

Not that I'd argue with Mr. Barger about anything, but we're in perfect agreement on the RT. It's a great traveling companion.

1984: THE EVOLUTION RUBBER GLIDES

This brings us back to where we left off at the beginning of the chapter, with the wonderful and then nearly new FXRS and FXRT, both powered by the wonderful and then really new V^2 Evolution engine.

If the FXRS had started out as an "engineer's bike" in 1982, for 1984 it was recast into a "marketeer's bike," with shorter forks and shocks that took away some of that ground clearance and lean angle that had originally been

This 1984 RT was upgraded with the gauges and radio from a later FXRT model. These newer pieces mount to the fairing, while the original 1984 speedo and tach mounted between the bars, just like those on the unfaired FXRS.

The basic RT came equipped with footpegs, but for 1986 Harley offered the deluxe FXRD Grand Touring version, featuring footboards (as shown on this upgraded RT), Tour-Pak, stereo, and extra gauges. This machine also has the police front fender and fairing lowers.

The FXR's one-piece, 4.2-gallon tank had the look of the old dual Fat Bobs, but was easier to manufacture and to fit to the motorcycle. The tank and center console shown were used on many of the FXR models, but others had their own, unique versions. In 1986 came the FXR Super Glide, a new low-priced model fitted with a different console, which held the filler cap and the speedometer. In 1987 came the FXLR Low Rider Custom, with no center console and one filler cap, on the right half of the tank.

engineered into it, in favor of a lower seat height that Harley's marketeers thought would revive its flagging sales.

Because the shorter suspenders still had to control the same load, fork and shock springs were made stiffer. The result was a great loss in cornering clearance (now less than that of the Wide Glide or Softail, but noticeable only by the few who actually tried to ride the new FXRS the way the original was meant to be ridden) and a stiffer ride (noticeable by anyone), balanced by a lower, more Harley-like feel. To emphasize the change in stature, the shorter FXRS was even given a new name: Low Glide.

The irony was, once the FXRS was given a motor as good as its chassis, the chassis was taken back a half-generation in function. A few noticed and complained, but the majority were pleased that their feet were now flat on the ground. Sales went up, too, though not by the 31 percent that Harley's overall sales went up that year.

The FXRT kept its longer suspenders and the Sport Glide name. With the new motor, it was finally the bike it was meant to be, and it got even better reviews. *Cycle* featured it in *two* full articles in the November 1983 issue. Predictably, the new engine got the bulk of the praise ("It never leaked a drop [of oil] while in our hands"), but the editors loved the chassis, too, commenting that "In our high-speed antics, we grounded the pegs only once. For such a large machine, that's amazing." Complaints were limited to the padding and shape of the seat, the too-tall windshield, high-effort front brake, and the high price ($7,699).

Overall, *Cycle*'s assessment was positive and right on, but I can't help applying some hindsight here, because they couldn't stop themselves from trying to predict the future. The editors predicted that the high-priced Milwaukee steeds were bad investments. Buyers of new Evo Harleys would have the last laugh in years to come when they were able to sell or trade them in for more than the original price.

True to Vaughn Beals' prediction, the RT was still contributing most mightily by converting riders of other makes. One notable "conversion" was that of Chuck Irwin, founder and president of the national Suzuki owner's group. In the

In 1988 came the restyled FXRS Low Rider, with a twin-filler version of the tank and a dual-instrument console, like that of the original Low Rider.

summer of 1983, Irwin had challenged Harley to a direct comparison of the then-new Evo-powered FXRT with the Suzuki GS1100G. After 3,000 miles of testing, Irwin concluded that the RT was the better bike, so he bought one and resigned from the club he had founded. Remembered Beals, "When he bought an RT, it boggled my mind, but it was the God's honest truth. We figured that was a real conquest!" Shortly thereafter Harley capitalized on the coup by featuring Irwin in two-page ads in all the magazines.

Sadly, neither the endorsement of the "nice guy" former Suzuki president nor the "bad guy" Hell's Angels president did much to raise RT sales. To help, Harley made a special offer to anyone who bought an FXRT before June 1, 1984: $900 worth of accessories, including a Tour-Pak trunk with liner, AM/FM cassette stereo with antenna, luggage rack, fairing pockets, and the engine gauge kit.

In 1988 Harley upgraded the forks on all FXR models to the 39-millimeter units used on the Sport and FXLR in 1987.

From two models in 1984 (FXRS and FXRT), the FXR chassis was "cut" into as many as six models by the early 1990s. For 1993, the FXRT was canceled, because of low demand. For 1994, all but the stripped FXR Super Glide and the FXLR Custom were replaced by similar Dyna models. For 1995, the Custom and Super Glide were replaced. Shown is a 1989 FXRS.

The RT was also offered in police trim, as the FXRP Pursuit Glide. After exhaustive testing, the California Highway Patrol (CHP) approved the FXRP, and Harley put in a successful bid to begin taking the business away from Kawasaki. Other police departments started buying Harleys again, too.

Like all the Harleys that year, the 1984 Rubber Glides were fitted with 11.5-inch brake discs (replacing 10-inchers) and new master cylinders and calipers with piston ratios juggled to lower lever effort. They each got only one of those discs on the front, so the overall effect was actually a slight reduction in braking power, though lever effort was reduced by a claimed 30 percent. The FXRS also lost its sissybar. Both RS and RT were fitted with the round air cleaner and the "deco marquee" tank emblems common to the line that year.

In midyear, two big things happened. First, all the Evo-powered models got a new clutch, a wet one with a diaphragm spring that was easier on the rider's hand. Second, the FXRS and FXRT got a new sibling that foretold lots of good things for the whole Harley line.

The FXRDG Disc Glide

That new bike was the limited-edition FXRDG Disc Glide. What did it contribute? Glitter. See, the marketing department saw gold in equipping Harleys with more and more chrome from the factory. Unfortunately, the process for chroming aluminum castings, in production-line quantities, day in and day out, was far more difficult than anyone realized. Hoping to perfect the process, while minimizing the risks of slowing down regular production, Harley's management decided that they'd experiment with a few limited-edition chromed models and gradually spread the chrome across the model line.

The Disc Glide was the first of these with the Evo engine. It was given 12 chromed covers on its engine (including timer, starter, valve covers, primary, and tranny top and side) that really gave the engine a more refined, custom, and finished look. Everyone (even magazine reviewers) who saw it commented on how much the chrome improved the looks of the engine. Despite this, and Harley's history of selling dressy customs, the editor of the Disc Glide review in the May 1984 issue of *Motorcyclist* predicted that it was "doubtful the company will apply its chrome-plating technology more widely." As Tweety said so often of Sylvester in the cartoons, "He don't know me very well, do he?"

The key to getting chrome for the whole model line was in getting its suppliers to eliminate hidden flaws and porosity in the aluminum castings and then to get its chrome platers to increase capacity. In 1985 came the FXRC and primped versions of the FLT and FLHT. Through that strategy, Harley was finally able to get up to speed enough to offer chromed and blacked-out engines on regular production models. First came the Softail Custom of 1986, and eventually the chrome-and-black engines became standard on almost the entire line.

By the end of the 1990s, the FXR had become one of the most popular platforms for outrageous customs, so Harley-Davidson decided to show the world how custom a bike could be right from the factory. The Parts and Accessories Division built the FXR^2, FXR^3, and FXR^4 models on a separate line, using all the chrome and billet goodies from the P&A catalog. Since the Evo engine was scheduled to get the axe at the end of the 1999 model year, this was Harley's last chance to use the FXR chassis without having to go through all the government recertification processes necessary if it were fitted with the new Twin Cam motor.

Disc Glide's name came from its aluminum disc-type rear wheel. In addition, it came with a laced front wheel and with special "Genuine Harley-Davidson" tank graphics that were actually embedded in the paint. All this for $8,199, about $750 more than for the regular Low Glide. Harley figures show that 853 were built, plus another 10 of what it lists as the "FXRSDG," but these may have been just an inside experiment.

FXRC "CANDY GLIDE" AND THE FXRS PERFORMANCE/SUSPENSION PACKAGE

For 1985, the FXRS Low Glide and FXRT Sport Glide were back, now with belt drive. In addition, the FXRT was given a second disc up front for much better stopping power, and the sissybar was made higher, to better pamper the passenger. Both wore bar-and-shield tank emblems for the new year.

Sport-minded riders had reason to rejoice, because the taller suspension was available once again on the FXRS. Low and stylish was standard; tall and sporty—the Performance/Suspension Package—cost an extra $150, and was one of the year's great motorcycling bargains. This package essentially took the Low Glide back to its old, sportier Super Glide II form, with longer forks and shocks and a second front brake disc. Nevertheless, the regular Low Glide outsold the sportier one by almost three and a half to one (3,476 to 1,008). If there was any question before, the issue was settled in 1985: Low really was what most of the customers wanted.

Harley Factoid, circa 1985: The FXRT (already with the performance suspension, plus bags and fairing) sold for $8,199, only $50 more than the FXRS Low Glide with the optional suspension. That's some cheap touring gear!

Two other FXR limited editions were run for 1985 (one official and one unofficial) both to gain extra sales and to help perfect the production line process for supplying more chrome. The official one was the FXRC Low Glide Custom, which in some locales was unofficially dubbed "Candy Glide," in honor of its delicious Candy Orange and Root Beer paint—paint that made the whole motorcycle seem to glow in full sunlight like a radioactive pumpkin.

Other special touches on the Candy Glide included unique tank graphics that were actually embedded in the paint, a root beer–colored seat, laced wheels, a sleeker front fender (like on the XLCR and XLCH), and the same package of chrome covers for the engine as on the Disc Glide, plus even more chrome, on the speedo and tach and other bits.

The Candy Glide wasn't for everyone, and in some parts of the country they were a tough sell. Why? The price was higher, for one. The biggest reason, though was that—especially in bright sunlight—it was too pretty for a man to be seen on. This was at a time when Harley-Davidson was just starting to get bold with color choices, and the black T-shirt crowd just wasn't fully ready for Candy Orange and Root Beer bikes with orange-brown seats. Only 1,084 were built.

The unofficial FXRS special was a version offered with the chrome covers of the FXRC, but without the candy paint. Only 299 were built.

Like all the Big Twins that year, they came with the diaphragm-spring wet

The FXR²'s tank and console are the twin-filler and twin-instrument units from the old FXRS Low Rider. Mirrors are carved from billet. Even the grips are chromed, with rubber pads.

clutch, 120-mile-per-hour speedometers, new throttle locking screws, evaporative emissions canisters on California-market bikes, improved starter relay, and chrome crossover on the exhaust. For those who didn't like the standard colors, different color options were available each month through Harley's new custom-paint program.

FXR SUPER GLIDE, FXRS LOW RIDER, AND FXRD GRAND TOURING

All the basic FX models except the Wide Glide were canceled at the end of the 1985 model year, so the FXR line was expanded to fill the resultant holes in the line-up. In addition, a more luxurious version of the FXRT was introduced (the FXRD Grand Touring Edition) and a second police FXR was also offered (the FXRP with windshield instead of full fairing).

Updates to the whole FXR line included a new oil tank, featuring a sight glass for checking oil in a hurry; turn signals that also operated as running lights; locking turn signal switches; a revised starter relay; powdercoated frame; and tuned intakes and revised exhaust systems for lower noise and emissions.

FXR Super Glide

Replacing the canceled Super Glide Fat Bob as the low-priced Big Twin for 1986 was the FXR Super Glide, a stripped version of the FXRS. For its low price of $7,349 ($950 less than the FXRS) the buyer of the Super Glide got a rubber-mounted five-speed Harley Big Twin with classic cruiser styling, but with a little less chrome and polish than on the higher-priced model. He or she also had to get by with a less-expensive seat, no highway pegs, and a chain final drive.

The Super Glide was fitted with the 4.2-gallon "turtle" tank, but with a new center console containing both the fuel filler and the speedometer, similar to the one that had graced the 1983–1985 XLS Roadsters. Contributing to the "clean bars" look, the turn signals mounted to the fork.

It also got the sleeker front fender used on some Sportsters and the FXRC before it. Like the rest of the new Super Glide, its tank emblems were unadorned by curlicues and other extras, with just the important basics: "Harley-Davidson Made in U.S.A."

Harley's brochure for the model billed it as "A basic, very affordable Harley-Davidson. For those who want a motorcycle they can believe in, not just ride on." It attracted some believers, too, because the new stripper sold well, with 2,038 going out the door.

FXRS Low Rider, Sport Edition, and Liberty Edition

Except for the new name Low Rider, the FXRS was little changed for 1986. The optional package with longer suspension and a second front brake disc was also given a rename for 1986, to FXRS Sport Edition. Sales of the regular FXRS were way down, from 3,476 in 1985 to 1,846 in 1986. Popularity of the FXRS models dropped as the Softail line expanded to dominate Big Twin sales.

The base FXRS was also offered in a special Liberty Edition to commemorate the restoration and 100th anniversary of the Statue of Liberty. The Liberty Low Riders featured laced wheels, Blackberry and silver paint, and "Ride Free" liberty graphics. Only 744 Liberty Low Riders were built, and $100 from the sale of each was donated to the Statue of Liberty-Ellis Island Foundation.

FXRD Grand Touring

Since the "upscale" Classic editions of the big tourers usually outsold the more basic models, Harley tried that approach with its smaller tourer for 1986 to create the FXRD ("D" stood for "dresser," according to Rit Booth) Grand Touring. The RDs were fitted with such luxuries as footboards for both rider and passenger, a wider and more plush seat, trunk with backrest for the passenger, chrome rails for the saddlebags, two-into-one exhaust, special paint and graphics, more gauges, and a standard AM/FM/cassette stereo with CB monitor, Dolby noise reduction, and controls for the system on the handlebars.

The FXRD was a great sport-touring bike, with all the handling, braking ability, ground clearance, and long-legged grace of the RT, but with more comfort and elegance. All that came with a steep price, however: $9,474, almost $1,00 more than an FXRT and actually an even $100 more than an FLHT!

Unfortunately, the RD wasn't a great seller. One thousand FXRDs were built and another 591 FXRTs that year. In general, the RTs sold, while the RDs sometimes languished on the show-room floors until they were discounted and finally sold, sometimes years later. As a result, the RD was canceled at the end of the model year.

FXLR LOW RIDER CUSTOM

Four of the 1986 FXR models from 1986 were back for 1987 (FXRS Low Rider, FXRS Sport Edition, FXR Super Glide, and FXRT Sport Glide), plus a new one, the FXLR Low Rider Custom.

Before we go through what was new to each, here's what they all got: powertrain changes listed in chapter 1, return to nonlocking turn signal switches, a new clutch cable with an adjuster in the middle of the cable, lighter cast wheels with 7 spokes instead of 10, and new tapered fender supports with a more forward mount for the shocks (to lay them down more) and a more rearward position for the back turn signals.

FXLR Low Rider Custom

The first Low Riders were the pair that Willie G. and Louie Netz rode to Daytona in March 1977. Put into production later that year, the original version of the Low Rider (with 3.6-gallon Fat Bobs featuring a center console with small speedo and tach, stretched front end, low bars, and blacked-out and polished engine) became one of Harley's landmark models. In later years, the name was tacked on to more ordinary models that bore little resemblance to the original.

To celebrate the 10th anniversary of the model, Willie and Louie created the Low Rider Custom for those who wanted the comfort of rubber mounts with all their chrome and polish. The new model was packed with custom touches from front to back. At the front, they added a laced 21-inch wheel and skinny tire; a slim fender; 39-millimeter forks; better-looking fork sliders, with chrome caps and the reflectors moved to the fender mounts; a chrome bullet headlamp mounted from below, without the "eyebrow"; chrome triple clamps; and a unique welded handlebar assembly that bolts directly to the top triple clamp, with all the wires run internally and carrying the chrome speedometer and idiot lights high and centered on the bars.

Further back, the chrome-and-black engine from the Softail Custom, was topped by a new version of the 4.2-gallon "turtle" tank, this one with the filler on the right half, a hand-laced leather strap down the center, special emblems on each side with 1917-style lettering, and special two-tone paint and striping.

In the center, it featured a special embossed seat with removable pillion pad and two-tone sidecovers with pinstriping. At the rear, the Custom had new fender supports that moved the top shock mount forward for a more laid-down placement of the shocks, and custom two-tone paint and stripes on the rear fender, over a disc wheel.

Harley-Davidson (and especially the Styling Department) was justly proud of the new Low Rider Custom and featured it in full-size poster form on the flip side of a fold-up brochure targeted at getting the owners of older Harleys to trade up to the new models. It worked, too. Harley sold 3,221 of the new customs, making it the second-best-selling Big Twin, behind only the Softail Custom. If the original FXR reflected the alter egos of the engineers who designed it, the Custom reflected the alter egos of the men in Styling.

Super Glide and Low Riders

Even the Super Glide was given the belt drive for 1987, the last of the Big Twins to get that feature. It also got new tank emblems with "Harley-Davidson" in outline script, underlined with bars and the "Super Glide" name. Despite the updates and the overall increase of Harley-Davidson sales, sales of the Super Glide fell by almost half, to 1,265.

Low Rider and Low Rider Sport Edition both were given the two-line "Harley-Davidson Made in U.S.A." tank emblems used on the FXR in 1986. They were also both fitted with the slimmer front fender from the Sportsters. For a limited time, laced wheels were available for the regular Low Riders.

The Sport was updated with new front forks, with 39-millimeter tubes (they had been 35-millimeter); new sliders without reflectors; chrome caps over the dust seals; and polished aluminum triple clamps. Turn signals were mounted to the top triple clamp. Atop these forks was a new, lower handlebar for a sportier riding position. Highway pegs were no longer standard equipment. To compensate somewhat for the higher seating position mandated by the Sport suspension, a new seat was fitted with a lower, wider rider section and removable passenger section.

With these updates, the Sport really stood apart from the regular Low Rider, and, for the first time, outsold the regular FXRS, 1,142 to 784. Overall, though, sales of all the FXR models were poor, except for those of the Low Rider Custom.

FXRT Sport Glide

Aside from the changes listed at the beginning of the section, the Sport Glide was little changed for 1987. It still had the larger front fender with dual support struts, the bar and shield on the tank, and 35-millimeter forks. Standard for the new year was the discontinued RD's sound system. Unfortunately, its sales plummeted yet further, to a low of 287.

NEW-LOOK FXRS LOW RIDER AND FXRS-SP SPORT EDITION

For 1988, all five FXR models (FXR Super Glide, FXRS Low Rider, FXRS-SP Low Rider Sport, FXLR Low Rider Custom, and FXRT Sport Glide) came with the 39-millimeter forks, which had been used only on the Sport and FXLR in 1987, as well as the engine updates listed in Chapter 1. A bunch of other updates for the FXR models included a new clutch cable with eyelet end, American-made Hayes brake calipers and master cylinders, wide-angle convex mirrors with ball-and-socket joint, and (for all but the Sport) turn signals mounted to the lower end of the mirror stalk.

Revamped Low Rider

For 1988, the Low Rider was revamped to make its styling much truer to that of the original Low Rider. Most striking was the new 4.2-gallon tank with a filler cap on each side of a new center console designed to mimic the one that had first been used on the 1977 Low Rider, with a small, tandem speedo and tach on the wrinkle-black housing. Only one filler was really needed, so the left filler cap housed a gas gauge and wasn't meant to be removed. On each side of the tank was a new emblem, with "Harley-Davidson USA" stacked in three lines.

Bringing it even closer in looks to the original, was the custom black-and-chrome engine first used on the Softail Customs, along with a lot of chrome and polish everywhere else and some new paint options. If the regular Low Rider wasn't dressy enough, a special 85th anniversary edition was offered.

The new look was popular, too. Sales more than quadrupled for the FXRS, totaling 2,637 of the regular model plus 519 Anniversary models.

FXRS-SP Low Rider Sport

The FXRS Sport Edition was finally given its own letter designation for 1988, now being called the FXRS-SP Low Rider Sport Edition. Its front suspension was improved by the addition of a simpler version of the air-assisted antidive system first used on the FXRT Sport Glide in 1983. Instead of a separate two-chamber reservoir with a rubber bladder between the chambers, the FXRS-SP system used the sealed handlebar as the system's air reservoir, and included an air valve on the left side of the bar as a means to adjust air pressure.

The new FXRS-SP was given the same tank emblems as the FXRS got, but little else was changed, other than those changes listed at the beginning of the 1988 section. Sales of the Sport fell almost 50 percent, to only 818 for the year.

These true factory custom FXR models are so detailed that about all the owner can really do to improve them is to fit a custom exhaust, as was done here. As you'd expect, the paint is amazing, too. To the human eye, the company name on the side of the tank glows in 3D. To the film in my camera, it disappeared.

The only Evo-powered Big Twin for model year 2000 was the FXR[4]. It was as custom as the two previous P&A FXR models.

FXRT Sport Glide

With sales so low for this model already, Harley didn't sink much money into changes for it. For 1988 it got an updated sound system with a digital clock. It also got the 39-millimeter forks (but still had the old braced front fender) and the new red-and-black version of the Harley-Davidson bar and shield, which was also used on the big baggers that year. Sales remained in the toilet, a total of 243.

FXLR Low Rider Custom

The Custom was back, with new paint options. Sales for the FXLR plummeted in 1988, even though Harley's overall sales were up by 13.5 percent.

After a great first year (selling 3,221), sales of the FXLR dropped by more than two-thirds in 1988, to a measly 902.

FXRS LOW RIDER CONVERTIBLE

For the start of the 1989 model year, all five FXR models from 1988 were back again, with few fundamental changes, other than nine-spoke cast wheels (except on the FXLR, which had a laced front and disc rear). Sales for

Curiously, the engines of the P&A FXRs were the plain silver engines, rather than the blacked-out versions.

all continued to slide downward, even as Harley-Davidson's sales rose 17 percent for the year. FXRT sales were actually up by a dozen to 255, but the Low Rider, Sport, and Custom sales fell to 2,096/755/1,016, respectively.

Midway through the year, however, a new model was released, the FXRS Low Rider Convertible. The Convertible wasn't so much a new model as it was a trim package added to the Low Rider Sport to create a spare sport-tourer. Included in the Convertible package were a quick-detach Lexan windshield, padded sissybar, semirigid leather-and-nylon saddlebags, taller handlebars, highway pegs, and turn signals mounted to the lower triple clamp so they would clear the windshield. Sales for the new model were very modest, at 292.

In 1990 the six FXR models (FXR Super Glide, FXRS Low Rider, FXRS-SP Low Rider Sport, FXRS Low Rider Convertible, FXLR Low Rider Custom, and FXRT Sport Glide) were all given the powertrain updates listed in chapter 1, along with revised brake rotors and pads and new tank emblems. Low Rider, Convertible, Custom, and Sport were given emblems consisting of "Harley-Davidson USA" in a circle with speed lines trailing back. Super Glide and FXRT were given a unique design with "Harley-Davidson" on a bar, trailing back from a circle with "Made in USA" inside. The FXRT got front crashbars as standard equipment.

Harley's sales were up by 7.5 percent and were now limited by the company's production capacity more than by demand. Some of the FXR models rose with the rest of the boat, but sales for the line still weren't good, at 304 for the FXRT; 1,143 for the FXLR; 989 for the Convertible; 762 for the Sport; 2,615 for the Low Rider; and 1,819 for the Super Glide.

FXRS-CONV. LOW RIDER CONVERTIBLE

For 1991, the same six FXR models were back. Little was changed, except that the Sport, Convertible, and FXRT were given the black-and-chrome version of the engine, leaving only the FXR Super Glide with the plain aluminum motor. Also, the front reflectors on all but the FXRT were moved from the fender stays to the frame down tubes, and the Convertible was finally given its own letter designation, "FXRS-Conv." (Yes, with the period, though in later years it was "CONV".) All rode on uprated Dunlop Elite tires.

Sales of all the FXR series remained mediocre: 272 for the FXRT; 1,197 for the Custom; 1,721 for the Convertible; 683 for the Sport Edition; 2,183 for the Low Rider; and 1,742 for the Super Glide. Release of the FXDB Dyna Sturgis, and steady low sales, sealed the FXR series' fate, though the models would soldier on for a few more years.

All six FXR models (FXR Super Glide, FXRS Low Rider, FXRS-SP Low Rider Sport, FXRS-CONV Low Rider Convertible, FXLR Low Rider Custom, and FXRT Sport Glide) were back for 1992, all with a new "letter-opener" tank emblems. (This was the first time they all carried the same emblems.) All got the engine changes listed in chapter 1, and on the Sport Edition, the turn signals were moved to the lower triple tree, as on the Convertible. At the end of the model year, the FXRT was canceled, going out as the last Harley to still use the old braced Sportster fender.

All but the FXRT were back again for 1993, with new low-profile clutch and brake levers, but few other changes. In midyear a new belt pulley with 50 percent more spline area was introduced.

Nineteen ninety-three was the company's 90th anniversary, so the FXLR Low Rider Custom was offered in 90th Anniversary livery, with special paint and cloisonné tank emblems. The factory boasted that only 800 FXLRs would be built in Anniversary trim. Given that average yearly sales of the Custom were about 1,200 in the early 1990s, most of that year's FXLR production must have been Anniversary machines.

The end was coming near for the FXR line. At the end of the 1993 model year, the FXRS, FXRS-SP, and the FXRS-CONV were canceled and replaced by Dyna models of similar names for 1994.

END OF THE LINE, 1994

Only two FXRs remained for the 1994 model year: the basic FXR Super Glide (the lowest-cost Big Twin) and the FXLR Low Rider Custom. Both got the drivetrain changes listed in chapter 1. Both got new tanks emblems with "Harley-" and "Davidson" on separate lines, in outline type. And both were replaced by Dyna models for the 1995 model year.

REVIVAL: 1999 FXR^2 AND FXR^3, AND 2000 FXR^4

Harley is known for bringing looks and features back from the dead, but the release of the FXR^2, FXR^3, and FXR^4 in 1999–2000 defied precedent. Here was a chassis that had been dead and gone for nearly a half-decade, powered by an engine that had been replaced in all models except the Softails.

Why this, especially when Harley-Davidson couldn't build enough bikes to meet demand, anyway? Many reasons, really, but three important ones.

First, since the demise of the FXR at the end of the 1994 season, the thing had become more popular than ever. Many of the best customs were being built on FXR chassis because they were cheaper and more available for chopping than the other Harleys were. Ever wonder why you rarely see any old FXRTs or FXRP police bikes any more? They were all chopped into customs. Same with the FXR Super Glides and on up the line. As the supply of those dried up, the aftermarket starting offering stock-type, as well as lowered and stretched versions of the FXR frame. Build an aftermarket motor to stuff in it, and the only one who loses is Harley-Davidson. The new FXRs were a way to get all that money flowing into Milwaukee rather than out to California, by offering what the big-name customizers offered: a "clean-hands," turn-key supercustom.

Second, many at The Motor Company loved the FXR and wanted to give it one last hurrah—and this was the very last chance to do so economically, for three reasons: (1) It still had the tooling to make the FXR chassis lying around. (2) The Evo motor was still in production for one last year. (3) It would take some work to fit the Twin Cam motor in the FXR frame, and once they had,the

combination would have to go through the whole (very expensive) process of EPA recertification of the old chassis with the new engine. Thus, once the Evo motor went bye-bye forever, so, too, would the FXR chassis.

Third, Harley was looking to develop its Parts and Accessories (P&A) division's ability to assemble complete bikes on its own production area, without interrupting the flow of the normal assembly lines, using parts already available through the P&A catalog.

The first result of P&A's work was the FXR^2. It was a chrome-covered beauty, taken about as far as you could go without raking or stretching the frame. This is one Harley that's not likely to get added chrome or billet parts because they're already part of the package. The list of Genuine Motor Accessories is too long to list here, but here are the really surprising items: chrome swingarm, chrome Bad Boy–type slotted disc wheel, chrome sliders, chrome handgrips, chrome carb cover, chrome voltage regulator, and even chrome spark plug covers! Painted parts were Arresting Red or Stone Cold Blue, with special "ghosting" tank graphics that appear and disappear as if by magic, depending on the angle of view and available light. All that's really missing is a custom exhaust, but the factory couldn't really supply that and still remain in good graces with the EPA.

The FXR^2 was the first factory supercustom, a bike chromed and customized beyond the call and yet is all-Harley, and thus will likely hold its value more than will all those customs built on aftermarket frames and engine cases. At $16,995 ($17,260 in California) it was a bargain, too. You could easily spend that much and more on a Softail and not have nearly the flash value or exclusivity offered by the FXR^2.

Following closely after the FXR^2 were the FXR^3 and the FXR^4, each taken further than the last, with various other mixes of P&A parts and different paint (including the aptly named Screaming Yellow Pearl or Candy Tangerine, both with Eclipse graphics, on the FXR^4).

REQUIEM FXR

So far as anyone outside the factory could guess, the FXR^4 was the last of the FXR models, and the last of the Evo-powered models.

Still, as Mark Tuttle said at the beginning of this chapter, many folks miss the sporting Big Twins. If you're among them, take heart. Although it's very unlikely that the FXR will return as a regular-production model, two strong trends are working in your favor:

First, Harley is hoping to surpass 200,000 sales by 2003, the 100th anniversary for the company, so it is going to need some new models to help reach that goal.

Second, as proved by the Dyna (designed to look like the old FX models), the Softails (designed to look like several older models), and the FLHT (designed to look like the old FLH), Harley often resurrects the looks and feel of discontinued old favorites.

You just may see a new sporting model along the lines of the FXRs, possibly featuring the double-balancer motor so no rubber mounts are needed, allowing an even stiffer and better-handling sporting Harley.

CHAPTER 5

The Evolution Sportsters

1 9 8 6 – 2 0 0 1

HARLEY'S "LITTLE TWINS" HIT THE BIG TIME

"I had many customers come up to me and say, "The 883 was the greatest thing you guys ever did because now I could buy a new Harley."

—**Vaughn Beals, former Chairman and CEO**

Harley-Davidson introduced the 883 Sportster in the summer of 1985. A few months later it introduced the higher-priced ($5,199) 1,000-cc Sportster. Shown is a 1987 model. The 1986 883s had the smaller fender shown. The 1986 1100s had the earlier and larger fender shown on the Dyna Glide Sturgis in the following chapter.

With apologies to Chairman Beals and the customer he talks about in the quote on the previous page, the greatest thing The Motor Company ever did for the Sportster crowd was when (at last) it released a Sportster engine that was the equal of its chassis—the 883 and 1100 Evolution Sportster engines for 1986.

As we've already seen, Harley's big baggers and sporting Big Twins only came into their own when they were finally fitted with the Evolution engine. So, too, did the Sportsters, because like the FLT and FXRS before it, the Sportster already had an improved chassis waiting for an improved motor when the Evo engine came along. Thus, the real story of the Evolution Sportster as a motorcycle begins long before the new motor was shoehorned into the frame.

"PRETTY COVERS," LESSON ONE: THE STORY OF THE "DISCO" SPORTSTER

In model year 1957, when the Model XL Sportster hit the streets, it was merely the old KH model updated with an overhead-valve engine. Thoroughly modern (for the day) it was, with a 55-cubic-inch (883-cc) engine and 7.5:1 compression, but it didn't really look or act the part of a sport machine (read "dirt bike," in those days). With a 4-gallon tank, stamped-steel triple clamp shrouds, two-into-one exhausts, and FL-style headlight, it was styled and marketed as a junior Duo-Glide. A version was even built for the U.S. Army, the XLA, which was the last Harley twin bought by the Army in any quantity.

The Sportster began to earn its name in 1958 with a second version, the XLH (H for higher compression, as in 9:1, plus bigger valves). Still, it didn't look the part. Then came the XLC (C for "Competition," which was listed as "low compression" on the dealer order blanks because it used the low-compression regular XL motor) and the XLCH (C for "Competition" and H for "high compression" because it used the hotter XLH motor), released during the 1958 model year. These were the true start of what we all know as the Sportster today.

Stripped of lights and battery for off-road and drag-race competition, the C and CH wore a small, 2.25-gallon "peanut" tank, a smaller version of the classic horseshoe oil tank used on the Big Twins, bobbed front and rear fenders, a separate "straight" (as in no muffler) pipe for each cylinder, longer shocks, Goodyear Grasshopper (dirt) tires, and a magneto ignition. Lean, light, and purposeful-looking, the C and CH were the start of the notion that Sportsters are "dirt bikes." Lights were also offered on the C and CH, for those who wanted to duke it out on the streets.

In 1959, lights became standard on the CH, and the C was dropped, because no one wanted a stripped performance machine with the low-compression motor. Instead of the shrouded light and triple clamps of the XL and XLH, though, the CH got a smaller headlamp (like that of the 1958 Hummer) mounted to the top triple clamp with an "eyebrow" mount. It also got a taillight on a fuller rear fender. Because the CH was now a real street bike, it had to wear mufflers, so it was given a unique two-into-one high exhaust with a muffler on the right, alongside the rear fender. Even with all the street gear, its

The first of the Evolution Sportsters to reach the dealerships in the summer of 1985 were the smaller, 883-cc versions, offered for the astonishingly low suggested retail price of $3,995. Shown is a later five-speed 883.

looks said "performance," and it lived up to those looks, too. Many think of it as the first real street Superbike. Though owners of Crockers and Vincent Black Shadows would rightly scoff at that part about it being the "first," few would deny that the 1959 XLCH was *the* Superbike of its day. It was also the best-selling Sportster.

That's where the Sportster line stood throughout the 1960s, with really two lines: the stripped, magneto-equipped XLCH and junior-FL XLH. In 1967, the XLH got an electric starter, while the CH kept its macho mag and kickstart-only.

Nevertheless, as the years went on, the XLCH got even more popular, while sales of the "junior-tourer" XLH dropped steadily. In 1970, the CH lost its mag, in favor of the points used on the XLH, and the lines became blurred as the XLH got the peanut tank, too.

About this time, the Sportster was losing its whole image. See, for about a decade, it had been the classic two-wheeled American hot-rod. But with all the large-displacement bikes showing up from Britain and the Orient, by 1970 it was just another also-ran. For 1973, Harley made a stab at regaining the performance image by boring the Sportster out to 1,000 cc, but it was too little, and far too late.

Nevertheless, sales were still good because the motorcycle market was booming. Then, after a record year in 1974, with sales of almost 24,000 Sportsters (compare this to Harley's *total* production of 29,620 Sportsters and Big Twins in 1984), Sportster sales began a precipitous drop every year thereafter.

Why the drop? The market was cooling, certainly, but Harley-Davidson suspected there was more to the story. Ray Tritten, group executive in charge of running Harley-Davidson for AMF at the time, commissioned a market study to find out why sales of the Sportsters specifically were suffering.

The results?

"People were complaining about handling, about shock travel, about seat comfort, a variety of things," remembered Vaughn Beals, who was hired as deputy group executive in 1975. "That was all done before I got there, and the result was a whole list of stuff that needed to be fixed. That evolved into making a new Sportster."

Shortly thereafter, Tritten and the newly hired chief of engineering, Jeff Bleustein (now CEO of Harley-Davidson), rallied the few engineers Harley had at the time, and then the many new ones he soon hired, and got them to work on a new chassis for the Sportster.

What came out of it all was a radically redesigned frame. Replacing the old 1950s-style frame of gently curved tubes, an open midsection, and

The Evo Sportsters were essentially the new motor fitted into the old chassis, so most of its features were familiar to Sporty fans. The key switch and choke were all on the left side, under the tank. The deluxe 1100 also had the chrome horn in the V of the motor.

forward-mounted shocks was a modern wonder of straight tubes, triangulated midsection, and rear-mounted shocks, with the lower shock mount right above the axle, as on the frame of the alloy-engine XR-750, released in 1972.

Cautious then as now, Harley-Davidson decided to test the waters with the new frame by using it on only one limited-edition model at first, the radically-styled XLCR Café Racer. "Café-racer" styling was hot then, and the XLCR was Willie G.'s take on the styling idiom, with a long "coffin" tank, solo seat with XR-style tail section, low bars, rearset footpegs, "bikini" fairing, oil tank and battery hidden behind triangular sidecovers, and radical "Siamese" (as in joined at the middle, like Siamese twins) dual exhaust with twin mufflers, left and right. Those who bought the XLCR, and some Sportster critics in the motorcycle press, raved about the improvements in handling and the boost in power provided by the Siamese exhaust.

Unfortunately, the XLCR wasn't the sales success many had hoped it would be. Nevertheless, Ray Tritten and others at Harley-Davidson thought they had a winner of a frame that could be the backbone of the whole Sportster line. They were quite taken with the exhaust, too. As the company would soon learn, to its regret, the CR wasn't really a fair test of the frame. See, the modern frame looked natural on the cutting-edge Café Racer. Also, the XLCR had been planned and styled to appeal to a new group of riders, rather than to the Sportster faithful.

Thus, for model year 1979, the Sportsters were restyled around the new frame and Siamese exhaust. Once the familiar Sportster bits, such as peanut tank and buckhorn bars were thrown back on, the differences between the old and new Sportsters were a bit subtle to the uninitiated, but they were definitely there. "I can remember very clearly when Willie G. wheeled in two Sportsters, the new one and the old one, into the conference room for a Product Planning meeting," said Vaughn Beals. "He was describing what was new and so forth. I finally said, 'Willie, I lost track. Which is the new one?' They

One of the things the buyer of an 1100 got for the extra $1,200 was a dual instrument console with a tachometer.

both seemed identical to me, which in retrospect shows what I didn't know at the time.

"Once I knew which was which, the new one looked pretty good to me. We showed it to our dealer advisory council, 10 or 12 dealers, and they thought it was dynamite. We went ahead with the program because, technically, it was designed to fix all the various chassis problems that the customers had identified."

Fix those problems it did, but it created a bigger one, too. Those who knew and loved the Sportster look thought the huge, flat-sided triangular sidecovers, way-to-the rear shocks, and Siamese exhaust made the new Sportster look "blow-dried" and "feathered." On the show-room floor, next to an older Sportster, the new one stood out like a lime green polyester leisure suit on a Brooks Brothers rack. Modern, trendy, and gaudy, it was a pair of Gloria Vanderbilt jeans to the old XLCH's Levi's 501s. You could see John Travolta or the brothers Gibb (as in the Bee Gees) riding it, but could you see Bronson (as in *Then Came . . .*) on it?

It was the Sportster for the disco age.

"It was [also] an utter fiasco," explained Beals. "Everybody said, 'Where's the oil tank? You can't see the battery anymore. It looks Japanese!'"

The "Disco" Sportster gave Willie G. and everyone else at Harley-Davidson Lesson One of three (see chapter 3 for Lesson Two and chapter 4 for Lesson Three) in how the design philosophy that former Harley engineer Rit Booth calls "pretty covers" would never work for Harley-Davidson. Booth explained: "What we learned through that Sportster, the FLT, and the FXR was that what the Harley customer wanted in a motorcycle was good-looking machinery—not good-looking covers."

"The only thing that Sportster did was clear the warehouses of the prior year's production," Beals remembered. "Usually, we had some left over at year end that we had trouble moving. Man, we didn't have any problem that year! People bought the old ones like crazy, but nobody bought the new ones. They really wanted more shock travel, but when the result was you could see daylight under the rear fender, heavens to Betsy, motorcycles don't look right that way."

"We, fortunately, learned from our screw-up on the Sportster not to screw with nostalgia," Beals added, laughing. "Even if it compromised function, you stuck with nostalgia. The tuition was very low, but the message got through loud and clear to all of us. We had to scramble to redesign and get that thing back to what it was."

SECOND SWING AND A HOME RUN

Scramble they did. At first, they reworked the sidecovers to give a peek at the battery again, for 1980. It probably helped some, but not much. The real solution was a complete redesign that made its debut at the buy-back festivities in York, in June 1981, for the 1982 model year.

The new frame kept the stiffness, good handling, and shock travel of the Disco frame, but gained back some of the pre-Disco Sportster good looks by once again exposing the battery and oil tank, and by moving the upper shock mount farther forward on the frame and laying down the shocks more. While they were at it, the Sportster engineers also made it cheaper to produce, by eliminating many of the cast-iron frame junctions and forgings. Overall, the post-Disco Sportster was popular, and its chassis was the basis for better things yet to come, most specifically, the 883, 1100, and 1200 Evolution Sportsters that are the subject of this chapter.

SILENT SPRING:
WHY CHEAPER IS BETTER

The post-Disco Sportster came along just in time to punctuate the buyback, but also just in time for the crash of the motorcycle market in model year 1982.

"When we bought the company in 1981, and closed in June," explained Beals, "spring hadn't yet come for us that year. The motorcycle market was in the doldrums. Usually, by June we had a handful of prior models and were just starting to switch production to the next year's models. We had never had a problem with carryover. In 1981 we had a problem. Essentially, the only way we could handle that was to discount. We had hardly gotten back from buying the company when we announced a 15 percent discount on our products. Nobody could remember when we last had a fire sale. That cleaned out our inventory and taught us a lesson: At the lower price, we noticed that we sold almost twice as many Sportsters in the same length of time as we would have sold otherwise.

"Next year, in 1982, it was worse. The market was now a disaster. We cut production way back, and our dealers still had inventory, so we repeated the program. We sold even more Sportsters. We thought, gee whiz, with a 15 percent price reduction, we nominally doubled our volume of Sportsters."

Taking quick action on that "cheaper is better" lesson, Harley-Davidson released a stripped and de-chromed base-model Sportster, the XLX-61 (61 for the displacement in cubic inches), for 1983. Gone were the buckhorn bars, speedometer, dual seat, and most of the chrome and paint options, in favor of just a speedo, low bars, a solo saddle, black shorty dual exhaust, and basic black paint with simple "Harley-Davidson XLX" tank graphics. It was given a little distinction, however, with a smaller, more modern-looking front fender (similar to that of the XLCR Café Racer), while all the other Sportsters (except the XR) had the braced fender.

Along with all the other Sportsters that year, the XLX was improved with a new electronic ignition with vacuum-controlled advance, higher compression, less restrictive exhaust, and a smaller air cleaner. The XLCH was dropped from the line-up.

The XLX was an instant hit because of its (briefly offered) introductory price of $3,995, and 4,892 were sold that year, making it the best-selling Harley by far. Needing every possible sale to get production back up to levels that would keep its bankers from foreclosing, Harley-Davidson also released the hot-rod XR-1000 that year, with heads, carbs, and pipes similar to those of the XR-750 grafted onto an XLX. The XLS Roadster was also restyled that year, with a new tank that was designed to look like the Fat Bob tanks on the Big Twins. Both of these were less successful than the XLX, but every sale *did* count.

Success of the XLX reinforced the lesson that, for Sportsters, cheaper really was better, and that lesson shaped the future of the Evo Sportster engine, because it had to be designed for economical production so that in 883-cc form, it could be sold at a sustainable profit for $3,995.

For 1984, the XLX and all the other Harleys were fitted with an 11.5-inch front disc (replacing the old 10-incher) and revised master cylinder. Meanwhile, its price had climbed to about $4,500, and it was fitted with a chrome-plated exhaust. With the increased price, sales dropped substantially. Partway through the model year came the real improvement, one that would carry forward onto the Evo Sportsters and help make them more civilized than the earlier Sportsters: a diaphragm-spring clutch and an alternator to replace the generator.

Not much changed for 1985, and Harley-Davidson curtailed Sportster production to clear showroom floors for The Next Big Thing in the Sportster line.

THE 1986 883 AND 1100 EVO SPORTSTERS

That Big Thing was the XLH 883 Sportster, released in early summer 1985 as an early-1986 model.

Except for the new engine, the 883 was XLX-basic—meaning solo seat, low bars, no passenger pegs, basic black paint (or Signal Red), basic "Harley-Davidson 883" tank graphics, smaller front fender, and speedo only for instruments—for $3,995 retail. Candy Blue or Candy Red paint cost $75 more. Everything else was familiar to the Sporty crowd: same peanut tank,

with ignition and horn on the left in the V of the motor and petcock (with reserve, but reserve really means "panic time" because the tanks only had a total capacity of 2.25 gallons to begin with) under the tank on the right. New on the 883 (and on all the other Harleys that year) were turn signals that double as running lights and new, locking turn-signal switches.

But you just can't say "except for the engine" because the new engine was the star of the show. Though it is covered in chapter 1, a few words about it are necessary here. With a bore and stroke of 3.00x3.812 inches, it emulated those of the first Sportster engine, and thus had the same displacement, 883 cc or 55 cubic inches. Those dimensions were chosen for reasons of both heritage and economy. Economy both of production and riding

Buyers of the basic 883 got only a speedometer. Shown is the electronic version on a 1999 Hugger.

For the extra money, the 1100 offered a dual seat, sissybar, more displacement, larger valves, blacked-out cylinders and heads with polished fins, higher bars, passenger pegs, and other features—but mostly it offered a bit more power.

because many insurance companies offered a price break for motorcycles of under 900 cc.

As covered in chapter 1, a major focus of the Evo Sportster engine design was in making it cheap enough to produce that Harley could offer the new machine at a retail price of $3,995. "We were really trying to get entry-level riders to buy a Harley," explained Vaughn Beals, "and we knew that the $3,995 price was critical to doing that."

As the "fire sales" of 1981 and 1982 had proved, and as the $3,995 (limited-time introductory price) XLX of 1983 had confirmed, the lower the price, the more Sportsters the company would sell. In the summer of 1985, three things made the lower price even more critical. First, the market, overall, in America for street bikes was still in a free-fall, contracting by about 20 percent every year. Second, the tariff that Harley had won in 1983 was starting to have an effect on the

prices and sales of the big-bore Japanese bikes. Third (and probably most importantly), the value of the U.S. dollar had fallen seriously compared to the Japanese yen. As a result, the prices of all the Japanese bikes had risen into Harley territory. Harley already knew cheap Sportsters would sell, but the question remained, how well would the new Sportster sell in a low-demand market, even if it was actually cheaper than many of the Japanese imitators (which it was—$500 less than the big Yamaha Virago that year). The answer was more gratifying even than Harley had hoped, but we'll get to that soon enough. Back to the engine.

Heritage didn't stop with the displacement and bore and stroke, either. Though its shiny aluminum heads, barrels, and cases flaunted its newness, the basic shape of all three were carefully styled to affirm its lineage.

Aluminum sheen aside, the most visible break with the past was the use of three-piece rocker covers, similar to those of the Evo Big Twin. These covers simplified maintenance, as did a number of other features, and this was all part of the effort to "sanitize" the Sportster and make it appealing to a new crowd of riders, while appealing to longtime fans, as well.

After removing the rocker covers one piece at a time, you could remove the cylinder heads themselves and then the barrels, all without pulling the motor from the frame. In fact, you can even leave the carb and pipes in place and remove and replace both heads and those parts all as an assembly without taking out the engine, as the flat-rate mechanics do. All this was possible because of the engine design, but also because the upper frame was revised to allow clearance for all this. Harley was thinking.

Though it had gained much displacement and convenience since the first XLCH Sportsters of the 1950s, the Evolution Sportsters still had the tall, slim look of the dirt bike the XLCH originally was.

Further simplifying maintenance was a feature new to the Sportster but that had been used on all the OHV Big Twins since the first Panheads of 1948: hydraulic lifters. No more valve adjustments were needed, and these lifters made the engine quieter, too. Unfortunately, Harley-Davidson didn't get them quite right the first go, and some of the early Evo Sportsters were plagued with a lifter or two that would collapse intermittently.

A key part of the sanitizing was the lack of oil lines. With the engine in the frame, you couldn't see any without looking closely. This made it look modern and nonintimidating to the neophyte and maintenance-phobic. It also helped keep oil leaks at bay. Sanitized though it was, the new Evo Sportster motor still had all the character that Sporty fans had always loved. That mostly meant that the 883 still had the Harley sound and vibes, though it was noticeably smoother than the old iron 1000, and was nearly identical in performance to the last XLH-1000s, too.

Little-noticed at the time but welcome nonetheless, the 883 came with a frame and other black parts protected by powdercoat paint. The baked-on powder paint sealed the metal in a thick, extremely tough cocoon that resisted water, corrosion, and chipping far better than the best paint. Not only was it a benefit to the buyer of a Sportster, but it eased production rework problems because a slip of the wrench or a dropped tool was less likely to chip a frame during assembly.

The modern, sanitized look wasn't deceiving, either. Except for the lifter problem, the new Sportster engine proved to be so much quieter, smoother, cleaner running, oil-tight, and trouble-free that it won the praise of owners, dealers, and the motorcycle press.

Cycle World tested a preproduction machine and reported on it in the August 1985 issue. Overall, the editors liked the new Sporty, deeming it quieter, smoother, and (surprisingly) just as fast or faster than the old XLH-1000.

A big part of the look was the "peanut" gas tank adapted onto the XLCH from the tank used on the Harley Hummer small singles.

From two at the start of the 1986 model year (883 and 1100), the Sportster line grew to three by the end of the year, when the Deluxe version of the 883 was released. The Deluxe featured laced wheels, dual seat and passenger pegs, dual instruments, and more color options. In 1987, a lowered version of the 883 was released, called the Hugger. A 1999 Hugger is shown here.

Nineteen eighty-seven was the last year of the 1100 Sportster, which was superseded by the 1200 Sportster in 1988.

This 1987 XLH 1100 was ordered in this custom color and with laced wheels.

Of its performance, the editors said, ". . . we can tell you that as far as acceleration, lugging ability, and overall engine performance is concerned, the difference between a 1,000-cc Sportster and an 883 isn't great enough to be detectable on the human dyno." Another interesting tidbit in the riding impression was a prediction by Vaughn Beals that the new Sportster would attract as much as 30 percent more sales. We'll come back to that in a moment.

Cycle gave a production 883 the full test in its September 1985 issue. The editors commented that it seemed down on power compared to the old 1000, but not by much. They also noted its smoothness and great gas mileage (54 miles per gallon overall), but were most impressed that a Harley this good

could sell for so little money, noting that it was "hundreds of dollars less than the current big-bore V-twin pretenders from Japan."

And with the service interval doubled from 2,500 miles on the old iron Sporty to 5,000 miles on the Evo, its owners kept on smiling because for the first time, they had a Sporty that required minimal wrenching, so they could do more riding.

When the rest of the 1986 model line came along in the early fall of 1985, it included yet another Evo-powered Sportster, the XLH 1100. If the 883 was the new XLX, the 1100 was the heir to the old XLH-1000's legacy. That is, it was the upscale Sportster, with more chrome, Buckhorn bars, dual seat and passenger pegs, both speedo and tach, larger front fender, wrinkle-black cylinders with polished fins, more stylish tank graphics, more paint options, chrome horn cover, and, of course, a larger-displacement engine.

Again, most of the discussion of this engine is in chapter 1, but a few words are warranted here. Harley got the extra displacement by simply using a larger bore and piston. To go with the extra displacement, the 1100 also got larger valves and ports, and the result was more horsepower—10 more, by Harley's figures, about 20 points more by percentage.

All these extra goodies and power came at a price, however: $5,199, or $1,204 more than for the 883. Also at a price in vibration too. The 1100 became known as a shaker, though it really was no worse than most of the old 1,000-cc Sportsters had been.

The 1100 was also offered in a special Liberty Edition to commemorate that 100th anniversary and restoration of the Statue of Liberty. The Liberty 1100 Sportsters featured laced wheels, a special paint job of Blackberry overall with maroon and silver pinstripes, and "Ride Free" liberty graphics on the gas tank and front fender. One hundred dollars from the sale of each was donated to the Statue of Liberty-Ellis Island Foundation to help pay for the restoration.

Later, a second 883 (the 883 Deluxe) was added to the Sportster fold to finish out model year 1986 with a three-Sportster line-up. The Deluxe included laced wheels, dual seat and passenger pegs, a tach to go with the speedo, and different paint options.

True to historical precedent, price proved the key to Sportster sales success. The basic 883 wrested the sales title away from even the Softail Custom, selling 8,026 copies in 1986. The upscale 883 Deluxe sold 2,322, and the XLH 1100 another 3,077, plus 954 in Liberty form.

Remember Vaughn Beals' prediction in the August 1985 *Cycle World* that the 883 could increase Sportster sales by 30 percent? In fact, they increased by 120 percent. If he'd have been that wrong in that direction more often, Harley would now be bigger than General Motors.

XLH 1100 30TH ANNIVERSARY EDITION, AND 883 HUGGER

For the start of its second year, the three basic Evo Sportster models (883, 883 Deluxe, and 1100) were all back, with some pretty substantial changes for second-year models, especially to the powertrains. Those changes are discussed in chapter 1.

Some things never change. The taillight used on Sportsters today is the same basic light used on the first Sportsters in 1957.

Wheels for the regular 883 and 1100 were cast in a new, lighter pattern, with seven spokes instead of nine. Those for the 883 were unpainted, while those for the 1100 were painted black, with polished edges. (The 883 Deluxe models still came with wire wheels.) Also, the 1100 was given the sleeker front fender used on the 883s.

XLH 1100 Anniversary

In the late 1980s, Harley-Davidson needed every possible sale it could get, so the company really didn't need much of an excuse to release a special edition. For 1987, the most convenient excuse was the 30th anniversary of the Sportster, so the company celebrated by releasing the XLH 1100 Anniversary. This special Sportster was dolled up in orange and black paint, with 30th anniversary graphics on the tank and front fender, a unique chrome-and-black treatment of the Sportster engine, and a serial plate listing what number a particular bike was among the 600 built.

XLH 883 Hugger

Partway through the year, a third 883 was released, the XLH 883 Hugger. The Hugger was touted as "A street motorcycle with a low profile," as in low seat height—1.75 inches lower, according to Harley's claims. This was accomplished by shortening fork tubes about 2 inches, lengthening the swingarm about a half-inch, revising the shocks, and giving the seat a looser cover so the foam would compress more. It also had pull-back buckhorn bars to bring the controls within reach of shorter arms, and to meet customer preference.

In the process of getting lower, the Hugger also got longer (by a half-inch) and the lowered rear resulted in more rake and trail for slower, more stable steering, at the cost of 2 degrees of cornering clearance on the right, but none on the left, according to Harley's figures.

Harley marketed the Hugger explicitly for the shorter rider, and implicitly for the female market. The Sportster was already pretty low, so why bother?

The answer came out of the same "fire sales" in 1981 and 1982 that ultimately gave us the 883. By lowering the price of the Sportsters, sales almost doubled, but something else also happened, according to Vaughn Beals: "Some months into [the first fire sale], somebody realized, 'Hey, usually we sell 2 percent of our Sportsters to women. Looky, we're selling 9 percent of these things to women.'" That got the planners at Harley-Davidson thinking about how they could sustain that increase in sales to women.

"We had and still have a lot of women inside the company who ride, so we did some very informal discussions among women riders in the company," he continued. "We had debated putting it out in pastel colors or something like that. They all laughed at us and set us straight real quick. They said, 'A lady who wants to ride a Harley wants a black Harley. We don't want any of these feminine colors you guys might think up.'

"What they wanted was a lower seat height and maybe lighter controls and stuff, so we pulled the bars back, lowered the seat a bit, and tried to soften the stiffness of the hand controls somewhat. It really worked, and now something like 15 percent of Sportster sales are to women. But we also never have publicly identified the Hugger as a lady's machine because there are some men out there who aren't all that big. It was helpful to them, and we didn't want to bias them against it."

Though it wasn't a pastel, there was a pretty new color exclusive to the Hugger that year: Bright Candy Plum. You know who that was aimed at.

Ride Free on an 883

During the year, the 883 was made an even more attractive package by a new program that guaranteed a trade-in value of $3,995 on any 883 traded in within a year of purchase on any Harley Big Twin. This program gave a whole new meaning to the "Ride Free" slogan.

This gutsy new program was the result of another observation made by the dealers and marketers. The 883s brought in a lot of new customers, and a fair percentage of them were so impressed with their new Harley that they were soon back to upgrade to a Big Twin. Clearly, this was a trend the company wanted to encourage, and the trade-in offer was the perfect way to do it. A customer could essentially test ride a Sportster for up to a year for little cost if he or she later upgraded.

"We were really trying to get entry-level riders to buy a Harley," said Vaughn Beals. "Sportsters were less intimidating, and they've always been that way, so the 883 made it easier for them to give our products a try. The Japanese were eager to copy our motorcycles, but that Ride Free program is one they haven't had the guts to follow. It's the only one we would have liked them to follow."

For model year 1991, the Sportster engine was given another update, this one more involved than the one that turned the old iron Sportster engine into the Evo. Nearly every piece was changed in turning the four-speed powerplant into the new-for-1991 five-speed powerplant.

Starting in 1988, the Sportsters were fitted with a stiffer, 39-millimeter fork to replace the old, willowy 35-millimeter fork. Starting in 1995, the ignition switch was moved from the left side to the right side, on the steering head, as shown here on a 1995 Hugger. Also that year, all but the 883 models got the larger, 3.2-gallon peanut tank.

Despite the trade-in program, sales were down drastically for the basic 883 in its second year (8,046 to 4,990) and down slightly for the Deluxe (2,322 to 2,260). Sales of the new Hugger (2,106) helped bring the 883 total near that of the previous year. The 1100 Sportsters fared better, though, increasing in total sales from 4,039 to 4,618, an increase of 14 percent, while sales of Harleys overall rose by 7 percent.

THE XLH-1200

Nineteen eighty-eight was celebrated as the 85th anniversary of the company with special editions of the Big Twins. Oddly, there were no 85th Edition Sportsters.

For 1988, the 1100 was bored out to create the XLH-1200. The bore job, plus a larger carb, and redesigned camshafts that were also added, resulted in 12 percent more horsepower and 10 percent more torque, according to Harley figures. While the power of the 1100 gave Sporty fans back their dignity by making it (just barely) quicker than the FXRS-SP, the 1200 sealed the deal.

In a nod to the past, the Sportster name was scrawled across each side of the 1200 Sportster's tank.

For the new year, all the Sportsters got their own versions of the 39-millimeter forks (with polished aluminum triple clamps on the 1200 but polished aluminum upper clamps and crinkle-black steel lower clamps on all 883s), better spring and damping rates, and better-looking sliders, with chrome dust-seal caps but without reflectors) that had been introduced the year before on the FXRS Sport and the FXLR.

Frames for all except the Hugger (the Hugger's was already a half-inch longer than those for the rest) got a slightly longer swingarm with longer shocks. This change gave slightly more travel, without noticeably lengthening the wheelbase, seat height, or changing the steering geometry.

Other updates to the Sportster line included American-made Hayes brake calipers and master cylinders; wide-angle convex mirrors with ball-and-socket joint; and, on 1200 and Hugger only, turn signals that mount to the lower end of the mirror stems. Turn signals on the 883 basic and Deluxe mount to the top triple clamp.

Overall, Harley sales were up almost 14 percent for the year. Most of the Sportsters kept pace, with sales of the Hugger leading the pace, more than doubling from 2,106 in 1987 to 4,501 in 1988. Sales of the basic 883 were up a bit to 5,387, while sales of the Deluxe fell, to 1,893. Sales of the new 1200 (4,752) stayed at about the same level as those of the 1987 1100 Sportster.

All four Sportsters from 1988 were back, with few changes. Most visible? New tank badges (with the Sportster name over a circle with "Harley-Davidson" and "883") and return to the nine-spoke cast wheels after two years with the seven-spokers. Most comical? A rise in the basic 883's retail price of four measly dollars, to $3,999 (in Vivid Black only). Later in the year, it was raised again, to $4,195.

Although the $3,995 price has steadily risen over the years since 1985, the 883 remains as the least-expensive path to the Harley experience.

Sales of Harleys were up 17 percent overall, but Sportster sales stayed relatively flat, as everyone was buying Softails.

Also in 1989, the AMA instituted a new race series, just for those basically stock 883 Sportsters.

For 1990, all four Sportster models were back, essentially without change (except for prices and color options) because Harley's engineering department was busy readying the next big update to the Sportster. Sales of all but the 1200 decreased slightly, but those of the 1200 rose just a bit.

1991: BELTS AND THE FIVE-SPEED SPORTSTERS

"Hell Freezes Over," announced the cover of the December issue of 1990 *Cycle* magazine.

For 1996, an even sportier Sportster was introduced: the 1200S. Among its features were a cartridge-type fork, piggyback shocks, a 3.3-gallon tank, and stickier tires. Shown is a 2000 1200S.

The Sport's shocks were gas-charged and included piggyback reservoirs. They are the best suspenders ever mounted by the factory.

The Sport had the larger, 3.3-gallon version of the classic peanut tank from the first year of production. Dual-plug heads and single-fire ignition were added to the Sport in 1998. The coils that spark the dual-plug cylinder heads reside under the tank on this 2000 model.

The occasion for the cold snap?

The first real upgrade to the Sportster transmission since before there was a Sportster. After all, when the Sportster was created by grafting on an OHV top end onto the old side-valve Model KH, the Sportster got the KH's four-speed transmission in the bargain. In the quarter-century since then, little had been changed, and all the Sportster's competition had gotten five-speeds long ago (and many were even on to six-speeds). Little wonder, then, that Sportster fans had long felt they'd get a five-speed when hell froze over.

The reason it took so long was that it was a really big job. As covered in chapter 1, everything in the tranny was new, and just about every major part of the engine, too. In fact, it would be easier to list what wasn't changed. The list is short, comprising little more than cylinders, pistons, and connecting rods. As a result, the five-speed 883 and 1200 Sportster engines were stronger, the charging systems more bulletproof, oiling and breather systems cleaner and more effective, the shifting was far smoother, and the whole powertrain was easier and less expensive to produce.

As motorcycles, the 883 and 1200 Sportsters were more fun to ride, too, courtesy of the new transmission and primary ratios. First through fourth gears were lower, for better acceleration, while the direct-drive (1:1 ratio) fifth gear was higher than the old fourth, reducing revs for less vibratory jaunts at cruise. In fact, the new Sportster five-speed powerplants were so good that they far outclassed the old chassis and suspension, which had seen only minor updates since 1982.

In addition to the new engine and tranny, the 1200 and Deluxe both were fitted with belt drive, which did for the Sportster all that it did for the Big Twin— smooth out the ride and eliminate the frequent lubing and maintenance required by chains. Because of the Sportster's lower weight and power, as well as advances in belt technology, Harley-Davidson was able to fit a narrower belt to the smaller twins—1.5 inches vs. 1.75 inches for the Big Twin. As a result, it wasn't quite the challenge to make room for the belt that it otherwise would have been. Even so, the shocks had to be slightly repositioned and a few frame tubes required strategically placed dimples.

All four Sportsters were fitted with rubber-mounted footpegs from the FXR models, which cut the vibration levels a bit. Front-end reflectors were moved from front-fender stays to the side of the frame rails, and both the 883 and 1200 were given new tank graphics that advertised the fifth gear.

As satisfying as the redesign was for the Sportster buyer, it turned out to be even more so for The Motor Company, once the sales results were in for that first five-speed year. Sales of the 1200 were up by nearly a third, to 6,282—making it the best-selling Sportster in the line. Sales of the 883 Deluxe more than doubled, to 3,034. Sales of the lower-priced 883 standard and Hugger were down slightly, to 4,922 and 3,487, respectively. Just as had happened earlier with the Big Twin line, Sportster customers were buying more of the upscale models than of the strippers.

After all the work of putting forth the new five-speed Sportsters for 1991, the Sporty engineers were on to better things for 1992, so little was changed in the Sportster line. Nevertheless, all were given revised swingarms (shorter for the Hugger and longer for the rest) and revised shocks. In addition, seats, tires, color combinations, brake rotors, and prices (the basic 883 was now up to $4,495, and still a bargain) were subtly changed. Drive chains for the Hugger and basic 883 were updated to O-ring types.

In January, a dedicated assembly line for Sportster engines entered service at the Capitol Drive engine plant.

BELTS FOR ALL, 90TH ANNIVERSARY, AND A SAFER FRAME

For 1993, the big news was belts. At last, both the basic 883 and the Hugger were fitted with the Gates belt drive. Also, all the Sportsters were given redesigned brake and clutch levers.

In celebration of the company's 90th anniversary, a special Anniversary edition of the 1200 Sportster was the star. Each of the numbered 90th Sportsters was given a special silver paint job with Charcoal Satin-Brite tank panels, red pinstripes, and enameled and plated cloisonné tank emblems.

For 1994, the frame received the bulk of the updates, and the change incorporated was long overdue, too.

See, the weak points of the whole chassis had long been the alloy fender supports that mount to the frame and sweep back along the rear fender. Their task was to support the whole seat-and-fender-and-rider assembly. They were well up to the task when all they were carrying was a rider and passenger.

People being what they are, some would add a sissybar and rack (which also had to be supported by those struts) and throw-over soft luggage (again, supported by those struts) and then load it all up with camping gear, climb aboard with a passenger, and head off to Sturgis. If the combined weight of rider, passenger, and luggage exceeded the design strength of those struts or you threw in a sudden side load from a stiff gust of wind, disaster sometimes happened. Those struts could crack, and the combined weight of rider, passenger, luggage, seat, and fender would then go crashing down onto the rear wheel, locking it up tight.

Heart-to-heart time for you owners of pre-1994 Sportsters: See that sticker on the side of that new luggage rack you bought? See that it says something like do not exceed 15 pounds, or some small weight figure? Listen. And go light on everything else back there, too. It could save you some skin.

To correct the problem (and for other reasons, as well), Harley engineers redesigned the rear section of the frame, strengthening it through the use of beefy forgings that extend farther back to support all the important stuff riding on the rear. Chrome-plated steel covers hid the forgings, and because the covers extended straight back instead of curving with the fender, they gave the whole rear end a lower, more modern look. The reflectors (which had been on the alloy struts) were moved onto the fender sides, just above the chrome covers, and the turn signals mounted farther back. All that strength came at the expense of weight, however, up about 20 pounds for all. A good trade-off.

As a result of the new frame, as well as the new seat designs, seat heights *were* actually lowered for the basic 883 and the 1200, but (despite appearances) they were *raised* for the Deluxe and Hugger. All the stuff under the seats were revised, too: electrics, oil tank, and battery tray.

On the left, inside the primary cover, a revised clutch-release mechanism that works with a new-design clutch cable to allow quicker changes of the cable. Easing the weight gain from the frame (somewhat) was the aluminum lower triple clamp fitted to all the 883 models (the 1200 had had it from the beginning).

Compared to 1994, all was quiet on the Sportster front for 1995. New colors and revised seats were fitted to all, as were new electronic speedometers and vacuum-operated petcocks (on the left side of the tank, so the ignition switch was moved to the right side of the steering head). The 1200 was fitted with the 3.2-gallon peanut tank, with a new "Harley-Davidson 1200" tank emblem. In the latter regard, 883s weren't left out either; all three sported new and stylish "Harley-Davidson Sportster 883" tank emblems.

1200S SPORT AND 1200C CUSTOM

The Sportster line expanded by two to fill two more market niches and contracted by one for a five-bike assault on showroom floors in 1996. New were the 1200S Sport and the 1200C Custom. Since laced wheels were now an option on the 1200, the Hugger and the regular 883, the 883 Deluxe was deemed redundant and cut out of the line-up.

1200S Sport

To attract the Sportster owners who were hell-bent on changing everything to raise the sporting potential of their machines, Harley offered the 1200 Sport, with everything they could ask for in the way of suspension and brake improvements. (More horsepower would have to wait.)

Triple discs were standard. Good ones, too, the same floating units fitted to the Bad Boy. Forks were the latest cartridge-type, with dual-rate springs and adjustments for spring preload and both compression and rebound damping. Shocks were deluxe units with the same adjustments, and they featured a remote piggyback reservoir, pressurized by nitrogen. Tires were upgraded, too, to Dunlop K591s in soft and sporty rubber compounds. On the new 3.3-gallon tank were unique checkered-flag tank emblems.

While all these changes didn't transform the old Sporty into a Ninja-killer, they did make the Sport the best-handling Harley since the late FXRS Sports, and one that's a quantum leap more fun in the twisties. Frankly, all the suspension adjustments can bewilder the unaccustomed rider at first, but once the fork and shocks are dialed in, they transform the Sport into a different breed of Harley.

1200C Custom

For the chrome set, Harley offered the 1200 Custom. Willie G. started with the shorter (in height and in length) Hugger chassis and added a bunch of parts similar to those of the Bad Boy. These included the slotted rear wheel, floating

Another new 1200 putted onto the scene in 1996: the 1200C Custom. Featuring a 21-inch laced front wheel, slotted disc rear wheel, and lots of chrome, the Custom took the Sportster chassis down a new path. Shown is a 2001 Custom.

For 1999, the Sportster Custom treatment was applied to the 883 to create the 883C. Forward-mounted foot controls and pegs were added to both Customs.

brakes, tall chrome-plated forged risers, and low bars with hidden wiring. The chrome goodies were similar to those of past models, such as the FXLR: 21-inch laced wheel, chromed speedo up high on the bars, and chromed bullet headlight with lower mount.

On the new 3.3-gallon tank were special chromed cloisonné emblems. Anchoring the look, Willie also specified a unique chromed and painted version of the Sportster engine.

Long, low, and high-style the Custom looked. It wasn't an illusion, either. The custom's seat height was 27.12 inches, the same as that of the Hugger.

The Rest

Of the other Sportsters, all but the Custom were fitted with new 13-spoke cast wheels as standard equipment, and all got recontoured switchgear for the year. Finally, the regular 1200 also got the new 3.3-gallon tank and new tank emblems (the 883s still got the old 2.25-gallon peanut). Harley announced that it was building a new plant near Kansas City and would shift Sportster production to the new plant in 1998.

The same five Sportsters were all back for 1997, with detail improvements. All got more freely breathing intakes and exhausts, which made the motors a little torquier, and sealed batteries for reduced maintenance. Eight eighty-threes were (at last) given the larger tank, with new tank emblems. And the regular 1200 got a new two-piece seat that was lower and better looking, and which nestled the pilot into a more comfortable riding position.

More horsepower and torque were what the 1200S Sport needed, and it got about 10 percent more of each for 1998, courtesy of new cams, higher compression (10:1 instead of 9:1), single-fire ignition, and dual spark plugs in each head to hold pinging at bay. Other updates include silver powdercoat on some of the engine castings, a diagnostics plug, and lots of bad black attitude. (Vivid Black was the only color offered, and the headlight eyebrow, handlebars, mirrors, and fender-mount covers were also black.)

All the Sportsters were given a new oil pump, for better scavenging of oil from the crankcase; revised ignition; and a fuse panel behind the cover on the left. In addition to color and seat updates for most of the models, the Custom was also available in 95th Anniversary livery, with special two-tone Midnight Red and Champagne Pearl paint and unique cloisonné tank emblems.

THE XL-883C SPORTSTER CUSTOM

For 1999, the custom touch was applied to the 883 to expand the Sportster line to six models. The new 883C Custom was an 883 with the 21-inch wheel and custom fork and handlebar assembly of the 1200C, plus the forward foot controls that were also added to the 1200C for 1999. Less expensive than the 1200C, of course, it had the 883 engine, without the black-and-chrome treatment given the 1200C's engine. The 883C was also given a unique "Harley-Davidson" emblem on its 3.3-gallon tank.

As already mentioned, the 1200C was made even more custom with forward controls. Drag bars were also new, as was the taller front suspension. The

The Sportster Custom front-end look comes from a special bar and riser, bullet headlight without the eyebrow mount, and lots of chrome.

1200S was now available in several pearl colors, as well as the Vivid Black of 1998. The rest of the line got only small detail improvements and new colors.

YEAR 2000 AND BEYOND

For the model years 2000 and 2001, all six Sportsters were back, essentially unchanged.

What's the future hold for the Sportster line? No one outside the company really knows, and those inside aren't saying. With Sportster buyers accepting more and more expensive Sportster models, the company eventually may decide it's worth the cost to fix at once the two last real shortcomings of the Sportster—vibration and the four-cam layout—through introduction of a Twin Cam "B" Sportster engine.

CHAPTER 6

The FXD Dyna Series

1991–1998

CLASSIC FX LOOKS WITH MODERN FUNCTION

The summary of all that research and discussion with Marketing was, "What the customer wants is a bike that looks like an FX." And this next part is very precisely worded: "If it doesn't vibrate, that's OK."

—**Rit Booth, project engineer for the Dyna chassis**

Even before the old FX series was canceled, people began to clamor for the classic FX look combined with some of the recent Harley updates, such as the five-speed transmission and maybe even rubber mounts. Most important, though, was the classic look. Harley stylists and engineers began work on the new machine in the mid-1980s, with the goal of introducing it with the updated "Optimum Evolution" engine, an early forebear of the much-altered Twin Cam 88 engine.

Hard times in the 1980s had one big lesson for all the motorcycle manufacturers: While they may have been in the business of *manufacturing* motorcycles, what they were in the business of *selling* was image—rolling picture frames for the rider, as *Cycle* magazine (January 1984) had said of the Softail. Didn't matter whether it was Ninja or Softail, race replica or cruiser, most of those who bought, bought because they could imagine themselves riding along in that picture frame.

Really, by mid-1984, the lesson had sunk in fully in Milwaukee. The Softail was all image and outsold everything else from the beginning. The all-function FLT was still in the line-up to reinforce the lesson as the more image-conscious FLHT outsold it by two to one or more. Even the sporty, high, and proud FXRS was lowered and customized for 1984 and sales went up.

Little wonder, then, that when a big new project was begun that year to refine and design the next-generation Harley, its styling was as much a part of the initial planning as were the engine's basic specifications.

DESIGN OF THE DYNA

Engineer Rit Booth pops up so often throughout the events in this book because during design of the FLT, FXR, Softail, and Sportster chassis, he was a project engineer in Applied Mechanics/ Design Analysis, so it was his job to use his design analysis and computer skills to help the project engineers design those chassis.

"Optimum Evolution"

Booth's last big assignment in Design Analysis, in 1984, was to begin work on a new chassis to go with a new engine then under development called "Optimum Evolution." Basically, the Optimum Evolution *engine* program was another concept developed by engineer Hank Hubbard, who had done the original concept

In late summer 1990, that new-old Harley thundered out of Milwaukee and York, Pennsylvania: the Dyna Glide Sturgis. Designed first to look like the old FX series, and second to function like a modern machine, the new Dyna Glide actually did both. The first Dyna model was the FXDB Dyna Glide Sturgis, released to simultaneously make its debut at the 50th anniversary of the Sturgis Rally and Races in Sturgis, South Dakota, and to commemorate the 10th anniversary of the original FXB Sturgis of 1980. Since the Dyna Sturgis was actually a 1991 model, seems H-D missed the 10th anniversary mark by a year.

for the Evolution engine (see chapter 1). The goal of the Optimum Evolution engine project was to finish the job started with the Evolution. That is, it would take the new top end that was the Evo and mate it with an updated bottom end to create a really new engine (see chapter 1 for more on the Optimum).

After brainstorming with the marketing and styling folks on what the chassis for the Optimum Evolution would look like, Booth left with a slogan that would carry him through the next five years in designing the new motorcycle: "What the customer wants is a bike that looks like an FX. And this next part is very precisely worded: If it doesn't vibrate, that's OK."

Don't understand? Here's what it all means: Nothing else mattered as much as making it look like the old FX models—not rubber mounts, not stiffness of the frame, not handling qualities, not comfort, not anything. *But*, if you can get the look *and* still squeeze in rubber mounts, go for it.

An obvious question springs to mind: If the FX look is what they really wanted, why didn't they just tell Booth to update the FX chassis for the five-speed tranny and new engine and be done with it? None of the participants interviewed for this book had a good answer to that, so I'll speculate here: They knew the FX chassis just wasn't good enough for the modern era, so they needed a new chassis and made a psychological ploy to ensure that the engineers put looks first this time, knowing those engineers would knock themselves out to get the rubber mounts, too.

In any case, that was the result— looks and rubber mounts. In keeping with the slogan, though, the design process started from a whole new direction. Said Booth, "For the FLT and FXR, we took some industrial rubber mounts and designed a motorcycle around them. For the Dyna, we designed the motorcycle we wanted and then figured out some mounts that would work with it. Really, that's the right way to do it."

After being promoted to product manager for the FX line in later 1984, Booth continued work on the Optimum Evolution chassis, with the help of the

Like the original FXB Sturgis of 1980, the Dyna version used low bars on tall risers for the drag-bike look, and it was fitted with the Low Rider's dual-filler Fat Bobs and dual-instrument tank cluster. Though the tank looks like the old dual Fat Bobs, it's actually a one-piece, 4.2-gallon tank designed just for the Dyna. The left filler cap includes a gas gauge and really isn't meant to be removed.

other engineers in the FX product group. For the purposes of this book, we'll refer to them as "Team Dyna," though the Dyna Glide name had yet to be coined. "We got to the point where we decided not to go ahead with the engine concept," said Booth, "but the frame looked pretty interesting so they decided, let's keep going on it."

Getting the FX Look

FX look? Easy to say, but how do you quantify all the things that contribute to that look? Turns out, that was one of the first major problems to solve. "We worked with Styling extensively," explained Booth. "To an extent, Styling knew something looked good when they saw it but could never really define it. So there was a period of time where I saw as my main function 'parameterizing' what Styling wanted. For smaller things, like a primary cover, they could get out their clay and show you exactly what they wanted. It was harder when it came to the big picture. We'd ask, 'Do you want the frame longer or shorter?' They'd say, 'I don't know; it just has to look like an FX.' So it was back and forth, and we went through a number of iterations, nonworking motorcycles using one set of parameters. They'd look at it and say, 'It doesn't look right.' Well, what doesn't look right? 'I don't know. Move this and move that.' They had the eye, you know."

What it came down to was long and low, or low and long, because one helps create the illusion of the other. So the team stretched things where it could and lowered other things where it could, and then changed just about everything else to balance out the look. Some stretches were easy, like adding an inch to the swingarm; others were more a matter of juggling geometry, like on the steering head, where Team Dyna designed in a 32-degree rake angle

(more than on any other Harley except the Softail Custom) and stretched the forks by about 2 inches.

Getting the required balance even meant changing the engine, transmission, and primary cases. Why all that work and expense, just for looks? The "Optimum" powertrain was originally designed to use a modified version of the shorter FLT and FXR primary case. Once they'd stuffed it into a prototype frame, it looked short and tall, rather than long and low. "From this exercise," said Booth, "we realized how important the long primary case length from the FL, FX, and Softail was to the look we were after."

The extra length in the primary meant pushing the motor forward, moving the tranny back, or lengthening the frame. In the end, the team did a bit of all those things, and a few more. One that's apparent if you look closely is that the engine's tilted backward 4 degrees so that a line drawn down the center of the V points 2 degrees to the rear of vertical. (The FLT and FXR had the engine tilted 2 degrees forward of vertical, and the Softail had its engine vertical.) This shortened the overall length of the engine-tranny package (while keeping the longer look provided by the primary) and lowered the aft edge of the rear cylinder head, allowing room to lower the frame backbone and lower the seat.

Problem was, the longer Softail inner primary was unsuited to use on a rubber-mounted machine because it was too flimsy (remember, Softail trannies and engines mount solidly to the frame, while on the new machine, neither did). That meant new inner and outer primary cases, too, to build in stiffness. This work was all done at the time Engineering was making changes to fit the five-speed transmission to the Softail, so a new set of inner and outer primaries was designed that could be used on both models.

Idiot lights and the number plate were part of the blacked-out "eyebrow" headlight mount. Again, though the FXDB was really a 1991 model, the plate commemorates the 1990 50th anniversary of the Sturgis meet. Also, the plate says this is number 122 of 1,600, but factory records list only 1,546 as having been built for 1991.

As said earlier, new engine and transmission cases were necessary to get the long, low look. Since both cases needed a redesign, the Dyna group made other changes, as well. The team redesigned both with bosses so they could be bolted together directly (based on the mounting pads used on Hubbard's "Optimum Evolution" concept), eliminating the bracket used on the FXR and FLT. They added a boss for a spin-on oil filter at the front of the engine, redesigned the oiling system so the oil was filtered before going to the engine (rather than on return), and added more internal passages to reduce the number of rubber hoses.

The longer primary was a subtle part of the FX look, but other parts were more obvious, such as the battery on the right side and the oil tank on the left. Putting the battery of the new machine where it was on the old was really no problem, but the oil tank was an issue. The problem? "You don't want the hoses going across the rubber mounts because the engine's always moving in the frame," explained Booth. "The only way to prevent that was to have the oil tank as part of the powertrain package."

"The other issue was packaging," Booth continued. "The FX had the battery on one side and the oil tank on the other. That space isn't really that big, and it could be used for other things. An oil tank can be down there where there's rocks and stones and it's dirty, but you don't want your electrics down there."

Booth's solution was to move the oil tank into a casting underneath the transmission, eliminating or hiding a bunch of oil hoses. Another benefit of this

From the factory, the front turn signals mounted to the top triple clamp. Signals on this example were moved by its owner.

The look H-D was after was long and low, and most everything on the Dyna was redesigned to get that look. Even the primary was stretched, compared to that of the other rubber-mount Harleys, to make it look longer. Front-end rake was a chopperesque 32 degrees, and the fork tubes were stretched about 2 inches. Seat height on the new machine was advertised at 26.6 inches, lower even than that of the 883 Sportster Hugger. Despite that, the Sturgis' seat was one of the most comfortable ever put on a custom-style Harley.

design was that it virtually eliminated any chance of the crankcase filling with oil if the oil-pump check valve malfunctioned. Yet another is that the whole powertrain could be assembled and the hoses hooked up before it was put into the frame. The filler hole for the oil tank was put on the right side, just ahead of the transmission, and its cap included a dipstick. Altogether, a tidy package.

Replacing the old oil tank on the left side was a new piece, with a familiar look but an all-new function. "Part of the look was to *not* have a triangular shape there or a cover there, but to have a real thing there, so that's where we put the electrics, and we styled the box to look somewhat like the old FX oil tank. The electrics would be built as a subassembly and tested as a subassembly, which could then be added to the bike and just plugged into the main wiring harness, which runs inside the backbone tube." Inside that box were the ignition electrics and circuit breakers, and the ignition coil attached to the front of the box so that it, too, was once again where it had been on the FX. Again, very tidy.

Another big facet of the FX look was the fuel tank. Actually, on the FX it was two tanks, the 3.5-gallon Fat Bobs with twin filler caps and speedo-and-tach

The Sturgis was one of only two Harleys in 1991 that was fitted with the old braced Sportster fender (the FXRT was the other). The Sturgis was also the only one with the orange-striped wheels shown.

center console first used on the Low Rider of late 1977. The main goals became to get that look but in a one-piece tank (like that of the FXR) to simplify assembly, and to be able to manufacture the tank from stampings put out by the ancient ring-and-die press that had been squeezing out Big Twin tanks since the 1930s. They also wanted a larger capacity of 4.9 gallons. "We worked real hard on the position of the gas tank. We made a bare shell and moved it around endlessly to find out exactly where we wanted it. Then, we had to figure out how to make it on the old tooling. That gas tank by itself was one guy's [Bob LeRoy's] project for nine months or a year."

Because there was just one tank, only one filler cap was really needed. Nevertheless, the FX look required two caps. Why go to one tank instead of the traditional twin saddle tanks? It would be easy to say "ease of production" or "cheaper," but I suspect the real reason was "liability." See, those saddle tanks looked great and had been part of the Big Twin style since the original Knucklehead of 1936, but they had one big fault. While the tanks are separate vessels, each with its own filler cap, they are also connected by a balance tube. Say you park your Softail Custom on its sidestand, pull off the right filler cap and top it off. As you're topping off, you notice the level keeps slowly going down, so you keep topping off 'til it's full and stays there. Then, you twist off the left cap (you only do this once), and fuel comes gushing out, and keeps gushing until you get the cap back on and sealed or lift the bike upright. If the engine's hot, you get clouds of gas fumes; if there's a spark source, you get a blowtorch. Not good for bike, rider, or corporate peace of mind. No worries of that on the Dyna. The left cap's a fake, there only for style and to hold the gas gauge.

Disappearing Frame Trick

Ultrastiff frames were starting to become all the rage in the motorcycle business in the mid- to late-1980s, and they still are today. To get the stiffness, most manufacturers made frames of large aluminum or steel spars and square tubing, or with triangulated trellis-type structures of round tubing that wrapped around to the outside of even wider four-cylinder engines and were so large they dominated the look of the whole machine. The FXR had this look in the underseat area, for stiffness and because the side structure had to be fairly wide to accommodate the rubber mounts on each side of the swingarm pivots. Some call this the "lobster" approach to frame design: The hard and stiff stuff's on the outside, and all the soft stuff's on the inside.

As usual, Harley-Davidson chose to swim against the flow and follow the model evident from the human body: The hard, stiff stuff's inside to support the basic shape, but the overall shape's determined by what's hung onto the frame.

"Collectively," said Booth, "we had come to the conclusion that the look of a Harley was an engine and two wheels. Although the engine and wheels need to be connected, the frame only adds to the look by being invisible. As much as possible, the Dyna frame is buried. At the same time . . . a few of us who were sport-bike oriented wanted the frame to be just as stiff or stiffer than the FXR's to provide good cornering and stability." Hidden, the frame would be, but everything hidden became Booth's playground. After all, this is the guy who

Long and low, the Sturgis wasn't meant to be a sport bike. That was the message of the single front disc brake.

rode to work and raced a Guzzi LeMans and later replaced the Goose with an XR-1000. You didn't really think he'd sacrifice everything for style, did you? Neither did Styling or Marketing, I'm sure—hence the "psychological ploy" theory discussed earlier.

To get that "internal" stiffness, Booth used a huge rectangular steel backbone sweeping back from the steering head, tightly over the engine, then bending down behind the transmission to join with two closely spaced rear down tubes. You have to look closely to see any of the backbone or the rear tubes on an assembled Dyna Glide. All the tubes that showed—limited to the lower cradle tubes—were round tubes, big and beefy on the Dyna to

Instead of the three rubber mounts and twin turnbuckles of the FLT and FXR models, the Dyna had only two mounts and one turnbuckle. To make the engine-transmission-swingarm unit more rigid, the transmission and engine cases were redesigned to bolt directly together. The new engine case was also revised to move the oil filter out front and hide more of the oil lines. The new transmission case also included a sump to hold the engine oil. Shown behind the battery box is the ignition switch with "Coke-machine" key lock.

Although the Dyna chassis was available only in the limited-edition Sturgis model its first year, the Dyna split to form its own line in the following years, replacing the FXR models one by one.

add stiffness. Booth did "dare to go square" (actually, rectangular) for the side rails of the swingarm, which helped make them stiff enough to hold flex at bay with the forward-mounted shocks that Styling insisted on. More on this later.

For the FLT, FXR, and latest Sportster frames, one of the goals had been to make them entirely from tubes and stampings, without the cast junctions or forgings used on the older Harley frames. Why? "[That was] influenced, I believe, by the competitive frames from Japan and Europe, and the low cost of the stampings themselves," said Booth. "Unfortunately," added Booth, "the gusset stampings are large to enclose a lot of volume, and there are an awful lot of inches of weld." Therein lay the problem. See, at Harley, those frames were welded by hand, not by some robot. More inches of weld meant more time to make each frame. More time to make each frame meant higher cost and fewer that could be made in a day, month, or year. By the late 1980s, fewer made meant more customers on the waiting list for their new machines.

With figures for the number of inches of weld, the cost for each inch, and the cost of the stamped gussets on the FLT and FXR frames, Booth had numbers to compare with the cost of castings and forgings. Using these, he struck the best possible balance—using some stampings and forgings and one big casting, in the places where each was most economical. Stampings were used

Now, there's a look that had been absent from the exposed-shock line for a while—the Wide Glide look, reintroduced in 1993 as the FXDWG on the FX-look Dyna chassis.

for the motor mounts and gussets under the backbone. Forgings were used at all the major frame junctions except the steering head, which was made from an investment casting.

The largest forging was used in the underseat area to link the rear down tubes, upper shock mounts, and side tubes from the backbone. It was designed so that it could be forged precisely enough to allow "self-fixturing," so that the tubes could be slipped into sockets in the forging and welded in place without the need for an elaborate frame jig.

Most innovative of all was the casting for the steering head. No crude iron sand casting that needed lots of machining to make it ready for use like the head on the old FX, the Dyna Glide steering head was cast of steel by the process known as investment or "lost wax" casting. This casting technique is expensive because it requires many steps for each individual part, but the resulting parts are precise, detailed, and clean. First, an exact replica (or "investment") is cast of wax. Then several investments are attached to the "tree" fixture. The tree and investments are then dunked in a ceramic slurry

With battery box on the right, the new Wide Glide looked much like the old, except this one had rubber mounts, a five-speed transmission, and all the updates of the 1990s Harleys.

Just like the original, the Dyna Wide Glide was a factory chopper, with tall fork, high bars, forward foot controls, and laid-back riding position.

The 21-inch laced wheel with tall, skinny tire and single disc were essential parts of the Wide Glide look, successfully recaptured on the Dyna version.

and the ceramic dries to a hard shell. The whole thing then gets heated to melt out the wax before molten steel is poured in to make the castings.

Expensive, yes, but Team Dyna calculated that the investment casting would actually be cheaper than the 13 pieces it replaced because the casting could be made precisely enough that it would be "self-fixturing" and only clean-up machining was required for the bearing races before welding it onto the frame. It was also precise enough that channels for a steering-head lock could be cast-in. More on the lock later.

Another atypical process was used for the front part of the swingarm. Since it wouldn't show and didn't need to be all that precise, it was made of sand-cast *steel* (iron is commonly used in sand castings, not steel) because that was the most economical way to get the stiffness and hollowness in the part. "It is kind of gnarly looking," admitted Booth, "but it is in a location where appearance is not too important."

Forward-Mounted Shocks and Rubber Mounts

From the beginning, there was never any real question: The Dyna would have forward-mounted shocks. The engineers had won that battle and gotten the better-handling rear-mounted shocks on the FXR (see Chapter 4), but there was no chance of that this time because the Dyna was supposed to be more of a "looker" than a "handler," and forward-mounted shocks were a big part of the FX look. Unfortunately, the forward shocks not only worked against having good rear suspension, they also made it much more difficult to use rubber mounts. Despite the last half of the Dyna slogan—"if it doesn't vibrate, that's OK"—Booth knew he'd find a way to fit rubber mounts into the styling of the new machine.

The problem?

Booth explained: "With laid-down shocks, bump inputs would transmit fore-and-aft motion to the engine and trans and load the rubber mounts. With the Dyna, I could see so clearly that the laid-down shocks were critical to the styling that I decided we would just have to make the mounts work with the laid-down shocks."

The related challenge was to control the engine movement in less space, so Team Dyna could pull in the frame rails for the "shrink-wrapped" look Styling insisted on. Working with the engineers from Barry Controls, over a long and difficult period, the team was able to develop mounts that were the right stiffness vertically to absorb the vibration with less actual engine movement, and that were very, very stiff laterally. Lateral stiffness was so good, in fact, that he could get the control he needed with just two mounts (rather than the three of

Give the Dyna Wide Glide flames on the tank and a Shovel motor, and it could easily pass for the original of 1980.

the FXR), front and back, both on the centerline, and only one (versus two on the FXR) of the turnbuckle Heim-joint control rods, in the center of the V.

In the end, the system set a new standard for rubber mounts. As on the FXR, vibration is almost amplified at idle. From there on up the rev range, the Dyna is relatively smooth (though not as smooth as an FXR or FLHT). And because the mounts can do their work in less space, the team wrapped the frame tubes tightly around the engine—some would say too closely. "I believe some guys still think I made a mistake in going along with Styling on laid-down shocks for the Dyna, because of the difficulties in development and because they still get an occasional customer complaint about the engine hitting the frame while motocrossing," he said.

Coke-Machine Locks

Steering-head lock, schmeering-head lock, right? Want to lock, your steering head, bring a padlock. That's been Harley's philosophy for some time. Unfortunately, it wasn't a philosophy that made friends in foreign countries,

The tank panels on the Dyna Wide Glides were shaped to mimic those of the 1958 Duo-Glides. Instead of the flames used on the original Wide Glides, the Dyna versions make do with flamed tank graphics, in two different versions. This style was used from 1996 on.

In 1993, Harley introduced another Dyna model: the FXDL Dyna Low Rider, with twin discs and the same 32-degree rake angle of the Sturgis. A new Dyna was released for 1994, the FXDS-CONV Dyna Low Rider Convertible, to take the place of the canceled FXRS Convertible and Sport. It featured a steeper, 28-degree rake angle for sportier handling. Shown is a 1998 Low Rider, lowered even further and fitted with an accessory shield and bags.

because the rules of some countries require an integral fork lock. Many of these same countries also required ignition locks with an arbitrary (and large) minimum number of available key combinations, and many of the ignition locks then in use on Harleys didn't qualify.

Harley had long wanted to increase its foreign sales, but had been held back by not having a real fork lock. To get what sales they did get, Harley welded on really hokey-looking fork locks. "Nobody liked them," said Booth. The result was that Team Dyna began looking at new types of locks for the new machine. Team member Bob Courtwright ended up selecting a ring-type lock because that type is much harder to pick and had literally thousands of available key combinations.

"People derided it as the 'Coke-machine' lock," said Booth, "but it's used on Coke machines because it's a high-security lock, with thousands and thousands of combinations and very hard to pick. Because of the high number of combinations, we were even able to get the Germans to agree that it met the security requirement."

It was a simple matter to design a space for the lock into the steering-head investment casting, but placement of the ignition key switch was the subject of much study. Traditionally, the FX machines (except the Wide Glide) had the key switch on the left side, under the gas tank. With the bike on the sidestand, the switch is on the low side and hard to see, particularly at night. After gathering lots of opinions, they settled on putting it on the right (high) side, under the seat, about where the rider's hand would be when his or her arm was hanging at his side.

Christening

With the bike nearing completion, no one knew what to call it. The "Optimum" tag had essentially died with that engine. It wasn't an FX, really, any more than it was an FXR, so everyone knew it needed its own name. Someone decided to turn the christening of the new machine into a contest, in which employees were encouraged to submit entries, and Marketing would pick the name it liked best. One employee suggested "Dyna Glide," and that was picked as the name for the new model. With FX looks and the Dyna name, the FXD series designator became a natural.

THE 1991 FXDB DYNA GLIDE STURGIS

While Booth and the engineering team were making the new design ready for production, Marketing and Styling were completing their work, too. The decision was made to bring the new machine out as a limited edition to simultaneously commemorate the 50th anniversary of the races and rally at

The Dyna Low Rider inherited the classic Low Rider dual-instrument console and twin-filler tank from the Dyna Sturgis. The Dyna Convertible carried its instruments between the bars, so it was given another version of this tank with a central filler and gas gauge.

Sturgis, South Dakota, and the 10th anniversary of the original Sturgis model of 1980. The new FXDB Dyna Glide Sturgis was released as a 1991 model, in time to be seen at the Sturgis 50th Anniversary Rally in August 1990, but since it was really a 1991 model, seems to me they missed the 10th anniversary of the original Sturgis model by a year.

Never mind that, though. At least it looked like the original Sturgis. As in black on black. Orange highlights on the tank, timer cover, wheels, and elsewhere. Low bars on high risers for the drag-bike look, without the back ache. It even got the old-style, dual-strut Sportster front fender, as on the original Sturgis. Front turn signals mounted to the top triple clamp, as on the FXRS-SP and the 883 and 883 Deluxe Sportsters.

In 1995, the least-expensive Big Twin was the new FXD Dyna Super Glide. To keep the price down, it was given the basic silver engine, one front disc, and a solo speedometer (no tach) mounted between the bars. It also shared the 28-degree rake angle used on the sportier FXDS-CONV.

its seat is actually comfortable enough that there's no need to go running to Corbin. It is perhaps the best Harley seat since the old sprung tractor seat went away. Through development of the seat, Booth also developed a philosophy that he still uses in his engineering: "I worked on that 'til half the people thought it was too hard and the other half thought it was too soft. Then, I knew it was right."

Like the seat, the rest of the bike was aimed dead down the middle at the Harley cruiser crowd, and it hit its mark. As a sporting machine, the Dyna was not an improvement on the FXRS-SP, but it was never meant to be. Rather, it was meant to give people the FX look they wanted, along with a useful level of improvements in handling and vibration reduction. From that standpoint, the Dyna Sturgis was an unqualified success.

Though issued only as a limited edition for 1991, the Dyna was destined for a larger role in the future, including that of the only remaining Big Twin sport bike once the FXRS-SP was canceled at the end of 1993. "The die was cast with the first Dyna," as then–vice president of engineering Mark Tuttle said. "Once we had the Dyna, the FXR models were going to be replaced by Dynas. It just didn't make sense to produce both platforms."

"This Ain't a Sport Bike"

The message had gotten through from Marketing and Styling to Engineering from the beginning that this ain't gonna be no sport bike, and that message was sent forth to the consumer by the choice of brakes: Single disc, front and rear, just like on all the other nonsport models, and they were just as weak and high effort. (It's only on the 2000 models that Harley has finally fitted good brakes.)

If the brakes didn't project the message strongly enough, a ride would. Within the dictates of style, Team Dyna had done what it could to make the Dyna handle and ride well. Still, there's only so much you can do when it's got to be long and low. The forward shock positioning and the need for a low seat height resulted in a paltry 3 inches of rear suspension travel—less even than a Softail has. The front suspension has more travel than the rear, but it doesn't work much better. That 32-degree rake angle guarantees more flex and stiction than when the same fork is used on a Sportster or FXR.

Also working against any sporting pretense was the 65.5-inch wheelbase, longer than that of any other Harley except the Softail Custom. The steering's slow and languid, but the Dyna's dead stable at speed. Its feel is spot-on for unhurried cruising.

Low seat heights and comfort generally are at odds. Dyna's seat height was 26.6 inches, lower even than that of the 883 Sportster Hugger. Despite that,

THE 1992 DYNA GLIDE DAYTONA AND CUSTOM

For year two of the new chassis, the Dyna Glide Sturgis was replaced by a new limited-edition Dyna. The new one had buckhorn bars, the smaller front fender of the recent Sportsters, dual disc front brakes, less menacing paint, a lot more chrome, and a new name: FXDB Daytona. The name commemorated the 50th anniversary of Bike Week in Daytona Beach, Florida. Though the bike made its debut at Daytona in March 1991, it wasn't actually available till later that year, as a 1992 model.

Painted in Indigo Blue metallic and Gold Pearlglo with special 50th graphics, the new Daytona was a stunner. The engine was black and chrome with polished fins. Covers for the electrics, coil, belt, oil filter, and battery were chrome. So were the headlight, triple clamps, risers, highway pegs, fender

Here's the tank and console shared by the Convertible and Super Glide, with central filler hole and gas gauge.

struts, and sissybar. Even the cast, nine-spoke wheels and rear belt pulley got a coat of gold paint, with polished highlights. It was all topped off with an embossed seat and a serial plate listing the particular Daytona as being one of the 1,700 built.

A third member of the Dyna family was also introduced for 1992, the FXDC Dyna Glide Custom. The Custom was based on the Daytona, with buckhorn bars, lots of chrome, and dual-disc brakes. However, the Custom featured a unique black-on-silver look, courtesy of the silver powdercoated frame; black and silver two-tone paint on the tank and fenders; chrome tank-top instrument cover; natural aluminum engine castings, but with all the chrome covers usually reserved for the wrinkle-black engines; and silver paint on the wheels and rear pulley cover.

Although not really planned as a limited edition, the Custom (as pictured in the catalog) actually proved to be more limited than any other Harley of the era. The reason? Harley, struggling to get its ambitious new paint facility on line

The forward-mounted shocks on the Dyna models were one of the FX styling cues Willie G. and Louie Netz insisted on having back on the Dyna.

189

as the 1992 models were in production, experienced great difficulty with the silver powdercoating for the frames. Only about 200 were built before the company gave up and switched to black frames.

Like all Big Twins in 1992, the two Dynas got revised brake discs and the engine updates listed in chapter 1. Once the new paint facility was up and running, paint jobs were finished off and protected by a powder clearcoat.

THE 1993 DYNA WIDE GLIDE AND LOW RIDER

First seen in 1980 and last in 1986, the Wide Glide, the first real factory chopper, returned in Dyna guise for 1993. Since the Dyna was designed from the start to mimic the look of the old FX chassis, it was a natural for an updated Wide Glide. Like the earlier Wide Glides, the Dyna version took its name from the widely spaced, heavily chromed front forks mated to a 21-inch laced wheel with skinny tire.

Add to that the Dyna version of the bobbed rear fender, factory Ape Hanger (yeah, Harley tried to trademark the name, after it'd been in use by others for decades) handlebars, a 5.2-gallon one-piece version of the old 5-gallon Fat Bob tanks (with one functional filler cap and one fake), tank-mounted FLH-type dash and speedometer, chrome bullet headlight, black-and-chrome engine, hidden-crossover exhaust, forward-mounted controls, sissybar, and 16-inch laced rear wheel with fat tire. All it really needed was a flamed paint job to truly mimic the original.

Instead of flames, Willie G. gave the Wide Glide a modern rendition of tank paneling used on the 1958 Duo-Glide, done in contrasting paint on two-tone machines or traced by pinstripes on solid-color machines. Tank emblems were a new design (suggestive of several older ones) with flames streaming back over the company name, hinting at the flames of the original Wide Glide. With the Wide Glide front end combined with the vibration-isolated, FX-look Dyna chassis, the new Wide Glide was a successful update of the old classic.

A special 90th Anniversary edition was also offered to commemorate the 90th anniversary of The Motor Company. Anniversary models came with silver and Charcoal Satin-Brite two-tone paint, formed-brass Anniversary emblems for the tank, and a serialized nameplate.

Curiously, with four versions of the FXR Low Rider still in production, Harley also gave the name to the new "standard" version of the Dyna, the FXDL Dyna Low Rider. The new Low Rider was based on the Daytona (meaning Dyna chassis, black-and-chrome engine, lots of chrome covers, buckhorn bars, black instrument housing, and 4.9-gallon tank), but without the Daytona's limited-edition paint and graphics. Tank emblems were a revised version of those used on the Dyna Custom of 1992, and the cast wheels were painted black, with polished edges.

Like all the Big Twins that year, the Dynas were fitted with new "low-profile" clutch and brake levers.

THE DYNA LOW RIDER CONVERTIBLE

As the FXR models were phased out one by one, new Dyna models were slipped in to replace the old models. Replacing the FXRS-SP and FXRS-CONV was one new Dyna model, the FXDS-CONV Dyna Low Rider Convertible. Convertible it was, in the Harley sense, with quickly detachable leather and nylon saddlebags and windshield. But there was much more to the package.

First, rake angle was reduced from the cruiser-spec 32 degrees to a sportier 28 degrees for quicker steering and a shorter wheelbase. Then, longer forks and shocks with more effective damping rates and dual-rate springs were added to give the Dyna Convertible better handling, ground clearance, and lean angle than anything else in the Big Twin line-up since the demise of the FXRS-SP. The black-painted cast wheels from the FXRS Low Rider were fitted.

Also new on the Convertible were a more comfortable seat with sissybar and backrest

By moving the engine's oil supply to a sump under the transmission, the Dyna engineers were able to completely eliminate a problem that had been plaguing Harleys since the 1930s—wet-sumping, caused by oil draining slowly from the high-mounted oil tank to the engine sump, and then puking out all over once the engine was started.

Even the basic, stripped Dyna Super Glide was a handsome machine, doing for the Big Twin line what the 883 did for Harley in general—giving customers a way to get "in" cheaply.

pad, a new version of the 4.9-gallon gas tank with fuel filler and gas gauge on the center console, and a tach-and-speedo instrument cluster on the handlebars. All these changes transformed the long, low cruiseresque Dyna Low Rider into a sport machine almost the equal in handling and cornering clearance to the discontinued FXRS Sport—hence the FXDS.

Dyna Wide Glide and Low Rider were carried over for 1994 with few changes other than to paint options and graph- ics and the changes discussed in chapter 1.

DYNA SUPER GLIDE

At the end of the 1994 model year, all the remaining FXR models were canceled. At the start of 1995 model year, a new Dyna was released to take over the low-price end of the Big Twin line, the FXD Dyna Super Glide.

The Dyna Super Glide was basically a stripped version of the Dyna Low Rider Convertible, with the unpainted and unplated version of the Evo engine, fewer chrome covers, 28-degree rake, unpainted cast wheels, center-filler gas tank, fuel gauge on the console, and only a speedometer (no tach) mounted to the bars. It was also given a unique tank emblem, consisting of the company name outlined and on two lines.

Dyna Low Rider, Wide Glide, and Convertible were all back, with only minor changes, such as vacuum-operated petcocks (moved more rearward on the tanks), and electronic speedometers. Unfortunately, the MTBE used in the gasoline in California and some other states caused problems with these petcocks, so new internal parts were designed and fitted under warranty to correct the problem.

The four Dyna models from 1995 were back for 1996 with a new frame that was reengineered to lower its height through the midsection, lowering seat heights by about an inch and giving them all a trimmer waist. New chrome fender-support covers jazzed up the rear end. Hand controls were revised. Cast wheels were also new 13-spokers (replacing 9-spokers), painted black (with polished edges) for the Low Rider and Convertible and left unpainted for the Super Glide. For the first time, laced wheels were an available option for the Convertible, Low Rider, and Super Glide.

In addition, the Convertible and Low Rider got new tank graphics, with the company name in old-style lettering; the Wide Glide got even more flames on its tank graphics; new paint options were available; the horn was moved to the center of the engine V on the left side; and all were fitted with new hand controls.

The same four Dynas were back again for 1997, with only minor changes, including new paint options.

1998 AND THE END OF THE EVO DYNAS

For the last year in Evo-powered form, the same four-bike Dyna line-up was back (Super Glide, Low Rider, Wide Glide, and Convertible). Clutches were revised to disengage with less lever effort, but little else was changed other than color combinations, which included a 95th anniversary trim option for the Wide Glide.

Thus, what began as one limited-edition model for 1991 ended at the close of model year 1998 as Harley's most versatile line, with four models that actually filled five niches in Harley's Big Twin line-up. Super Glide was the entry-level Big Twin. Low Rider was the top-of-the-line exposed-shock cruiser. Wide Glide was the factory chopper. And Convertible was the Big Twin sport bike and sport tourer. Best of all, they were all back the next year with the Twin Cam motor, a greatly updated and revised version of the engine the Dyna was meant to debut with, Hank Hubbard's "Optimum Evolution."

Index